Fishing For Dummies™

Temperature Counts

Fish, like people, respond to temperature. When it's too hot or too cold, they don't feel like doing much, so there's no use fishing for them. Using this guide, you can decide when it's time to fish and when it's time to stay home and clean your gear.

Type of Fish	Lower Limit	Optimum	Upper Limit
Freshwater			
Bluegill	58°	69°	75°
Brook Trout	44°	58°	70°
Brown Trout	44°	56°– 65°	75°
Channel Catfish	55°	82°– 89°	na
Coho Salmon	44°	54°	60°
Lake Trout	42°	50°– 59°	na
Largemouth Bass	50°	65°– 75°	85°
Muskellunge	55°	63°	72°
Northern Pike	56°	63°	74"
Rainbow Trout	44°	61°	75°
Smallmouth Bass	60°	65°– 68°	73°
Walleye	50°	67°	76°
Saltwater			
Cod	31°	44°– 49°	59°
Bluefish	50°	62°– 72°	84°
Bonefish	64°	75°	88°
Dolphin	70°	75°	82"
Fluke	56°	66°	72°
Redfish	52°	71°	90°
Red Snapper	50°	57°	62°
Snook	69°	70°– 75°	90°
Speckled Trout	48°	72°	81°
Tarpon	74°	na	100°+

BUSINESS AND
GENERAL
REFERENCE
BOOK SERIES
FROM IDG

Fishing For Dummies™

Quick Reference Card

Match Your Lure to Your Rod and Line

Your rod has a limit to how much weight it can cast effectively. So does your line. Freshwater anglers, use this chart as a guide to what's just right and what's too heavy.

Lure (and/or Sinker) Weight	Rod	Line
1/4 oz	Light or Ultra Light	6–12 lb test
3/8 oz	Medium Light	12–14 lb test
1/2 oz	Medium	14–17 lb test
5/8 oz	Medium Heavy	17–20 lb test
7/8 oz	Heavy	20–30 lb test

Gee Whiz! Did I Fry Up the World Record?

You may not ever get close to a world-record fish, but it could happen. Keep this reference chart for some of the world's most popular game fish, and if yours beats the record, go to the nearest tackle shop, register it, and wait for the endorsements to roll in.

Fish	Weight	Where and When
Brown Trout	40 lb 4 oz	Little Red River, Arkansas, May 9,1992
Largemouth Bass	22 lb 4 oz	Montgomery Lake, Georgia, June 2, 1932
Smallmouth Bass	11 lb 15 oz	Dale Hollow Lake, Kentucky, July 9, 1955
Northern Pike	55 lb 10 oz	Lake of Grefeern, Germany, Oct. 16, 1986
Muskellunge	65 lb	Blackstone Harbor, Ontario, Oct. 16, 1988
Walleye	25 lb	Old Hickory Lake, Tennessee, April 1, 1960
Striped Bass	78 lb 8 oz	Atlantic City, New Jersey, Sept. 21, 1982
Bluefish	31 lb 12 oz	Hatteras, North Carolina, Jan. 30, 1972
Weakfish (sea trout)	19 lb 2 oz	Jones Beach Inlet, New York, Oct. 11, 1984

IDG
BOOKS
WORLDWIDE

Copyright © 1997 IDG Books Worldwide, Inc.
All rights reserved.

Cheat Sheet $2.95 value. Item 5028-4.

For more information about IDG Books,
call 1-800-762-2974.

...For Dummies: Bestselling Book Series for Beginners

Praise for Fishing For Dummies

"I've been fishing for 60 years and I've found this book to be the most informative and entertaining I've ever read."
— Art Laursen, Sr., Fire Chief, Greely Hills, CA

"I recommend this book to any fisherman, whether they like to hook and cook, catch and release, or both!"
— Art Laursen, Jr., Danville, CA

If you are a beginning angler, this is the first book you should read. Pete Kaminsky has a keen reporter's eye and the sensitivity of your favorite teacher (the funny one who understood how you felt as a stranger). Here he draws on his vast experience, covering all kinds of fish and fishing, but in small bites, easily digested. . . . This is the most personal text book you are ever likely to find. Even the know-it-all angler will find something new. So, if you are not a fishing nut now, don't worry, Pete will get you there.
— Joan Stoliar, Director, Project Access

I've known Peter for years and am a big fan of his writing style. *Fishing For Dummies* taught me some new tricks — and made me laugh along the way. Buy this book — you'll enjoy it.
— Tom Rosenbauer, Vice President, Merchandising, The Orvis Company, Inc. and author of *The Orvis Flyfishing Guide*

After decades of technically overarching, "how-to" angling literature that turns off as many people as it instructs, we now have a book that provides meaningful advice to those who have always wondered, but were probably afraid to ask. As with Kaminsky's other writing, this is truly first-rate. Readers will appreciate Kaminsky's mastery of the subject matter and the humor with which he presents it.
— Charles F. Gauvin, President & CEO, Trout Unlimited

With his trademark blend of supreme scholarship and keen wit, Peter Kaminsky has commited an act of true piscatorial worth.
— Gary Soucie, Editor, *American Angler* and author of *Traveling with Fly Rod and Reel* and *Hook, Line and Sinker: The Complete Angler's Guide to Terminal Tackle*

TM

BUSINESS AND GENERAL REFERENCE BOOK SERIES FROM IDG

References for the Rest of Us!™

Do you find that traditional reference books are overloaded with technical details and advice you'll never use? Do you postpone important life decisions because you just don't want to deal with them? Then our *...For Dummies*™ business and general reference book series is for you.

...For Dummies business and general reference books are written for those frustrated and hardworking souls who know they aren't dumb, but find that the myriad of personal and business issues and the accompanying horror stories make them feel helpless. *...For Dummies* books use a lighthearted approach, a down-to-earth style, and even cartoons and humorous icons to diffuse fears and build confidence. Lighthearted but not lightweight, these books are perfect survival guides to solve your everyday personal and business problems.

> *"More than a publishing phenomenon, 'Dummies' is a sign of the times."*
> — The New York Times

> *"A world of detailed and authoritative information is packed into them..."*
> — U.S. News and World Report

> *"... you won't go wrong buying them."*
> — Walter Mossberg, Wall Street Journal, on IDG's ...For Dummies™ books

Already, hundreds of thousands of satisfied readers agree. They have made *...For Dummies* the #1 introductory level computer book series and a best-selling business book series. They have written asking for more. So, if you're looking for the best and easiest way to learn about business and other general reference topics, look to *...For Dummies* to give you a helping hand.

7/96r

FISHING
FOR
DUMMIES™

FISHING FOR DUMMIES™

by Peter Kaminsky

IDG Books Worldwide, Inc.
An International Data Group Company

Foster City, CA ♦ Chicago, IL ♦ Indianapolis, IN ♦ Southlake, TX

Fishing For Dummies™

Published by
IDG Books Worldwide, Inc.
An International Data Group Company
919 E. Hillsdale Blvd.
Suite 400
Foster City, CA 94404
http://www.idgbooks.com (IDG Books Worldwide Web site)
http://www.dummies.com (Dummies Press Web site)

Library of Congress Catalog Card No.: 97-70365

ISBN: 0-7645-5028-4

Printed in the United States of America

10 9 8 7 6 5 4 3 2 1

10/RX/QU/ZX/IN

Distributed in the United States by IDG Books Worldwide, Inc.

Distributed by Macmillan Canada for Canada; by Transworld Publishers Limited in the United Kingdom and Europe; by WoodsLane Pty. Ltd. for Australia; by WoodsLane Enterprises Ltd. for New Zealand; by Longman Singapore Publishers Ltd. for Singapore, Malaysia, Thailand, and Indonesia; by Simron Pty. Ltd. for South Africa; by Toppan Company Ltd. for Japan; by Distribuidora Cuspide for Argentina; by Livraria Cultura for Brazil; by Ediciencia S.A. for Ecuador; by Addison-Wesley Publishing Company for Korea; by Ediciones ZETA S.C.R. Ltda. for Peru; by WS Computer Publishing Company, Inc., for the Philippines; by Unalis Corporation for Taiwan; by Contemporanea de Ediciones for Venezuela. Authorized Sales Agent: Anthony Rudkin Associates for the Middle East and North Africa.

For general information on IDG Books Worldwide's books in the U.S., please call our Consumer Customer Service department at 800-762-2974. For reseller information, including discounts and premium sales, please call our Reseller Customer Service department at 800-434-3422.

For information on where to purchase IDG Books Worldwide's books outside the U.S., please contact our International Sales department at 415-655-3023 or fax 415-655-3299.

For information on foreign language translations, please contact our Foreign & Subsidiary Rights department at 415-655-3021 or fax 415-655-3281.

For sales inquiries and special prices for bulk quantities, please contact our Sales department at 415-655-3200 or write to the address above.

For information on using IDG Books Worldwide's books in the classroom or for ordering examination copies, please contact our Educational Sales department at 800-434-2086 or fax 817-251-8174.

For press review copies, author interviews, or other publicity information, please contact our Public Relations department at 415-655-3000 or fax 415-655-3299.

For authorization to photocopy items for corporate, personal, or educational use, please contact Copyright Clearance Center, 222 Rosewood Drive, Danvers, MA 01923, or fax 508-750-4470.

is a trademark under exclusive license to IDG Books Worldwide, Inc., from International Data Group, Inc.

About the Author

Peter Kaminsky caught his first fish, a 30-pound grouper, on a party boat in the Florida Keys. It was the first time he went fishing, and that grouper won $45 for the big fish of the day. Kaminsky was hooked. He was Managing Editor of *National Lampoon* at the time. Soon after, he began to write for *Outdoor Life, Field & Stream,* and *Sports Afield.* In 1985, he began his regular contributions to *The New York Times* "Outdoors" column. Kaminsky also writes "The Underground Gourmet" in *New York* magazine and is a frequent contributor on food and dining in *Food & Wine* magazine. As a television producer, Kaminsky has created many prime-time specials with Jerry Seinfeld, Mary Tyler Moore, Bob Newhart, and a fellow angler who is sorely missed, John Candy. Kaminsky is a graduate of Princeton University and lives in Brooklyn with his wife and two children, all of whom fish.

ABOUT IDG BOOKS WORLDWIDE

Welcome to the world of IDG Books Worldwide.

IDG Books Worldwide, Inc., is a subsidiary of International Data Group, the world's largest publisher of computer-related information and the leading global provider of information services on information technology. IDG was founded more than 25 years ago and now employs more than 8,500 people worldwide. IDG publishes more than 275 computer publications in over 75 countries (see listing below). More than 60 million people read one or more IDG publications each month.

Launched in 1990, IDG Books Worldwide is today the #1 publisher of best-selling computer books in the United States. We are proud to have received eight awards from the Computer Press Association in recognition of editorial excellence and three from *Computer Currents*' First Annual Readers' Choice Awards. Our best-selling *...For Dummies*® series has more than 30 million copies in print with translations in 30 languages. IDG Books Worldwide, through a joint venture with IDG's Hi-Tech Beijing, became the first U.S. publisher to publish a computer book in the People's Republic of China. In record time, IDG Books Worldwide has become the first choice for millions of readers around the world who want to learn how to better manage their businesses.

Our mission is simple: Every one of our books is designed to bring extra value and skill-building instructions to the reader. Our books are written by experts who understand and care about our readers. The knowledge base of our editorial staff comes from years of experience in publishing, education, and journalism — experience we use to produce books for the '90s. In short, we care about books, so we attract the best people. We devote special attention to details such as audience, interior design, use of icons, and illustrations. And because we use an efficient process of authoring, editing, and desktop publishing our books electronically, we can spend more time ensuring superior content and spend less time on the technicalities of making books.

You can count on our commitment to deliver high-quality books at competitive prices on topics you want to read about. At IDG Books Worldwide, we continue in the IDG tradition of delivering quality for more than 25 years. You'll find no better book on a subject than one from IDG Books Worldwide.

John J. Kilcullen

John Kilcullen
CEO
IDG Books Worldwide, Inc.

VIII WINNER
Eighth Annual
Computer Press
Awards ≥1992

IX WINNER
Ninth Annual
Computer Press
Awards ≥1993

1995 COMPUTER CURRENTS READERS CHOICE

X WINNER
Tenth Annual
Computer Press
Awards ≥1994

XI WINNER
Eleventh Annual
Computer Press
Awards ≥1995

IDG Books Worldwide, Inc., is a subsidiary of International Data Group, the world's largest publisher of computer-related information and the leading global provider of information services on information technology. International Data Group publishes over 275 computer publications in over 75 countries. Sixty million people read one or more International Data Group publications each month. International Data Group's publications include: **ARGENTINA:** Buyer's Guide, Computerworld Argentina, PC World Argentina; **AUSTRALIA:** Australian Macworld, Australian PC World, Australian Reseller News, Computerworld, IT Casebook, Network World, Publish, Webmaster; **AUSTRIA:** Computerwelt Osterreich, Networks Austria, PC Tip Austria; **BANGLADESH:** PC World Bangladesh; **BELARUS:** PC World Belarus; **BELGIUM:** Data News; **BRAZIL:** Annuário de Informática, Computerworld, Connections, Macworld, PC Player, PC World, Publish, Reseller News, Supergamepower; **BULGARIA:** Computerworld Bulgaria, Network World Bulgaria, PC & MacWorld Bulgaria; **CANADA:** CIO Canada, Client/Server World, ComputerWorld Canada, InfoWorld Canada, NetworkWorld Canada, WebWorld; **CHILE:** Computerworld Chile, PC World Chile; **COLOMBIA:** Computerworld Colombia, PC World Colombia; **COSTA RICA:** PC World Centro America; **THE CZECH AND SLOVAK REPUBLICS:** Computerworld Czechoslovakia, Macworld Czech Republic, PC World Czechoslovakia; **DENMARK:** Communications World Danmark, Computerworld Danmark, Macworld Danmark, PC World Danmark, Techworld Denmark; **DOMINICAN REPUBLIC:** PC World Republica Dominicana; **ECUADOR:** PC World Ecuador; **EGYPT:** Computerworld Middle East, PC World Middle East; **EL SALVADOR:** PC World Centro America; **FINLAND:** MikroPC, Tietoverkko, Tietoviikko; **FRANCE:** Distributique, Hebdo, Info PC, Le Monde Informatique, Macworld, Reseaux & Telecoms, WebMaster France; **GERMANY:** Computer Partner, Computerwoche, Computerwoche Extra, Computerwoche FOCUS, Global Online, Macwelt, PC Welt; **GREECE:** Amiga Computing, GamePro Greece, Multimedia World; **GUATEMALA:** PC World Centro America; **HONDURAS:** PC World Centro America; **HONG KONG:** Computerworld Hong Kong, PC World Hong Kong, Publish in Asia; **HUNGARY:** ABCD CD-ROM, Computerworld Szamitastechnika, Internetto online Magazine, PC World Hungary, PC-X Magazin Hungary; **ICELAND:** Tolvuheimur PC World Island; **INDIA:** Information Communications World, Information Systems Computerworld, PC World India, Publish in Asia; **INDONESIA:** InfoKomputer PC World, Komputek Computerworld, Publish in Asia; **IRELAND:** ComputerScope, PC Live!; **ISRAEL:** Macworld Israel, People & Computers/Computerworld; **ITALY:** Computerworld Italia, Macworld Italia, Networking Italia, PC World Italia; **JAPAN:** DTP World, Macworld Japan, Nikkei Personal Computing, OS/2 World Japan, SunWorld Japan, Windows NT World, Windows World Japan; **KENYA:** PC World East African; **KOREA:** Hi-Tech Information, Macworld Korea, PC World Korea; **MACEDONIA:** PC World Macedonia; **MALAYSIA:** Computerworld Malaysia, PC World Malaysia, Publish in Asia; **MALTA:** PC World Malta; **MEXICO:** Computerworld Mexico, PC World Mexico; **MYANMAR:** PC World Myanmar; **NETHERLANDS:** Computer! Totaal, LAN Internetworking Magazine, LAN World Buyers Guide, Macworld Netherlands, Net, WebWereld; **NEW ZEALAND:** Absolute Beginners Guide and Plain & Simple Series, Computer Buyer, Computer Industry Directory, Computerworld New Zealand, MTB, Network World, PC World New Zealand; **NICARAGUA:** PC World Centro America; **NORWAY:** Computerworld Norge, CW Rapport, Datamagasinet, Financial Rapport, Kursguide Norge, Macworld Norge, Multimediaworld Norge, PC World Ekspress Norge, PC World Nettverk, PC World Norge, PC World ProduktGuide Norge; **PAKISTAN:** Computerworld Pakistan; **PANAMA:** PC World Panama; **PEOPLE'S REPUBLIC OF CHINA:** China Computer Users, China Computerworld, China InfoWorld, China Telecom World Weekly, Computer & Communication, Electronic Design China, Electronics Today, Electronics Weekly, Game Software, PC World China, Popular Computer Week, Software Weekly, Software World, Telecom World; **PERU:** Computerworld Peru, PC World Profesional Peru, PC World SoHo Peru; **PHILIPPINES:** Click!, Cerebro/PC World, Computerworld Philippines, PC World Philippines, Publish in Asia; **POLAND:** Computerworld Poland, Computerworld Special Report Poland, Cyber, Macworld Poland, Networld Poland, PC World Komputer; **PORTUGAL:** Cerebro/PC World, Computerworld/Correio Informático, Dealer World Portugal, Mac*In/PC*In Portugal, Multimedia World; **PUERTO RICO:** PC World Puerto Rico; **ROMANIA:** Computerworld Romania, PC World Romania, Telecom Romania; **RUSSIA:** Computerworld Russia, Mir PK, Publish, Seti; **SINGAPORE:** Computerworld Singapore, PC World Singapore, Publish in Asia; **SLOVENIA:** Monitor; **SOUTH AFRICA:** Computing SA, Network World SA, Software World SA; **SPAIN:** Communicaciones World España, Computerworld España, Dealer World España, Macworld España, PC World España; **SRI LANKA:** Infolink PC World; **SWEDEN:** CAP&Design, Computer Sweden, Corporate Computing Sweden, Internetworld Sweden, it.branschen, Macworld Sweden, MaxiData Sweden, MikroDatorn, Natverk & Kommunikation, PC World Sweden, PCaktiv, Windows World Sweden; **SWITZERLAND:** Computerworld Schweiz, Macworld Schweiz, PCtip; **TAIWAN:** Computerworld Taiwan, Macworld Taiwan, NEW ViSiON/Publish, PC World Taiwan, Windows World Taiwan; **THAILAND:** Publish in Asia, Thai Computerworld; **TURKEY:** Computerworld Turkiye, Macworld Turkiye, Network World Turkiye, PC World Turkiye; **UKRAINE:** Computerworld Kiev, Multimedia World Ukraine, PC World Ukraine; **UNITED KINGDOM:** Acorn User UK, Amiga Action UK, Amiga Computing UK, Apple Talk UK, Computing, Macworld, Parents and Computers UK, PC Advisor, PC Home, PSX Pro, The WEB; **UNITED STATES:** Cable in the Classroom, CIO Magazine, Computerworld, DOS World, Federal Computer Week, GamePro Magazine, InfoWorld, I-Way, Macworld, Network World, PC Games, PC World, Publish, Video Event, THE WEB Magazine, and WebMaster; online webzines: JavaWorld, NetscapeWorld, and SunWorld Online; **URUGUAY:** InfoWorld Uruguay; **VENEZUELA:** Computerworld Venezuela, PC World Venezuela; and **VIETNAM:** PC World Vietnam. 1/24/97

Author's Acknowledgments

There are many people to thank, but first an anonymous thank you to all the anglers — men and women who have shared their knowledge, companionship and, often, their tackle with me over the years. I would especially like to acknowledge the late Gene Calogiero (forgive me, Gene, I'm just guessing at the spelling, and you're not around to correct me anymore), who first taught me how to tie flies and fish the Esopus Creek. Nick Lyons for his generous counsel and support as I tried to learn how to write about this wonderful sport. John Culler for buying my first fishing piece in *Outdoor Life*. Duncan Barnes for years of putting up with my aging-hippy-writer's ways. Susan Adams for making a home for me at *The New York Times* (and Joe Vecchione for getting me started there). Tom Akstens for being an exemplar of a passionate and joyful angler. A debt beyond measure to the unsung Everglades guide Jack Allen, the most complete angler I know, who, by his example, has taught me that one can make a life out of angling, not rich in money, but face it, for most of us, the money isn't going to happen anyway, so we might as well enjoy the fishing.

Dedication

For Grandpa Jan.

Publisher's Acknowledgments

We're proud of this book; please send us your comments about it by using the Reader Response Card at the back of the book or by e-mailing us at feedback/dummies@idgbooks.com. Some of the people who helped bring this book to market include the following:

Acquisitions, Development, and Editorial

Project Editor: Tim Gallan

Acquisitions Editor: Sarah Kennedy, Executive Editor

Copy Editors: Diana Conover, Felicity O'Meara

Technical Editor: Nicholas P. Sita

Editorial Manager: Kristin A. Cocks

Editorial Coordinator: Ann Miller

Production

Project Coordinator: Debbie Stailey

Layout and Graphics: Brett Black, Cameron Booker, Angela F. Hunckler, Drew R. Moore, Brent Savage, Kate Snell, Michael A. Sullivan

Proofreaders: Kathy Layng, Rachel Garvey, Nancy Price, Robert Springer, Ethel Winslow

Indexer: David Heiret

Illustrator: Ron Hildebrand

Special Help

Jamie Klobuchar

General and Administrative

IDG Books Worldwide, Inc.: John Kilcullen, CEO; Steven Berkowitz, President and Publisher

IDG Books Technology Publishing: Brenda McLaughlin, Senior Vice President and Group Publisher

Dummies Technology Press and Dummies Editorial: Diane Graves Steele, Vice President and Associate Publisher; Judith A. Taylor, Brand Manager; Kristin A. Cocks, Editorial Director

Dummies Trade Press: Kathleen A. Welton, Vice President and Publisher; Stacy S. Collins, Brand Manager

IDG Books Production for Dummies Press: Beth Jenkins, Production Director; Cindy L. Phipps, Supervisor of Project Coordination, Production Proofreading, and Indexing; Kathie S. Schutte, Supervisor of Page Layout; Shelley Lea, Supervisor of Graphics and Design; Debbie J. Gates, Production Systems Specialist; Tony Augsburger, Supervisor of Reprints and Bluelines; Leslie Popplewell, Media Archive Coordinator

Dummies Packaging and Book Design: Patti Sandez, Packaging Specialist; Lance Kayser, Packaging Assistant; Kavish+Kavish, Cover Design

◆

Contents at a Glance

Cartoons at a Glance

By Rich Tennant • Fax: 508-546-7747 • E-mail: the5wave@tiac.net

page 169

page 305

page 5

page 119

page 271

Table of Contents

● ●

Introduction

● ●

*F*amous non-dummy Mark Twain once said, "Fishing is a jerk at one end of the line waiting for a jerk at the other end." I'm not sure that I totally agree with him, but if you substitute the word "dummy" for "jerk," it's a pretty accurate description of the beginning of everyone's angling career (including mine).

Within the context of this book, "dummies" is a term of endearment that refers to people who realize that they don't know much about a given topic but are smart enough to get themselves help, preferably by buying a book like this one. Some people look like they were born with a rod in one hand and a stringer full of fish in the other, but the fact is, they all started out life not knowing a rod from a reel or a fish from a football. You're already one step ahead of them because you bought (I hope) this book.

We are all born with an ability to *learn* how to fish because fishing, like hunting or picking fruit, is as basic as the search for food. And all human beings are born with pretty sophisticated food-finding genes. Thousands of generations of our grandmothers and grandfathers spent their whole lives seeking food, and we have inherited their abilities. So we may start out as dummies, but we don't start out stupid.

Right now, if I put you on a stream or by the shore of a lake, you might not be able to tell me where *all* the fishy-looking spots are, but every one of you could tell me *some* of them. It's an ability you are born with.

This book will help you develop that ability. In a very short while, you beginners will be catching fish. Those of you who already know a little about catching fish will be catching more fish. Once you have a few basic pointers, it's as easy as falling off a log (which is something you want to avoid, as the splash will scare the fish).

I am not promising that you will catch fish all the time. Fish, after all, would just as soon never taste a hook or feel the sizzle of a frying pan. For as long as we have been catching fish, fish have also been outsmarting us. "That's why they call it fishing and not catching," goes the old saying. This book will help you fish, and it will help you catch, too. No matter how much you know, there are still a couple of tricks that even the oldest angler can pick up.

As a writer for major outdoor magazines and an outdoor columnist for *The New York Times,* I've had the opportunity to learn from great fishermen and fisherwomen all over the world. They have made fishing both easier and more rewarding for me and, through this book, they will do the same for you.

Fishing is a great joy and a lifetime sport. I have found that there are successful fishing days and unsuccessful fishing days, but there is no such thing as a bad fishing day.

Ten Reasons Why You Should Fish

1. Good fishing only happens in a pretty place.
2. Teddy Roosevelt and Calvin Coolidge fished, and they got to be President. (As did Herbert Hoover, Jimmy Carter, and George Bush). Wendell Wilkie, on the other hand, didn't.
3. It's a chance to get out of the house early and buy candy bars.
4. You can do it with your kids.
5. You can do it without your kids.
6. You can spend a lot of time looking through neat catalogs.
7. You can get away from phones, TVs, and stereos.
8. On the other hand, you can take a phone with you, and no one needs to know you're calling from the stream.
9. People don't think less of you if you lie. In fact, they expect it.
10. It's fun.

What I Assume about You

There are three kinds of people who can use this book:

- People who have never fished
- People who have done some fishing
- People who have fished a lot

For those of you who have never fished, you will find enough to get you started. You don't have to learn everything all at once. If you are already an angler, there are plenty of tips and techniques that you can turn to right away without going through the basics all over again. And you master anglers will also find this book a handy reference for all kinds of fishing questions. So depending on where you fit on the scale of never fished, fished some, or fished a lot, you can skip those parts of this book that aren't important to you right now.

How to Use This Book

This book is a reference; you don't have to read it from cover to cover. I suggest that you find a topic that interests you in the table of contents or index and go from there. I've peppered the chapters with cross-references to related topics in other chapters (and even other books). If you want to read this book from front to back, feel free, but like I said, skipping around is good too.

How This Book Is Organized

No mystery here: Each chapter in this book presents self-contained coverage of a specific subject. Related chapters are grouped into parts. Here are summaries of each part:

Part I: Starting Out

The first chapter of this part is for those of you who have never fished. The rest of the chapters cover your equipment: lures, bait, flies, rods, reels, and so on. If you're a beginner, you'll want to read every word. More experienced anglers should skim these chapters for tips and tricks, but you can also skip right over all of Part I if you want to get into some of the deeper stuff right away.

Part II: What You're After

There are a whole lot of fish in the sea, but most of them are of absolutely no interest to the sport-fisherman. The two chapters in this part tells you about the fish that people fish for, what they look like, and where they're found. Chapter 9 covers freshwater fish, and Chapter 10 covers saltwater fish.

Part III: Now You're Fishing

There's a lot of great info in this part. After an enlightening and important chapter on knots, I cover the basics of bait-casting, spinning, and fly-casting. I also discuss fighting, landing, and releasing fish. I help you decide the right times and right places for fishing, and I even provide some insight on how to get to the best fishing holes.

Part IV: Eating

Depending on your point of view, this part covers a lot more or a lot less than what you might expect from the title. I don't teach you how to use a knife and fork, and I don't talk about chewing and digesting. What I do cover are topics like storing, cleaning, and cooking fish. So if you thought that Part IV is just about eating fish, I actually cover a lot more than that.

Part V: The Part of Tens

Every ...*For Dummies* book ends with a group of chapters that are, in essence, top-ten lists, and this book is no exception. In this part, I present some interesting Internet sites, my favorite fishing books (besides this one), and a bunch of great places to fish.

Icons Used in This Book

This icon flags information that will save you from making the same mistakes that took the rest of us years to unlearn.

Having the right fly, lure, rod, hat, shoes, and so on can make all the difference between success and a miserable day. This icon flags the stuff you *really* need.

From a hook in your finger to a dip in a stream, text next to this icon will show you how to stay dry, comfortable, and safe.

With more and more people pressuring fewer and fewer fish, we all need to learn some basic rules of the road.

Part I
Starting Out

The 5th Wave   By Rich Tennant

RICHTENNANT

FISHING TACKLE

"What kind of line do I use when I go fishing?
Usually, 'I'm only doing this to save money
on our food budget, Honey'."

In this part . . .

Most of this part is devoted to the coverage of equipment: rods, reels, bait, lures, and whatnot. Chapter 1 is an introduction to the whole concept of fishing, so it geared mostly for beginners. Chapters 2 through 8, however, are great reading for beginners and experienced fishermen alike.

Chapter 1
Some Basic Basics

• •

In This Chapter

▶ What fish *really* want

▶ What information you need (and where you can *find* it)

▶ Why you *need* a license

• •

*1*f you have read this far, you probably have some interest in catching fish. Perhaps you have never tried to catch one, or you may have caught many and would like to improve your skills. Either way, whether you're a novice or an experienced angler, the equation remains the same — catching a fish requires three things:

✔ A fish

✔ A fisherman or woman

✔ Some fishing gear

What Is a Fish?

A *fish* is a cold-blooded animal that lives underwater, has fins, and breathes through gills. Some fish, such as eels, may not look as if they have fins, but they do. Other fish, such as manta rays, may look more like futuristic designs for jet fighters, but they, too, live in the water, navigate with fins, and breathe through gills.

As far as the angler (that's you) is concerned, fish eat other fish, insects, and the occasional unlucky mammal, reptile, or other animal that finds itself in the water. Although some fish subsist on a diet of plants, *fishing* is the art of convincing a fish that the thing at the end of your line is an edible animal (or part of one). Whether you use a bait, a lure, or a fly, a fish usually strikes because it thinks that your offering is an easy meal. At other times, a fish, like any protective parent, may strike because it thinks that your imitation animal endangers its young (and very few species can stand to see their babies eaten).

What does a fish look like?

A fish biologist may need to know hundreds of parts of the anatomy of a fish. As an angler, you're only interested in a few — the parts that are illustrated in Figure 1-1.

The torpedo shapes of most game fish allow them to move easily through tides and currents. The *fins* propel and guide their movements, and sometimes, as in the case of spiny rays, fins serve as protection. *Gills* enable fish to breathe by extracting oxygen from the water. The *lateral line* is a special sensory organ that enables fish to detect vibrations in the water (like the kind of vibrations that are made when you clank an oar on the bottom of a rowboat or when you tramp along the rocks in the bottom of a stream). Most fish that you are interested in catching face upstream so that they can spot food as the current carries it downstream toward them.

What does a fish want out of life?

On an average day, a fish has only two requirements:

✔ Finding something to eat

✔ Avoiding being eaten

In other words, food and shelter are at the top of the priority list of every

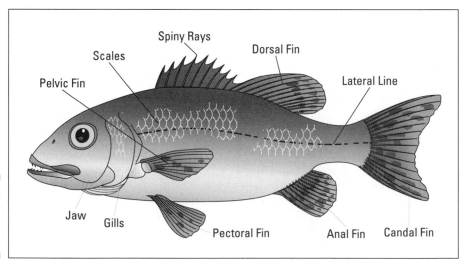

Figure 1-1:
Your
average
fish.

fish. At certain times of the year, making babies also acquires some importance. But by and large, in looking at any fishing situation, you should ask
yourself these two questions:

- ✔ What will the fish be looking for in the way of food?
- ✔ How will the fish avoid danger from predators while it is looking for food?

Figuring out the food

Answering the first question can tell you a great deal about what kind of
bait, fly, or lure to use to trick a fish into biting down on your hook. Often,
when you see a fish feeding, a close look at the water can tell you what food
is available. After you have figured out what food is available, your job is to
tie something on your line that looks like that particular type of fish food. If
a fish is taking something big, such as herring or shrimp, guessing the right
food isn't very hard. However, as any frustrated trout fisher can tell you,
four or five kinds of food — little insects, bait fish, crawfish, worms, and the
like — are often in the water at any given time. In these cases, some concen-
trated observation should help you to figure out what the fish are eating.
Most of the time, fish seem to follow this unwritten rule: "If a choice between large food and small food can be made, then pick something to eat
that is so small that it is invisible to any angler."

Finding a safe hideout

All other things being equal, a fish would spend all of its time in a safe place,
where predators can't see it or reach it. But to get food, fish, like people,
need to get out of the house and go shopping, and that time that a fish is
away from home is when the angler has an opportunity to catch the unwary
fish. Although a fish in pursuit of a juicy meal may be a little less cautious
than a fish lying under a rock, safety is always a prime concern; and no fish
worth his (or her) fins *ever* chases food without having some kind of escape
route close at hand. After you know what and where these escape routes
are, you are well on the way to knowing where and — more importantly —
where *not* to fish.

A fish can use one of three ways to escape being caught:

- ✔ **Hide in the dark.** Look for fish in or near shadows. Also, expect fish to
  be feeding when the light is low (at dawn and dusk — and sometimes
  even at night).

- ✔ **Hide under something.** If no food is around, expect to find fish under
  nearby rocks, fallen trees, and undercut banks.

- ✔ **Get down.** If you are a bear, a bird of prey, or an angler, chances are you
  are not going to go very deep into the water to chase a fish. Therefore,
  even on a bright, sunny day with no tree limbs or rocks to crawl under,
  a fish may stay in plain view in deep water.

Fishing versus Angling

A *fisherman* or *fisherwoman* is a person who fishes. People catch fish by using all kinds of gear (from spear guns to nets to bare hands). An *angler* is a fisherman or woman who angles (an Old English word for *fishing*) with a rod and reel. This book is about angling. Figure 1-2 shows two anglers who are pretty much ready for any situation.

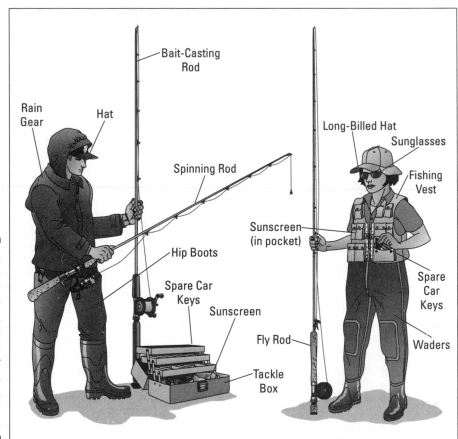

Figure 1-2: The almost-complete angler. Two anglers, well equipped for spinning, bait casting, or fly-fishing.

Bait-Casting Rod

Rain Gear

Hat

Spinning Rod

Hip Boots

Spare Car Keys

Sunscreen

Tackle Box

Long-Billed Hat

Sunglasses

Fishing Vest

Sunscreen (in pocket)

Spare Car Keys

Fly Rod

Waders

It started with Adam (or shortly thereafter)

Although no one is sure exactly when people started to use fishing rods, we do know that Stone Age people used pieces of flint, bone, or wood to make fishing implements called *gorges*. Basically, a gorge was a double-pointed, bait-wrapped, narrow piece of flint, bone, or wood that was tied around its middle to a line. The fish would eat the bait, and (when the angler pulled on the line) the gorge would stick in the fish's throat. It's probably safe to assume that these cave folk made these tools for fishing (otherwise it would have been a pretty big waste of time when they could have been out there chasing mammoths or giant sloths). The first real proof we have of people actually fishing with rods comes from drawings of the ancient Egyptians. Whether the "Phishing" Pharaohs used bait or lures is an open question. We do know that the ancient Greeks fished. Homer, the author of *The Iliad* talks about people using an ox horn to catch "little fishes."

Those anglers of old used a wooden rod with a line attached to the end. It was very much like today's cane poles that many young anglers first use to fish for panfish at every lake and dock. We know that people were using reels by the 12th Century because pictures of rods and reels appeared in China shortly before Marco Polo visited there. And the art of fly-fishing was already well advanced in England when, in the 15th Century, the most famous fisherwoman of all time, Dame Juliana Berners (an English nun), wrote her *Treatise On Fishing With An Angle*.

By the time that Izaak Walton wrote *The Compleat Angler* in the 17th Century, fishing knowledge about the fish that lived in the rivers of Europe was very advanced, but Walton never saw a rainbow trout, a largemouth bass, a bonefish, or a bluefish (all of which were first seen in the New World). Many of the fishing tools that are taken for granted today (such as more-advanced reels and rods made of newer materials) did not appear until the 19th and 20th Centuries. In the early 19th Century, the precision watchmakers of Kentucky perfected the modern bait-casting reel. A few decades later, in England, Holden Illingworth invented the spinning reel. The 20th Century has introduced such wonderful rod materials as fiberglass and graphite, which enable the modern caster to achieve distances that only a champion could have dreamed for in Walton's day. This century also saw the birth of the outboard motor, which works even better than the strongest rod in getting you within fishing range.

Your main tool: A fishing rod

Rods come in all sizes, and they are made from many different materials. Some rods are made of graphite or other space-age composites. Some rods are made of fiberglass. Other rods are made of bamboo. Which rod is best for you?

Your choice of rod depends on the type of fishing you do. Figure 1-3 shows the three basic types of rods. Like everything else these days, you can spend a little or you can break your piggy bank. Take my word for it: If you're a novice, you don't need to break your piggy bank. Buying the most expensive rod would be like buying the great racehorse Secretariat so he could pull your milk wagon: You'd wind up with more horse than you need, and you probably wouldn't know how to get the most out of Secretariat anyway. Save the expert gear for the experts and start off with a good, serviceable starter kit. Reputable manufacturers (such as Berkely, Shakespeare, Orvis, and the like) have very good beginners' kits that contain rod, reel, and line. At 1997 prices, such a conventional spinning or casting outfit may run you between $50 and $75. You can get started fly-fishing in the $150 range. After you use a beginners' outfit to get the feel of fishing, you are ready to move up from the entry-level kits to the more sophisticated and pricier stuff.

GEAR

Avoiding the heartbreak of rodbreak

Although both cars and fishing rods are products of modern technology and use similar materials, I've noticed that cars have a nasty tendency to break and/or lose fishing rods. The minute your rod gets near a car, the rod is in danger of being mugged. If you put a rod on top of the car while you take off your boots, I promise you that one day you will drive off with the rod on the roof and that it will fly off and be lost forever (if not crushed by the truck in back of you). If you lean a rod against your car's tailgate or rear bumper, it will someday find a way of wedging itself into the hinge of the trunk or tailgate. When you close the trunk or tailgate, you will be reminded of the rod's location by the crunching sound that it makes as it breaks in two. If you try the old standby of putting the rod on the vehicle's floor beside the front passenger seat and placing it so that its tip is pointing toward the back seat, I can almost guarantee you that you will break off the rod tip someday. Basic rule of thumb: If a rod *can* be broken by putting it in or near your car, the rod *will* be broken.

The cure for your rod catching "Car Disease": *Break down* (disassemble) your rod and put it in a case; or if you are placing your rod in the back of a pickup truck, lay the rod down flat on something soft.

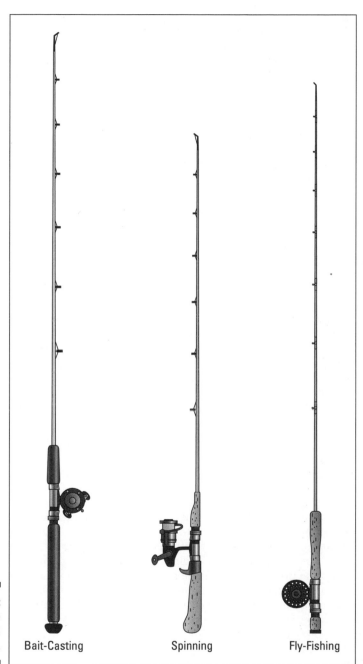

Figure 1-3:
Some
standard
rods.

Bait-Casting   Spinning   Fly-Fishing

How Do I Learn? Who Do I Ask?

If you never fished at all before you began to read this book, you may have started fishing a little bit later than most. If so, don't worry. (I didn't really start to fish until I was in my twenties.) Still, the best time to begin to fish is when you are a little kid and a parent, grandparent, uncle, or big brother or big sister gets you started with a simple rod and a worm or some balled-up bread on a hook.

But if you weren't lucky enough to begin fishing as a very young youngster, you can become an angler (or a better angler) in any number of ways.

Parents

Fishing with Mom and Dad is a good place to start, but Mom and Dad need to be patient. Type-A parents who hover over their children, correcting and criticizing, are not very good fishing instructors. Parents who stop teaching and start fishing the minute that they see a fish to catch are better off not teaching. Jack Hemingway, oldest son of the late American author Ernest Hemingway, is a fishing fanatic. Jack's dad, Ernest, was a famous fisherman as well as a great writer, so you would be inclined to think that Papa Hemingway was one heck of a fishing teacher. Well, Jack once said that in all the years that he went marlin fishing with his dad, he (Jack) was actually allowed to hold the rod exactly once! Before you decide to teach your child to fish, make a resolution to let your youngster do the fishing and you do the watching.

Friends

Friends are great teachers. Or maybe it is more accurate to say that you can learn a great deal from friends. I have always learned (and continue to pick up tricks) from fishing buddies. The thing to remember about friends, like the thing about parents, is that fishing is not a competition between anglers. Fishing is a contest between an angler and a fish. Many people have difficulty accepting pointers and advice from friends. If you want to be a good angler, learn to accept help. This *doesn't* mean that you have to listen to every opinionated gas bag who comments on your style. After you pass the beginning stage, you can always go off by yourself. It's perfectly fine to say, "I'm going to try that next pool for a while. I'll meet you later by the big rock," and, in so doing, getting out of earshot of any self-appointed font of wisdom.

But not your boyfriend

Guys have as about as much patience teaching fishing to women as they do teaching driving. You may luck out and have a terrific, unselfish guy to learn from, but just as often, asking your boyfriend to teach you to fish is as good as asking for an argument. If any of your women friends know how to fish, this is a much better route. I think of myself as a pretty liberated guy and a patient teacher. I have taught my eldest daughter a lot about fishing, but I was amazed one summer afternoon on the Lamar River in Yellowstone Park to watch how rapidly and easily she picked things up from a woman angler who joined us that day. There wasn't a whole lot of competitiveness, and I have to admit that my daughter learned more in that session than I could have shown her in five afternoons.

Guides

Wherever you find good fishing, you can usually find professional guides to take you fishing. Many anglers try to impress their guides with stories of the places they've been and the fish they've caught. They bristle when their guides try to improve their fishing techniques. This is downright silly. A good guide is on the water from 200 to 300 days per year. Any guide can teach amateur anglers something. Apart from listening for a guide's advice, anglers can also learn by keeping their eyes open. As the great Hall of Fame catcher, Yogi Berra, once said, "You can observe a lot just by watchin'."

Guide service can cost anywhere from $50 to $600 per guide per day. Some guides are patient, but others are like Marine drill sergeants who feel that they have to subdue every angler into an obedient zombie. To find a good guide, personal endorsements are best. Articles mentioning good guides often appear in outdoor magazines. Many guides advertise. Professional outfitters can also give you references to guides. Tackle shop owners often have relationships with guides, so if you like and/or trust a tackle shop owner, that owner can also be a good source for recommendations.

Because people usually hire guides for special trips, I strongly advise you to take the time and effort to check out your prospective guide before you end up in a boat with someone who makes your skin crawl. Before you book a guide, talk to him or her on the phone if you can. Ask about the guide's policy if you have to cancel your booking. Ask the guide how he or she deals with bad weather. (Some guides cancel because of wind, rain, or cold. Other guides go fishing no matter what the weather and expect you to pay in full.) Finally, remember this: Only a rare guide *guarantees* fish. Don't expect the guide to feel sorry and give you a refund if you don't catch anything. If the fishing is crummy, you may get a discount or a refund, but that practice is the exception rather than the rule.

Schools

These days, you can take lessons for all the things that people just used to pick up somehow as part of everyday living: cooking lessons, parenting lessons, personal trainer sessions, and (most importantly for this book) fishing lessons. Fly-fishing, being a pretty pricey sport, is taught at all kinds of schools. If you use conventional tackle (spinning and bait-casting), schools are available to teach you how to use it, too. You need to look for two kinds of fishing knowledge in a fishing school:

- **Fishing technique:** How to cast. How to hook, fight, land, and sometimes release a fish. When I began fishing, I went to a casting clinic for two days, and attending that clinic was the most valuable thing I ever did on the way to becoming an angler.

- **Fishing lore:** How does one read the water? What are the fish taking? What different lures, flies, or baits should you try and when? These questions are the kinds of questions that a beginner's course can start to answer. That being said, I find that people are more often frustrated by lack of technique than they are by lack of lore. After all, you can usually get a friend or relative to take you fishing. But if you can't use your rod and if you don't know how to tie your hook to your line, your fishing session isn't going to be very productive.

Magazines and books

"The Big Three" North American outdoor magazines (*Field & Stream, Sports Afield,* and *Outdoor Life*) have all been around for more than a century for a good reason. They are good and readers know it. They are full of useful information for both anglers and hunters. They deliver many how-to and where-to stories. I still pick up tips from all of them. Other specialty magazines are available for bass fishermen, fly fishermen, saltwater fishermen, and the like. And, of course, I recommend some books that I think most people would agree are good for the beginning angler. (See Chapters 24 and 25 for a complete listing.)

Prime learning directive: Use your eyes!

I can probably give you no more valuable piece of advice than this: *Watch the water!* Can you see fish feeding? How are they feeding? Are they slashing through a school of bait? Are they lazily cruising, looking for the odd bit of food? Are birds feeding on bugs or bait fish in the water? Where does the current go? Does the water contain currents within currents, and are fish feeding in the seams between currents? What places look as if they would provide the best protection for a fish who wants to be near food and feel safe at the same time?

No matter how good an angler you become, you can always be more productive on the water if you stop to look first. We all want to rush from the car and immediately heave our lines into the water, but you can do a million percent better if you study the water *before* you start fishing.

Four Things That I Wish Somebody Had Told Me About When I Started

So now you know what a fish is, what it likes to eat, and where it lives. You have your brand new rod and reel, and you are ready to go. Let me clue you in to a few things to avoid in *all* fishing situations!

1. Bad vibrations

When it comes to fishing (with apologies to any Grateful Deadheads who may be reading this), there are no such things as "good vibes." In fishing, all vibrations are bad. I am talking about clanking oars on the bottom of your aluminum boat, running your motor near feeding fish, or wading through a quiet pool like a 250-pound fullback busting through a gang of linebackers. Check out the special sensory organ called *the lateral line* shown in Figure 1-1. This organ basically enables fish to "see" vibrations.

Why would a fish want to see vibrations? Predators make vibrations. To a fish, vibrations mean that danger is nearby (like, for example, an angler).

2. Lures that look as natural as Godzilla

Some lures are designed to catch fish, and other lures are designed to catch fishermen. Often, the ones that look best to you don't have a prayer of catching a fish. Realistic paint jobs, eyes that blink, fins that wiggle in your hand look as real as a Barbie doll and work about as well (in fact, though I have never tried it, Barbie or Ken might work even better than some lures if you're going for a shark or some other major meat eater). Stick with the tried and true experience-tested lures. You won't catch fish *all* the time, but you will catch fish *some* of the time.

3. Shadows of evil

Hawks throw shadows on the water. So do bears, eagles, ospreys, otters, alligators, raccoons, fishermen, and anything else that eats fish. Through thousands of generations of breeding, those fish that weren't afraid of shadows were eaten. In this way, natural selection had bred extreme caution into any fish that you will be interested in catching. So take note of the sun (or on bright nights, the moon) and be careful to keep your shadow away from the fish.

4. Your Budweiser hat

Don't get me wrong. I have nothing against loud, garish clothes. After all, if you can't escape the Good Taste Police when you are out fishing, you need to find a new pastime. However, Day-Glo fishingwear on a stream or lake is not the ideal camouflage. If you're out for a day trolling on the ocean, well, go ahead and wear whatever you want.

The Dog Ate My Homework (Or Why You Need a License)

I do not pay many taxes happily. However, I don't have a problem with paying for my fishing license. Clean streams, public access, stocking, disease eradication, senior citizen programs, juniors programs — all are paid for, in large part, by fees paid by anglers. In this age of downsizing and trimming of government programs, you can be sure that some legislators would go after funds now spent on fishing if sportsmen and women were not on the pay-as-you-go system of yearly fishing licenses.

Rules change from place to place; but in general, only small children and senior citizens are exempt from license fees. Some states do not require them for saltwater fishing, but many — a growing number — do. Almost every state requires that you have your license in your possession when fishing.

If you are fishing as an out-of-stater, chances are, you must pay a higher fee for the privilege of fishing than in-state residents. I have no idea why this isn't considered unfair gouging, but it is the law, so don't fight it. After all, who needs hassles on a fishing trip? The point, or at least one of the points, of going fishing is to leave those kinds of problems back in the everyday world.

Chapter 2

The End of Your Line: Bait

You may have the world's most expensive rod, the greatest reel, and the fish sense of an osprey, but whether you fish with fly, bait, or lure, none of these assets matter if the thing at the end of your line does not *look* or *act* like something the fish wants to eat or chase from its territory.

A fish will go for your hook for two reasons:

✔ It's hungry

✔ It's angry

In general, fish strike because they are hungry. Fish, like humans, want something for nothing, and in most cases, they take whatever you have on your line as an easy meal, *provided you're using what they want.* Often, simply offering food isn't enough. A stream, lake, ocean has many types of potential fish food. Your job is to figure out what the fish is in the mood for. Or, if the fish isn't in the mood, then your job is to bring off an irresistible seduction.

Bait: Real Food for Real Fish

In all likelihood, the first fishermen did not use bait. They used sharp sticks, spears, or their bare hands. Bait fishing came along when some smart human had the idea that there had to be an easier way: Instead of you chasing the fish, why not make the fish come to you by offering it something to eat?

What qualifies as bait?

Anything that works. Although many anglers, especially young ones, have had good luck with cheese bits, corn kernels, and bread balls, some kind of meat from the fish's environment is always the best bait. Anglers use craw-fish, minnows, crickets, leeches, and hundreds of other animals — alive or dead, whole or in pieces. Still, if you had to choose one, it may as well be the earthworm.

Can live bait be dead?

The short answer is yes. Many game fish take bait that is dead. I guess the theory is that fish consider it fresh meat that won't try to escape. "Live" really means "recently alive." In saltwater fishing, for example, you may fish chunks of mossbunker or strips of ballyhoo. This bait is anything but live, but it's still called *live bait*. The real consideration is *fresh* versus *spoiled* bait. Go for the fresh. The fish will.

Freshwater Bait

At one time or another, somebody, somewhere, has tried just about every-thing to catch a fish: peaches, candy corn, leftover lamb chops, dead (and sometimes not dead) goldfish from the aquarium. But for the most part, fish like to eat things that they find in their natural environment: insects, worms, other fish, and fish eggs. And, through centuries of trial and error, anglers have narrowed their bait choices to a few reliables. This section covers the most popular bait for freshwater fish.

By the way, the reason you find certain baits in bait shops is that they really work.

Why do they call them night crawlers?

No big mystery here. The big juicy worms called night crawlers like to crawl around above ground at night. They are far and away the most popular bait in the world for at least four reasons:

- ✔ They are easy to find. You'll come across them in leafy piles any time of day or squiggling around on the front lawn at night.

- ✔ They are easy to catch. There is no such thing as a racing worm. They may wriggle out of your hand, but still, it doesn't take a lot of skill and speed to pick up a worm.

✔ They are cheap to buy if you don't feel like running around a wet lawn at night.

✔ They catch fish. I don't know why it is that fish who have never seen an earthworm will attack a worm on the end of your line. Maybe the reason is that there are so many other creatures that look like earthworms in the fish's environment. Little eels, snakes, and other kinds of aquatic worms live in the water, and fish feed on them readily. Not to say that earthworms don't get washed into the water as well: A big mud-producing rain can wash a decent number of worms into the water, where it's fair to say that "a worm in a stream is like a fish out of water." In other words, it's easy prey.

How to hook a worm (and not say ugh!)

There are three standard ways to put a worm on your hook. Each is illustrated in Figure 2-1.

✔ The simplest is to push the hook through the smooth or *collar* section of the worm (A).

✔ It takes a little more finesse, but another method is to put the point through the top of the head and then out through the collar. It gives the worm great action when you move it through the water (B).

✔ *Texas rigging* is just like the preceding method, except that you turn the hook around and bury the point in the collar so that the worm doesn't hang up in weeds or rocks (C).

As far as being grossed out is concerned, get over it. My daughter can do it, and so can you.

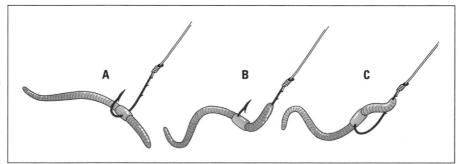

Figure 2-1: Three ways to hook a worm.

How to store your worms and stay married

Nothing smells as bad as bait that has been cooking in the car for a few days. And the smell *never* comes out of the car, your clothes, or your garage. You can only do two things with unused bait: Store it properly or heave it. With worms, a cool, dark place and a can or bucket filled with loosely packed earth does the trick. If you want to keep worms for a few days (or if you get really attached to them and want to keep them as pets), you need to feed them with some crumbled up cereal, hard-boiled eggs, or maybe some suet.

Minnows and other midget fish

When people talk of minnows, they are usually talking about a whole range of small bait fish. In addition to true minnows, some of the fish that are lumped in this category include chubs, shiners, suckers, smelt, sculpin, and alewives. The important thing for you to remember is that big fish *love* to eat little fish. If you open the belly of any trophy-sized fish, you'll find that small fish account for most of the food in its stomach.

There is something very exciting about casting a minnow into the water and watching your line as the minnow swims around. When a large fish approaches, the minnow gets very excited (you would too if you were in the minnow's shoes). Let the fish take the minnow for a few moments before you try to rear back and set the hook.

Rigging a small bait fish

Two of the most common ways of rigging a minnow are to run the hook through both lips or to pass the hook through the top part of the body just behind the dorsal fin (see Figure 2-2). Be careful when you cast. If you really muscle it, all you will succeed in doing is ripping the minnow off the hook and watching it fly into the water without doing you any good.

Rattlin' worms, Cajun style

Of all the ways I have seen for catching bait, the most surprising was shown to me by two Cajun fishermen in the little town of Washington, Louisiana. I was going to a catfish dinner with Herman Biedstrop and Reynard Soileau when they said, "Wanna see us rattle up some worms?" Since I was a guest, I said, "Sure," and they pulled their pickup truck to the side of the road. Reynard grabbed two sticks from the back of the truck. One of them had a line of notches running up its whole length. He rubbed the smooth stick over the notches and it made a rattling sound. Within seconds, the ground erupted with hundreds of wriggling worms. Something about the vibration of the notched stick just drove them to distraction. So if you know a place where there are worms, this trick is a pretty foolproof way to get a mess of 'em.

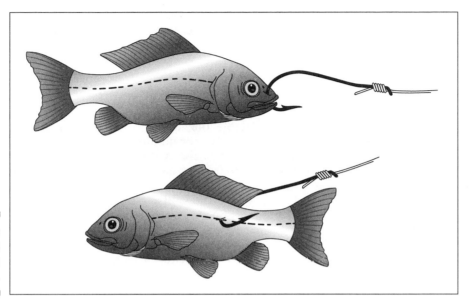

Figure 2-2:
Two ways
to hook a
minnow.

Alewives

This small herring, sometimes known as a sawbelly, is a prolific food and a spectacular bait. Fish them just like a minnow. I have caught many small-mouth on them in the reservoirs of the northeast U.S., and in the midwest, you have a real shot at enormous (upwards of 10 lbs.) trout in the Great Lakes.

I remember fishing in float tubes on the coast of Door County, Wisconsin, some years ago with a pioneer of Great Lakes fly-fishing, Bob Nasby. It was autumn, when the big brown trout congregate at the mouths of small streams, in the hope of getting them to spawn. We were using a fly tied to look like a sawbelly. Although the fishing was tough, as it often is when fish have spawning on their mind, they did take the occasional fly. Mostly what they did was jump out of the water right in front of you. They sounded like a Labrador retriever jumping into a swimming pool. It gets you so excited you can hardly cast. They tell me that in midsummer, the huge trout pen up the sawbellies in a murderous feeding frenzy. If you can get to the Great Lakes at this time of year, try some alewives on your hook.

Icing before driving

Live bait fish are hard to keep alive for very long. Usually, the water heats up and is depleted of oxygen. If you put a trayful of ice cubes in the bait bucket before you set off on a long drive, you improve the chances of your bait surviving. It's best to put the cubes in a plastic bag instead of taking a chance of having the chlorine in the tap water poison the fish. Also, go easy on the ice. You are trying to keep the fish active and spry, not flash freeze them.

Hellgrammites: major league ugly

There are a lot of unpalatable looking things in the water, but if forced to make a decision for the title of Ugliest Bait Alive, it would have to be a toss-up between the bloodworm favored by the striped bass and the hellgrammite used in streams for trout and bass. This larva of the Dobson fly (don't ask me what it looks like 'cause I've never seen one) is dark, with pincers and many legs. I have never caught a fish on a hellgrammite, but they are sold everywhere, and most books mention them, so perhaps it's just me.

Figure 2-3 shows you how to hook a hellgrammite. You place the hook right behind the head to avoid being pinched. This rig allows the hellgrammite to move freely.

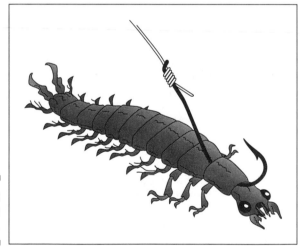

Figure 2-3:
Hooking a
hellgrammite.

Crawfish

Cajun food has become very popular among humans in the last ten years, but crawfish have been a favorite of fish for a very long time. It is the best smallmouth bait I know. Look for crawfish under rocks in the riffles of a stream. You can catch them with a seine, or net, that you position a few feet downstream. Stir up the bottom where the crawfish live, and when your debris floats down to your net, you will probably find a good number of crawfish ready to be harvested. Crawfish keep well in damp moss. If you put them in still water, they use up the oxygen very quickly and die.

To rig a crawfish, place the hook in the tail, as shown in Figure 2-4. Hooking it in this location allows the crawfish to move around freely so that it can attract the attention of foraging fish. In deep lakes, to get the crawfish down to where the fish are feeding, use a sinker that pulls off easily when it becomes lodged in subsurface rocks. The sinker will pull off if it hangs up so that you can keep fishing without losing your crawfish.

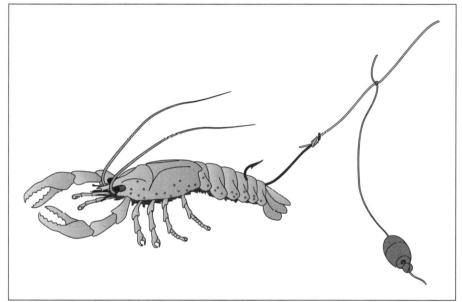

Figure 2-4:
A hooked crawfish with a sinker on the line.

Grasshoppers and crickets

Crickets and hoppers are terrific bait for bass, trout, and all kinds of panfish. They move around a lot, attracting attention when they hit the water, and they are big enough for a fish to expend the energy required to leave its lair, rise to the surface, and eat. In summer, when the fields are full of hoppers, game fish are particularly tuned on to them. Crickets were pretty much designed to be cast with a cane pole. The touch and mechanics required for cane pole fishing can be instantly translated to handling a fly rod. This may explain why all through the southern U.S., wherever one sees bank fishermen with cane poles, there is often a flyrodder or two thrown in fishing for such unsnobby fish as bluegill, crappie, and goggle eye.

You hook a grasshopper through the collar just behind the head, as illustrated in Figure 2-5. You need to cast delicately because a hard cast may rip the collar away from the body.

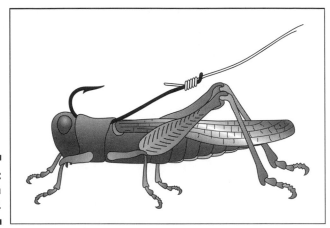

Figure 2-5:
Hooking a
grasshopper.

Leeches

Dark and slimy, leeches are pretty ugly and guaranteed to turn off small children. They are, however, a good bait for many species, including my favorite, walleye. I don't have a whole lot to say about leeches other than don't worry about them attacking you and sucking out all your blood. They are not that interested, especially when you are sticking a hook through them.

Hook a leech through the sucker as seen in Figure 2-6 and it will try to swim away. This is a good thing. Its body stays fairly straight when its trying to swim, which helps counteract the leech's tendency to ball up on your hook. Notice the word "helps": Sooner or later, most leeches ball up.

Salmon eggs

When the great runs of Pacific Salmon make their spawning journey up the rivers of the northwestern U.S., both the grizzly bears and the rainbow trout are very happy. The grizzlies love it because the streams are full of spawned-out, weak, easily caught salmon. The rainbows love it because the streams are full of delicious, easy-to-catch salmon eggs. (Of course, those rainbows that get eaten by the aforementioned grizzly bears are probably not that happy.)

The eggs of salmon are delicate, and casting them requires the kind of soft touch that you use for crickets and grasshoppers. Figure 2-7 shows how to hook one.

Figure 2-6:
A leech
hooked
through the
sucker.

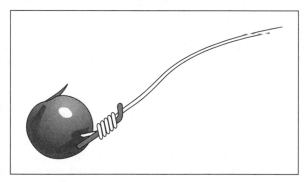

Figure 2-7:
Hooking a
salmon egg.

You have to use a special hook, a short-shanked, rounded-gap brass hook, which you bury completely in the egg to give the hook maximum holding power and castability.

Saltwater Bait

If it is alive and in the ocean, chances are, there is something in the ocean that will eat it. Saltwater fish are great opportunists, which means that if you give them an opportunity, they will eat. Like their freshwater cousins, however, saltwater fish do have some preferences, and the biggest tarpon or striped bass might prefer a tiny two inch worm to that big juicy herring. Just because saltwater fish are big doesn't mean they are stupid. What follows are some of the baits that I like — because I catch fish with them.

Clams and mussels

Fish, like people, find shellfish easier to eat once the shells are removed. There's not a whole lot of technique to discuss here. I recommend cutting your bait into bite-sized pieces, particularly for flounder or fluke. A big piece of soft bait allows the fish to pull the bait off the hook without your knowing it.

Worms

Fishermen use a number of worm species for bait, but the most common is the bloodworm. Cut a piece off of one and the liquid that squooshes out looks like blood. These many-sectioned, pincer-headed worms give hellgrammites a run for their money in the ugly department, and they can be very effective bait. As with mussels and clams, use small pieces for small fish. For bluefish and stripers, use a whole worm hooked right behind the head.

Bunker

The bunker or Atlantic menhaden is a prolific bait fish off the east coast of the U.S. They arrive in huge schools, and one can often see equally large schools of bluefish and bass slashing through them as they feed. It is a sight that never fails to excite the angler. When the bunker are in, you can snag them with weighted treble hooks expressly manufactured for this purpose. All you do is heave your hook in the middle of a school of bunker. Then reel in and really haul back on your rod as you do so, and you will probably snag a bunker. Put it in a live well, and when you have a half a dozen or so, you are ready to go fishing for stripers and blues, weakfish, and even tuna.

Squid

It's hard to fish a squid incorrectly. Fresh or frozen, whole or in pieces, they are a preferred food for everything from tuna to striped bass, sea bass, and flounder.

Grass shrimp

In many tidal flats, grass shrimp thrive in the underwater vegetation. When they get swept up in moving tides, they are a very good bait for striped bass, weakfish, redfish, bonefish, and just about anything else that feeds around beds of seagrass in shallow water.

You hook a shrimp by carefully threading the hook through the tail (see Figure 2-8). With this rig, the shrimp may still move about, attracting the attention of feeding fish.

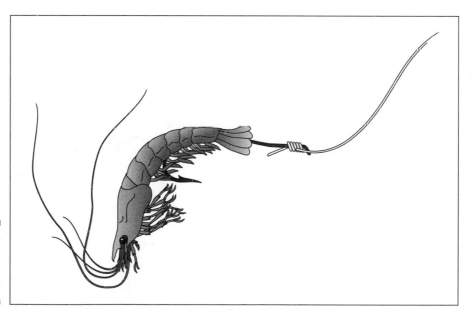

Figure 2-8:
Hooking a
grass
shrimp.

Mullet

These good-sized bait fish move in huge schools. They make quite a distur-bance and never fail to distract me from concentrating on what's on my line. You'll be standing there on some jetty and the mullet will all break the surface with a loud "whoosh." You think it's a big fish breaking water and you turn to see all these little rounded mullet snouts sticking out of the water like seals in the zoo begging for a snack. Many fishermen capture their mullet by casting a round, weighted net into a school. This method requires a good deal of skill and practice. Often it requires holding one end of the net in your teeth. If you get a good strong cast going, I'm sure you can set a new distance record for heaving your dentures. Insert a hook into a live mullet the way you would a minnow or alewife. Redfish, bass, blues, marlin, and tuna all take mullet.

Eels: the ultimate slime

On the east coast of the U.S., especially in the northeast, eels are about the best striper bait going. They move about and make a lot of commotion. And they're big enough to make a nice meal. They are also the slimiest thing since Jiffy Lube. If a live eel drifting in the tidal current doesn't call up a bass, chances are there are none around — or at least none that are interested in food.

To hook an eel, while holding it with a towel or rag, insert the hook through the jaw and nose, as shown in Figure 2-9.

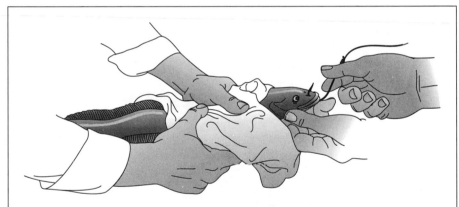

Figure 2-9: Hooking an eel.

Stay put, you little bugger! In addition to being slimy, eels are very strong, and they wriggle like crazy. Put some ice in the bucket with your eels, enough to keep the water chilled in the bottom of the bucket. The cold calms them down so that they don't squirm out of your hand and wriggle all over the boat.

Chapter 3

Lures

• •

• •

*B*ait is great, but many times *lures* are better. True, you can just heave your bait out there and sit back and relax until something bites, but some anglers (I am one of them) prefer to be doing something other than waiting for the tap-tap-tap of a fish on the line. When you'd rather be actively fishing than just waiting for action, lures (sometimes called *artificials*) are the hook vehicle of choice.

I never argue with another angler about his or her preference of bait versus artificials: I mean, fishing is supposed to be a hassle-free pastime, and my philosophy is "fish and let fish." Still, lures, in general, present two advantages over most baits:

✔ You can reuse a lure many times. A bait is usually shot after one fish has chomped it to pieces.

✔ You can cover a great deal more water with a lure than you can with a bait. Therefore, many more fish are likely to see your offering.

Many Are Chosen, but Only a Few Will Do

Whenever I walk into a tackle shop, I think of a comment that Abraham Lincoln once made about poor people, except I substitute the words *fishing lures* for *the poor:* "God must love fishing lures because he made so many of them."

Literally thousands of lures are available. From dual-propellered, double-jointed rattlers as big as a Humvee (or at least they seem that way) to tiny lead-head bucktail jigs and from little scale models of trout that look absolutely lifelike to floating salads of rubber legs and metal blades that look like something that came to life in the junkyard of a toy factory — so many lures are available that you could go bankrupt buying them all. But you can do very well without 99.9 percent of them. Many are just endless variations on a single theme. Others have been improved upon by new technologies.

You don't need that many lures to handle most fishing situations. I probably have fewer than two dozen; and if I were absolutely ruthless, I could reduce this total to a dozen and still catch as many fish.

When you are considering buying and using a lure, ask the following eight questions:

How deep does the lure run?

If you want your lure to catch fish, then you have to put it in a place where the fish are. If the fish you're hoping to catch are hanging out five feet below the surface in cool water, you're probably going to have to go to them (that is, you must fish at their level) rather than have them come to you at the surface. On the other hand, if they are busy feeding on the surface, a deep-running lure won't be very effective.

What kind of action does the lure have?

When you retrieve the lure, does it wobble and shimmy, does it dive and surface, does it burble and pop, or does it chug and sputter? Any of these characteristics can serve either to excite a fish or to turn it off. The same noisy lure that may entice a bass out of its shadowy hole on a hot day is guaranteed to send a bonefish on a beeline for the Continental Shelf. Different actions suit different fish. Different water also dictates different action. (The pronounced action that spurs a bite in off-color water can be a real loser in clear water.)

How fast is the lure designed to move through the water?

Because of the advances in reel-making technology, a few cranks of a reel's handle can move a lure through the water more swiftly than was possible in the old days. This fast response is good because sometimes a fish (like a pike or muskie) flashes after a swift-running lure while it ignores a slowpoke. However, many old standby lures act very erratically when you crank up the speed. What you want to know is the range of speed that is optimum for any lure.

How big should the lure be?

Although the general rule of "big bait, big fish" is usually a good one to follow, the optimum size of a lure is important and it may vary from place to place. In one place, for example, trout may grow fat on grass shrimp. In another, trout may be keyed in on alewives. Whatever the case, you want to use the right size lure to attract them. This rule of thumb doesn't mean that your lure must always slavishly imitate the size of a fish's food. Sometimes, a little bigger lure works well. At other times, a *much bigger* lure works better. The theory is that after a small lure has got them "out of the house" and feeding, they are really going to take notice of that nice big mouthful that you throw at them. I can't tell you what the right size lure is in any given situation, but fish can and do.

Does the lure raise a ruckus?

In the sense that sound consists of vibrations and all fish sense vibrations through their lateral lines, *all lures make a sound.* The question that you need to answer is this: What sounds turn fish on, and what sounds turn them off? As with everything in angling, no hard-and-fast rule applies, although certain tendencies apply under certain conditions. For example, in the bright light of day, a big, noisy lure (such as a Jitterbug) may not do very much to attract bass. At night, however, the gentle chugging of a Jitterbug can be just the thing to attract a bass in low-light conditions.

Does a lure's color count?

Yes and no. Fish *respond* to color, but they don't see color in the same way that you and I do. Take the color red. Red is the first color of lure that many people pick out, but after a red lure goes very deep in the water, that vibrant scarlet turns to dark gray. The thing to remember about color is that *water absorbs color differently than air,* so the brilliant hues of a lure in the air of a tackle shop may not even be visible to a fish in the water. Also, sunlight makes colors appear differently at different times during the day. Some anglers follow a system called fishing the spectrum, that takes account of what fish see and when they see it.

- ✔ **Dawn and dusk:** Use silver, blue, and green.

- ✔ **Late morning and afternoon:** As the day progresses, use yellow, orange, red, orange, and then yellow again, in that sequence.

- ✔ **In full sunlight:** Use red in shallow water, yellow in medium-deep water, and blue, green, or silver in deep water.

Look at color from a fish's point of view. Some years ago, I was fishing on the Esopus Creek in the Catskills, one of the historic streams of American trout fishing. Late in the afternoon, the fish were taking pink mayflies with purplish wings. I caught one of the mayflies in my hat and held it up to the sky. Seen, in silhouette, the mayfly had no color but black. I didn't have any purple and pink flies with me, but I picked an orange and yellow fly out of my box that was the right size and shape. I held it against the background of the sky. Seen against the backlight of the sky, its color was black too, and its silhouette was similar to that of the pink mayflies. What I learned was this: If you are fishing on or near the surface, color doesn't make much difference if the fish's view is from below.

Is a glittery lure good?

Glitter is good, and so is the contrast between light and dark, and so is iridescence. All of these qualities of light reflection suggest the play of light shining through water on the scales of a moving fish. For example, the Daredevle lure, which is probably the all-time fish taker in American waters, is nothing more than a spoon (with alternating wavy bands of red and white) that wobbles like a frantic fish. The shape, the wobbling motion, and the optical effect of the contrasting colors all trigger a feeding response in many game fish. In my opinion, lure colors could be black and white or green and white and still be as effective, but red seems to trigger a buying response among anglers.

Do taste and smell matter?

No. I know that this flat statement sounds a little curt, but I have never seen evidence that the taste or smell of a lure has much to do with anything. Actually, come to think of it, catfish do respond to stinky baits, but that's about it.

So Many Lures, but Only a Few Types

A lure is supposed to do any or all of the following:

- ✔ Look like a fish
- ✔ Move like a fish
- ✔ Splash like a fish
- ✔ Look or act like something that isn't a fish but that still is something that fish eat

Different lures emphasize some of these qualities but not others, but in one way or another, all lures share some of them. Lures may exhibit these qualities on the surface, a few feet down, or on the bottom. Ultimately, the lure you choose depends on what the fish want or what you can convince them that they want.

In putting together the following description of lures, I have given an example of my favorite in each category. Other anglers swear by other choices, but the ones I have chosen have worked for me; and I think that everybody (no matter what their personal preferences) would agree that the ones I have chosen are all great lures.

Plugs

A *plug* is something that looks like a fish that other fish want to eat. Plugs can swim, dive, pop, or burble, but they are all alike in that they look and act like bait fish. Before the big explosion in the use of spinning equipment that occurred after World War II, plugs had to be big enough to put a bend in the stiff bait-casting rods of that time. The mechanics of the spinning reel (you really don't want me to get into the physics of it, and even if you did, I would never get it right) allowed for much lighter lures than bait-casting reels.

One of the things that I really love about plugs is the *ka-chunk* sound they make as they hit the water. I'm sure that this sound has little to do with one's success as an angler other than the fact that it sounds like something ought to sound when you go fishing. A good cast and a seductive ka-chunk somehow give me confidence, and confidence breeds success in all sports.

Popping plugs

Because consistency has been called the hobgoblin of petty minds, let me begin by contradicting what I just said about *all* plugs imitating bait fish. Some lures, I am convinced, are seen as frogs, mice, little birds, and other nonaquatic creatures who find themselves out of their own element and in the fish's element. When cast to a weed line tight against a bank or under an overhanging bough: Sometimes a popper (such as those shown in Figure 3-1) can pull a nice fish from its lair even at high noon on a sunny day.

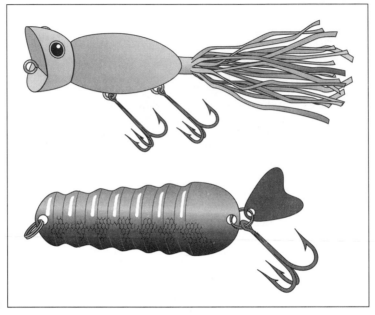

Figure 3-1:
The Hula
Popper
(top) is
great in
freshwater,
and the
Atom
(bottom) is
good in the
surf.

Plunking a Hula Popper beside a lily pad and giving it an occasional burble has lured many bass (and quite a few pike) over the years. The key here is not to be a blabbermouth with your lure. Fish don't like small talk. Let the Hula Popper hit the water and wait until the concussion rings subside. Then give it another pop. Wait again. You want to practice getting the maximum burp out of your popper with a minimum of commotion on the water. By using the plug that way, the Hula Popper stays in the fishy zone longer.

While pond fishing often calls for restraint with a Hula Popper, casting an Atom into a wolf pack of marauding bluefish calls for a different understanding of fish psychology. When a great deal of bait is in the water, you want to draw attention to your plug so that the fish keys in on it and ignores the thousands of other bait fish all around. A loud, splashy plug, fished very fast with a jerky motion, often works in this situation.

TIP

If I had only one lure

My favorite lure is the Rapala, which is a plug made by the Rapala company of Finland. I love the way this plug lands in the water; and even more, I love the way that it moves in the water. I have caught bass, trout, pike, bluefish, and even tarpon on the Rapala. *Outdoor Life* once sent me to Finland to research the story behind these phenomenal plugs that had become so popular all over America. What I found was an unusual story for a sport-fishing lure.

At the turn of the 20th Century, Americans began to make a plug called a *wobbler.* The wobbler was a little wooden fish that wobbled like a distressed minnow. Some of these plugs found their way over to Finland where a woodsman and fisherman named Lauri Rapala began to fish with them. By *woodsman and fisherman,* I don't mean a guy who worked in a factory all week and went fishing on the weekends. I mean a guy who chopped wood and caught fish for a living.

You have to be a pretty fair fisherman to keep your family fed and clothed on your take from the lakes of Finland. These lakes are not very rich, and the fish — mostly trout — are few and far between. A good lure meant more to Lauri Rapala than a nice fishing trip. Lauri *had* to catch fish.

The plug that he devised, the one that came to be known as the Rapala, was designed for trolling. Not trolling behind a big powerful boat, but trolling behind a canoe-like boat paddled by Lauri. After a great deal of trial and error, Rapala's wobbler minnow began to wiggle and wobble behind him in a very tantalizing way. It caught fish better than anything ever had in those hard-fished northern lakes, and the Rapala went from being a commercial fisherman's preferred tool to one of the most effective weapons in the sport-fishing arsenal. That *Life* magazine published a story about the Rapala plug in an issue that featured Marilyn Monroe in a nude swimming sequence didn't hurt either.

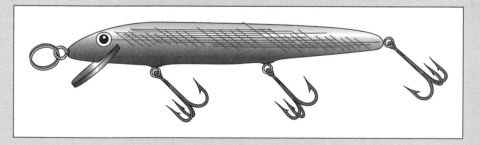

Plugs that swim

Swimmers (swimming plugs) do just that: They swim, just as bait fish swim. Swimmers can swim on the water's surface, just under it, or even deeper. Some swimmers make a big commotion, and some move sleekly through the water.

A number of fine plugs swim at or near the surface. The Rebel is one of these, and the Lazy-Ike is another. Most swimmers float until you begin to reel them in. With many swimmers, the faster you reel, the deeper they dive (although even deep-running plugs have a cutoff depth beyond which you cannot fish them).

Plugs that go a little deeper

Some plugs dive deeper than others. In many cases, this deep diving is a function of the angle of the lip. The sharper the angle of the lip and the faster the retrieve, the deeper the plug dives. With this in mind, you might cast your plug over a submerged weed bed that you know lies three or four feet below the surface. Weed beds provide a number of food sources, and game fish know this. As your plug travels over the weeds, you want to get it down to the level of the fish. If they don't see the plug, they ain't gonna bite it. By experimenting with a few different retrieval speeds, you can see (and eventually feel) the depth at which your plug runs. Plugs in this go-a-little-deeper category include the Countdown Rapala, the Flatfish, and the Rebel Deep Runner (shown in Figure 3-2).

Many diving plugs dive only when you retrieve them. When you stop the retrieve, they float to the surface (which is a good thing to bear in mind when your plug is passing over submerged rocks and stumps). Instead of reeling furiously, let the plug rise to the surface, and you will avoid hanging up on underwater hazards.

Deep divers

Some years ago, *Outdoor Life* sent me up to the Saint Lawrence River in pursuit of muskellunge. Common wisdom has it that you have to fish 10,000 hours to catch a muskie. I wasn't counting, but I must have fished only 9,999 hours because I finished the trip muskie-less. I did catch a large number of northern pike and both smallmouth and largemouth bass on the deep-running plugs that I was using for muskies, the Bomber and the Waterdog (shown in Figure 3-3). These plugs are also known as *crankbaits*.

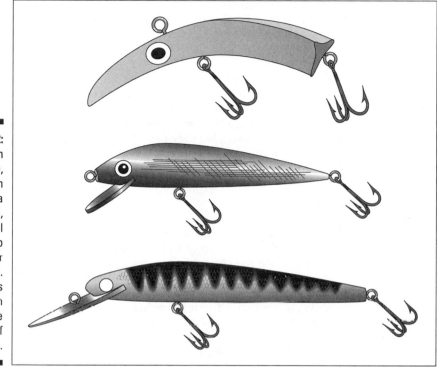

Figure 3-2:
The Flatfish (top), Countdown Rapala (middle), and Rebel Deep Runner (bottom). Three plugs that work in the middle range of depth.

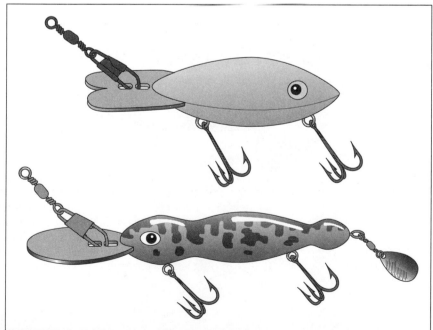

Figure 3-3:
The Bomber (top) and Waterdog (bottom). Their long "wobble plates" enable them to dive deeply, and these plates also help keep the hooks from hanging up on snags.

Depending on design, crankbaits work well at different depths, although no lure runs very well beyond 35 feet deep unless the lure is weighted. Crankbait design allows them to move well through weeds and around obstacles.

Suppose that the fish in the lake are *suspended* (hanging out) at seven feet below the water surface. So you run to the tackle store and buy a lure that says that it runs at seven feet below the water surface. Next year, you return to the lake, and you have no idea which lure in your box is the seven footer. The solution is simple: Take a laundry pencil and write the optimum running depth on the belly of the lure.

Chuggers

The ka-chunk of a plug hitting the water is one of those things that just *sounds* like fishing. To that group of sounds that induce a sense of angler well-being, I would add the *chug-chug* of a Jitterbug making its way across a bass pond on a warm summer night. A Jitterbug sounds like an old car engine, sputtering far in the distance. This plug has been used almost forever, and it catches fish without requiring a great amount of finesse on the part of the angler. I would recommend the Jitterbug (shown in Figure 3-4) right up there with the Rapala as a newcomer's tool: The appropriate action has been designed into the Jitterbug — all you have to do to attract a bass to it is reel it in at a few different speeds.

Figure 3-4:
The Arbogast Jitterbug, a great American bass lure.

Stickbaits: Some take some skill, and some do the work for you

A *stickbait*, until you do something to it, just lays there on the water like — you guessed it — a stick! A stickbait needs to be jerked, twitched, and popped by the angler before it has any action. For this reason, I don't know if a stickbait is the kind of lure that a beginner would want to use. *However* — and this is a big *however* — somebody had the bright idea of putting propellers on stickbaits, and (all of a sudden) fishing aficionados had a lure with built-in action and fish-attracting commotion. Modified stickbaits, like the Devil's Horse shown in Figure 3-5, *chug-plop-gurgle* and wobble around, all of which are good features that might gain the attention of any predatory fish in the neighborhood. The propellers move in two different directions, so they don't twist your line. This is not something you'd want to see in an airplane's propellers, but it works fine for fishing lures.

Figure 3-5: The Devil's Horse is a stickbait with fore and aft propellers.

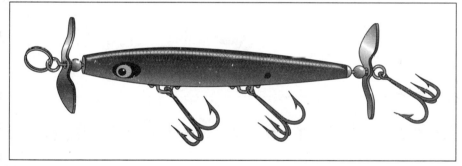

Jerkbaits

Jerkbaits (shown in Figure 3-6) get all their action from the way that the user retrieves the plug: fast jerks, erratic jerks, or trolling. Many anglers think that the action of these plugs resembles the action of a distressed or injured bait fish, the kind of bait that muskies and pike, for example, find very attractive. While I'm on the subject, let me clear up one thing: Jerkbaits are not necessarily used by jerks. (Although if people don't jerk the jerkbait while retrieving it, then you can draw your own conclusions.)

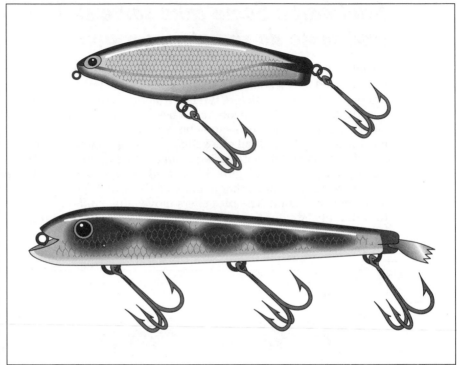

Figure 3-6:
High-
buoyancy
jerkbaits,
such as the
Bobbie Bait
(top), have
a lip to help
them dive.
Low-
buoyancy
jerkbaits,
such as the
"B" Flat
Shiner
(bottom),
are
weighted to
help them
sink deep.

Spoons (And Why They Call Them That)

This is a question that I asked when I started fishing. The answer is: In the old days, people fished with real tablespoons with hooks attached.

When you look at the business end of a tablespoon, you see that it's shaped somewhat like a fish. It also has some metallic sheen, and (by the nature of its design) it has shaded portions as well, so it presents that contrast between light and dark that is characteristic of many successful lures.

Spoons come in all sizes and colors. You can fish them just as they are (as fans of the Phoebe lure do), or you can attach a strip of pork rind as the partisans of the Johnson Silver Minnow lure do.

The champ came from Detroit

Back at the turn of the century, kids in the working-class neighborhoods of Detroit would take a trolley car to the end of the line and fish in the Detroit River. One of those kids, Lou Eppinger, grew up to run a small taxidermy and tackle shop. In 1906, he went on a fishing vacation in Ontario, where he spent a month by himself fishing. He brought a new spoon that he had designed. It was heavy — two ounces — so he could cast it with the clunky bait-casting rods that most anglers used in the days before spinning made light lures a possibility. Eppinger hammered out the metal so that it was thinner in the middle and thicker at the edges. This imbalance gave his spoon a pronounced wobble. The lure *almost* turned over when it was reeled in, but it *always* righted itself. Eppinger caught a great number of fish with the spoon, and when he returned from his vacation, he began to sell the lure that he first called The Osprey.

When World War I came along, the United States Marines made quite a name for themselves and began to be known as daredevils. Eppinger admired the Marines, but being a God-fearing man, he couldn't bring himself to write the word *Devil*. So, in honor of the Marines and in keeping with the teachings of his Lutheran pastor, Eppinger called his new spoon the Daredevle. Shown in the following figure, the Daredevle is one of the most successful lures for all kinds of fish. Midwestern pike fishermen swear by it, but so do Ozark smallmouth anglers, Louisiana redfishers, and even tropical bonefishers.

Spinners

The advent of spinning tackle enabled anglers to use much lighter lures than the heavier lures required with bait-casting equipment. There are a number of reasons, both practical and as a matter of preference, why light is nice.

- Light lures, when they land, make less disturbance that do bait-casting lures; and light lures, therefore, provide less chance of spooking fish.

- Light lures are smaller, as a rule, than bait-casting lures, and sometimes small is what game fish are looking for.

- Light lures require light line — that is, line that breaks more easily if you pressure it. Many anglers enjoy the challenge of landing a hard-fighting fish on light line because doing so takes more skill than "just horsing it in" with heavy line. Look at it this way: After you hook a 1-pound trout on 12-pound-test line (line that breaks when subjected to 12 pounds of pressure), the end of the battle is a foregone conclusion. The angler wins. Hook the same fish on 2-pound-test line and you'd better have a good touch if you don't want to lose it.

Your basic spinner has a little blade that looks like a miniature spoon. The blade is attached to the lure in such a way that the lure can spin and wobble as it is pulled through the water. Quite often, a piece of *bucktail* (deer hair), pork rind, or rubber is attached to the spinner to give it some extra length and wiggle. A basic spinner is shown in Figure 3-7.

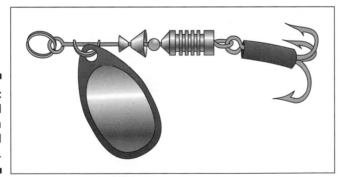

Figure 3-7:
A typical spinner: a hook and a blade.

Spinners enable you to cover a great deal of water in order to locate fish. If the fish rush your spinner but don't strike, try a different type of lure; but at least your use of a spinner has helped you to locate your quarry.

Spinners spin, and a spinning lure that spins the way it was designed to spin *always* twists your line. This line twisting can lead to all kinds of backlash problems. The solution to these problems is simple: When using a spinner, always use a swivel.

The Three Ages of the Fisherman

When he wants to catch all the fish he can.

When he strives to catch the largest fish.

When he studies to catch the most difficult fish he can find, requiring the greatest skill and most refined tackle, caring more for the sport than the fish.

—Edward Ringwood Hewitt

(from Charles F. Waterman, *A History of Angling,* Winchester Press)

Spinnerbaits

If spinnerbaits had mothers, even they would be hard pressed to say their little ones were good-looking. The spinnerbait is one of the most gizmo-like lures. But remember: It's not how a lure looks to you that's important. What's important is how a lure looks to a fish. A *spinnerbait* moving through the water looks like a bait fish or other animal doing its best to get away in a hurry. This rapid action often triggers an attack response in game fish.

One tip that I learned from Gary Soucie's fine book, *Hook, Line, and Sinker,* is how to make a spinnerbait (like the one shown in Figure 3-8) weedless. All you need to do is loop a rubber band between the eye of the lure and the barb of the hook.

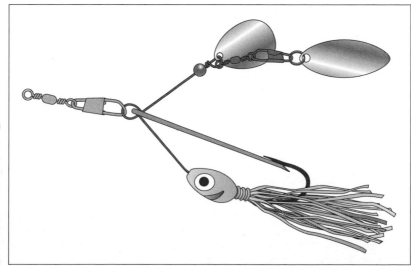

Figure 3-8: A spinnerbait with a rubber band that makes it weedless.

Buzzbaits, a special kind of spinnerbait

Some anglers call all spinnerbaits buzzbaits, and some anglers use the word *buzzing* to describe what they do with any topwater lure when they retrieve it rapidly. Technically speaking, a *buzzbait* is a spinnerbait with bell-shaped blades, like the Clacker (shown in Figure 3-9).

You can buzz with a buzzbait. You can also buzz with a spinner. The idea of buzzing is to retrieve a lure so rapidly that it skims along the surface of the water, creating a great deal of commotion and leaving a bubbly wake. The advantage of this technique is that you can use it to cover a large amount of water, and fish are often attracted by all the fuss. You can use the buzzing technique to locate fish. Then you can begin to fish more deliberately with other lures. Or you may get lucky while buzzing and actually hook something. The downside of buzzing is that it is the least weedless form of fishing — short of attacking a stand of lily pads with a garden rake.

Figure 3-9:
A true buzzbait has turbine-like blades like the ones on this Clacker.

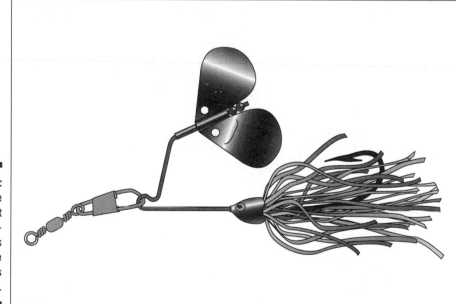

Jigs

A *jig* is a piece of metal, usually lead, with a hook attached. Jigs cast well in the wind, and they sink rapidly. With the addition of feathers, plastic tails, and pork rinds, jigs (such as the Hammertail shown in Figure 3-10) can imitate all kinds of bait. I think, though I have no data to back this up, that more fish have been caught on jigs than through any other method of fishing with artificial lures. Sometimes fish take a jig as it drops to the bottom. Or more commonly, the angler *jigs,* which means raising and lowering the rod tip to bounce the lure off the bottom. This motion stimulates a response in many fish.

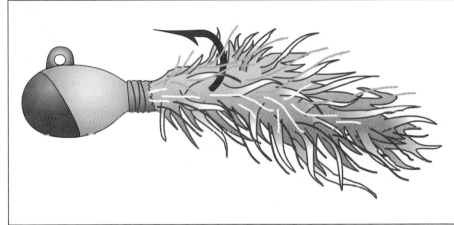

Figure 3-10:
The
Hammertail,
a typical
bucktail jig.

Bright lights, big city, big bass

Nothing ever convinced me of the value of jigs more than an experience that I had with an Argentine sportsman named Carlos Sanchez. I met him while I was on a *Field & Stream* assignment in the mountains of Patagonia (which is the closest thing to Trout Heaven that I have ever found). Carlos was such a good guide that I invited him out to Montauk Point, at the tip of Long Island. It was fall and the bluefish were running strong.

We fished hard for three days, running up and down the beaches and we caught diddly-squat. I kept telling Carlos, "Fishing for blues here at this time of year usually is great." And he kept giving me a look of flagging faith. When we got home to Brooklyn, the answering machine had a message from Dr. Gary Sherman that promised big bass; better still, his message advised that after we fished, he would drop Carlos and me at a pier in Manhattan and that we would still be back at my office by 10:00 a.m.

Sherman gave Carlos and me poles with 2-ounce lead-head bucktail jigs. He lined up our position by taking a reading from the World Trade Center and two church steeples in Brooklyn, and every time we passed over a little depression in the bottom of the harbor — *wham!* — we were into 15-pound striped bass. So it was the best striper fishing I had ever had up to that point, and it was a two-minute walk from my house and an equally short boat ride into New York harbor!

They call them jigs, but they look like spoons

A whole family of jigs (universally used in saltwater but also popular in freshwater, too) look more like spoons but technically are jigs. Why? The main answer is that "Somebody called this family *jigs* in a book, and every writer since then has followed the leader."

Actually, lures like the Hopkins, the diamond jig, and the Kastmaster (as shown in Figure 3-11) are all jig-like in that they are heavy metal, they cut through the wind, and they sink fast. However, on the retrieve, they are fished more like spoons, where their shine and bait-fish-like motion attracts game fish.

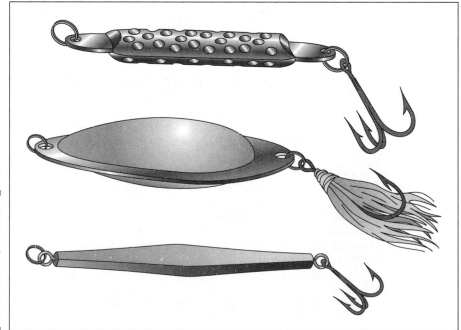

Figure 3-11:
A Hopkins (top), a Kastmaster (middle), and a Diamond jig (bottom).

The Hopkins is a descendant of the old tin squids (so-called, I guess, because somebody thought they look like squids). These lures were used by commercial surfcasters in the good old days before World War II when all the fish were as big as ponies, or so the yarn spinners would have us believe. The Kastmaster is one of the most beautiful designs of anything since the Great Pyramids (I mean it), and it is great for bluefish and the occasional striped bass. The diamond jig, especially when fished with surgical tubing, is a very effective surf lure if you fish it slow and hop it along the bottom. The tubing is soft on the fish's mouth, has the outline of an eel or a small fish, and comes in fish-attracting colors.

If You Had Only One: The Plastic Worm

Notice I said *you*. I personally prefer the Rapala to all other lures, but most fishermen will tell you that the plastic worm is the greatest thing since sliced bread. In fact, having tried both sliced bread (balls) and plastic worms, I think that plastic worms are even better than sliced bread. Plastic worms have become such a mainstay over the last 30 years that often the question one angler asks another is not "What lure are you using?" It could just as well be "What color are they taking?" That you are asking about the color of a plastic worm is understood.

Like a jig, a plastic worm can be taken as it lands, as it drops, or while it is bounced along the bottom. It can also be slithered off a lily pad or pulled off a log. In short, if you can think of a new way to fish a plastic worm, try it: Some fish somewhere may like it.

Rigging a plastic worm:
Texas versus Carolina

You can rig plastic worms in many ways. However, two ways that may get you through most situations: the Texas rig and the Carolina rig. First, the rig from Texas:

1. **If you want to fish deep down, put a lead-head sinker on your line before you tie the line to the hook.**

2. **Push the point of the hook through the head of the plastic worm about $1/2$ inch.**

3. **Pull the hook point out through the head of the plastic worm.**

4. **Push the hook through the plastic worm until the eye of the hook comes up against the head of the worm.**

5. **Turn the hook so that the point faces the body of the worm and bury the hook point in the worm as shown in Figure 3-12.**

Figure 3-12:
Use the
Texas
rig for
weedless
maneuvering.

Now for the Carolina rig, which allows the worm to float off the bottom:

1. **Put a slip sinker on the line above a swivel.**

2. **Tie a leader to the other end of the swivel.**

3. **Tie the leader through the eye of the hook.**

4. **Thread the plastic worm on the hook (see Figure 3-13) in the same way that is shown for the Texas rig.**

Figure 3-13:
Use the
Carolina rig
to stay
above
trouble.

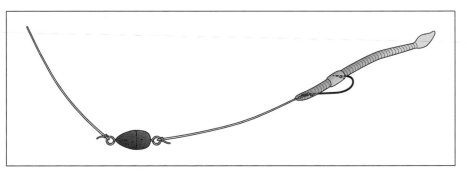

Avoiding Hook Salad: Tackle Boxes and Other Equipment

Lures cost money. The longer you fish, the more lures you have and the bigger your investment in gear. Lures, especially the treble-hook variety, have a way of getting caught up with other lures in the most unholy nest of prickly metal that you ever saw. A tackle box to store your lures, bobbers, hooks, and the like is an absolute must.

How big a tackle box should you buy? The answer to that question is the same as the answer to the question "How powerful a computer should I buy?" Figure out how much storage you could possibly need and then double it. You will eventually grow into your tackle box. A tackle box with many compartments is nice, but equally important is having enough big compartments to hold some oversized plugs. Otherwise, you may put those big plugs in the bottom of the box where they can snarl in your maps, bandages, leaders, and the like.

There are many good tackle-box manufacturers around, but a fairly universal brand that I recommend is Plano.

Things to include in any tackle box

In addition to basic fishing supplies, I recommend that you include the following in every tackle box:

- ✔ Matches (in a waterproof container)
- ✔ A small bottle of sunscreen
- ✔ Bandages (also in a waterproof container)
- ✔ A flashlight and extra flashlight batteries
- ✔ An extra car key in its own little box, which is attached to a *large* red-and-white round bobber (large enough so that the little box with the key won't sink)

Things not to include in any tackle box

Here's my list of never-includes for your tackle box:

- ✔ **Food:** I guarantee it to melt, crumble, and do everything it can to mess up your gear.
- ✔ **A whole mess of plastic worms and jelly grubs, all in the same compartment:** They can melt, possibly eat through the plastic of the box, magically attract treble hooks, small spinners, dog hair, and everything else until you have a useless, gloppy mass of stuff.

For surf fishermen

It is impractical — make that impossible — to run up and down the beach, chasing feeding schools of game fish while holding on to a tackle box. The *surf bag* — usually a canvas bag with some plastic cylinders inside to hold saltwater lures — is a great invention. Most surf bags hold about a dozen lures with side compartments for a hook sharpener, leaders, and the like.

Although surf bags are not that clumsy to carry, you may feel as if you want to take your bag off and lay it on the sand next to you while you fish for a close-to-shore school. *Don't.* One of two things can happen:

✔ The tide can come up all of a sudden, and it can take your surf bag on a never-to-be-seen-again voyage. Given the price of saltwater plugs, this loss can be a major bummer.

✔ If you find yourself in one spot for a while, chances are, you are into fish. The chances also are that some dune jockeys may come roaring down on you in their four-wheel-drive vehicles. I have learned from *crushing* experience that in the battle between four-wheel-drive vehicles and surf bags, the four-wheel-drive vehicles always win.

Chapter 4

Flies

• •

• •

*F*ly-fishing has a great deal of mystique — some people would say mumbo-jumbo — about it. Because fly-fishing was once practiced only by rich English gentlemen, it was thought to be a little bit of a closed club, the kind of club that only snobs could join. In fly-fishing, more Latin has been thrown around, more books have been written, and more choices have faced the angler (more than 2,000 recorded fly patterns exist!) than in any other kind of fishing. Clearly there is a lot to learn if you want to be a complete fly-fisher. But all fly-fishing gets down to a few basics; and after you learn them, the rest is just a matter of practice.

If you are like most flyrodders, you will start out wanting to know everything about fly-fishing and end up trying to clean out your mental file cabinets as you get down to a few favorite flies and a few techniques that work for you. Remember this: You can catch your first fish on a fly within hours of your first attempt at a cast.

Where Is the Fly in Fly-Fishing?

Once upon a time, when the only fish you fished for with a fly was a trout, a *fly* was a bit of feather and fur on a hook. It was always meant to look like an insect, a very particular kind of insect, the mayfly. But these days, fly-fishers angle for trout, bass, striped bass, redfish, bluefish, blue marlin, bluegill, dolphin (fish), ladyfish, tarpon, fluke, flounder, salmon, and on and on. The list gets longer every year as more and more people take up this challenging and satisfying sport. So a *fly* no longer means "something that looks like an insect." In the same way that someone who makes CDs is still called a record producer (or the way that a person who makes videos is called a filmmaker), anglers who use a fly rod to deliver concoctions that look like shrimp, eels, bait fish, baby robins, frogs, mice, and crabs still refer to the thing on their end of their line as a fly.

So even though a *fly* once meant just that — something that looked like a winged insect found in trout streams — it may be more accurate to give a fly a wider definition so as to take into account where the sport is today and where it is going. If you say "a fly is something you fly-fish with," you would be right, but you wouldn't be shedding much light on the subject.

The key thing about a fly is its *weight* or lack thereof. Bait and lures all have some weight to them. The minnow, or Daredevle, or plastic worm and sinker that you cast with a bait-casting or spinning rod is heavier than the fishing line. The weight of the thing at the end of your line bends your rod and is catapulted to where you want to fish. A fly, on the other hand, has almost no weight. Using a heavy fly line in a bullwhip motion carries the fly to your target. When a fly lands, there is no *plunk* or *plop* that you have come to expect from bait or lure. The fly, when properly delivered, seems to sail to the target and to land as softly as a snowflake. This feature, I believe, is one of the chief attractions of angling with a fly rod: the ability to enter silently into the world of the game fish and to deceive it into striking your fly. Fly-fishing is, to my way of thinking, up-close-and-personal fishing. This is not to say that fly-fishing is better, or more challenging, than any other kind of fishing. But when stealth and delicacy are required, a fly may work well when nothing else seems to do the trick.

Having said that considerable mouthful on the unspoken question of "What is a fly?" it remains true that during the past three or four hundred years, *fly-fishing* meant *trout fishing*. Only in the last century or so have other fish attracted the attention of flyrodders. So although it is true that a fly is no longer just an imitation of a mayfly, it is also true that the vast majority of flies and all the terminology in fly-fishing came out of trout fishing; and even today, most flyrodders are trouters, and most artificial flies were originally devised to entice trout to the hook.

Following is a look at the mayfly, which, from birth to death, is of paramount interest to the trout and the fisher of trout. The point to bear in mind is that wet flies, dry flies, and nymphs — terms that you come across again and again in fly-fishing — all have their origin in the life cycle of the mayfly.

The short, happy life of the mayfly: Swim, eat, fly, mate, and die

I have often envied the mayfly. Not that I'd want to be one; they only live about a year. However, when you compare the way a mayfly's life goes with the way your average human gets in and out of this world, I like the mayfly script better. A mayfly starts out as an egg on the bottom of a stream. (So far no great shakes; but stick with the story until the end, and you can see what I am talking about.) Soon, the egg hatches, and out crawls a many-legged little critter known as a *nymph* — or immature mayfly. When you see trout with their noses down, rooting about on the bottom of a stream, they are often feeding on nymphs.

About one year to the day from when it began life as an egg, the nymph is ready to hatch and become a full-fledged mayfly. When flyrodders talk about a *hatch,* they don't mean what happens when the egg becomes a nymph. Technically speaking, this change is a hatch, but this type of hatch isn't of much interest to trout; therefore, it is of even less interest to trout fishermen.

The *trout fishing hatch* occurs when all the mayflies of a particular species — and millions of mayflies may be in a single stretch of a stream — shed their old skin, rise to the surface, sprout wings, dry themselves off, and (for the first time) fly. This process, which takes a few minutes for each individual fly, normally takes a few days to play itself out for all of the flies of a given type on any given stream. Usually, a hatch begins in the warmer waters downstream and moves upstream, which has relatively cooler waters.

In this period of time, between when they begin to shed their skin and when they first take flight, the mayfly is at its most vulnerable. Look at it this way: If I were the trout and you were the insect, you'd have a pretty hard time defending yourself just as you were trying to pull a sweater over your head (or better yet, just as you were trying to wriggle out of a wet suit). Fly-rodders sometimes call this shedding stage *the emerger stage.*

When a hatch is on, the trout know that plenty of easy-to-catch food is around, just for the taking. When the mayfly has broken out of its old nymph case and is in the wriggling-out-of-the-wet-suit phase, it is often known as a *wet fly.* Many mayflies never make it to full-blown, flying-around mayflydom. For one reason or another, they cannot shed their cases and they just float on the surface as stillborns — stillborn but still tasty to the trout.

Most of the time, the mayfly does make it out of the case; and most of those that do rest for a while on the surface of the water, drying their wings and just generally getting their bearings. You can easily tell if an insect is a mayfly at this point because its two wings are folded back and stick up in the air like the sail of a sailboat. To the hungry trout, this is the sitting-duck phase. The insect is now a full-fledged mayfly or *dun.* And the artificial fly of choice at this time is often the dry fly. The mayfly may beat its wings every now and again in order to dry them. This further attracts the attention of the trout.

Because the mayfly instinctively knows that it may be gobbled up at any moment, it is in a hurry to get off the water. Because the trout knows this too, it will feed purposefully as long as there are mayflies on the water.

As a general rule, most flyrodders find dry-fly-fishing the most satisfying way to take a trout. I think that this attitude has a great deal to do with the fact that when a trout eats your dry fly, you get to see the whole thing. As with topwater lures, a visual-surface take is incomparably exciting. Many writers and many more anglers run off at the mouth about all the extra skill and smarts you need to be successful with the dry fly. Baloney! Dry-fly-fishing is just more fun because you get to see all the action.

A different kind of spinner

If our mayfly manages to survive the hatching stage and the wing-drying stage, it is ready for one last change into the *spinner phase*. Shortly after hatching, a mayfly flies around for the first time and heads for a streamside bush or tree. After it reaches that sanctuary, its tail grows longer and its wings lose their milky translucence and become clear. Then, that evening or possibly the next day, the spinners fly over the stream and mate in midair. The male, having done his assigned job, drops to the surface of the stream and dies. The female deposits her eggs in the stream (where they cling to a rock, hatch, and start the nymph cycle all over again). Following this, the female joins her husband-for-a-day on the surface of the stream. At this time, a trout sees a huge amount of fresh mayfly meat that has no chance of escaping. At this stage of the hatch, known as a *spinner fall,* an angler can encounter some amazing fishing. In the case of some flies — the biggest mayfly, which is called the Green Drake, and the smallest mayfly, the *tricorfithydes* or *trico* — the best fishing in the whole hatch is during the spinner fall.

So much for the life of the mayfly (shown in Figure 4-1): It begins life as a little crawler on the bottom of the stream; then on the last day of its life, it sprouts wings, flies up into the bright summer sky, and, in a grand climax, mates for the first time while in midair, following which it immediately dies and falls to the surface of a clear-flowing stream. See what I mean about the mayfly having a better life script than most folks?

The one with the most flies wins

"Artificial flies are all named. There are the 'Professor,' the 'Hackle,' the 'Ibis,' the 'Yellow Sally,' and several other breeds. Whenever a bilious angler has no luck and nothing to do, he sits down and concocts a new swindle in feathers, and christens it with a nine-jointed Indian name, and at once every angler in the country rushes in and pays $2 a dozen for samples."
—Henry Guy Carlton

Figure 4-1:
The mayfly
begins at
the nymph
stage and
then
hatches to
become an
emerger, a
dun, and
finally a
spinner.

Which Fly Do I Use?

During any hatch, the trout may be keyed in on one phase of the mayfly's life cycle. If you can figure out what the trout are taking, you have a fighting chance to "match the hatch." This match-the-hatch principle is one of fly-fishing's deeply held articles of faith: You try to give the trout a fly that looks like the food that it is currently eating. Just as mayflies have different stages of life, different artificial flies represent each of those stages.

High and dry

For most trout anglers most of the time, the dry fly is the preferred method of taking trout. However, a dry fly (shown in Figure 4-2) is not always the most effective method, and it doesn't always pull up the biggest fish (although there are times when it does both). I think that this preference exists because of the thrill of anticipation experienced when watching the fly floating down the stream, knowing that a trout may take it at any moment. And if and when the trout takes your fly, it engenders one of angling's great feelings (just as the plug fisherman gets a happy jolt when watching a largemouth slam a popping plug).

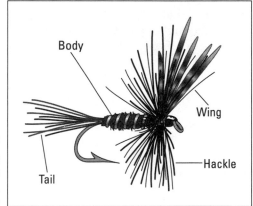

Figure 4-2:
The classic
dry fly.

The traditional dry fly has the following features:

- ✔ The tail is as long as the body.

- ✔ The tail is usually made of stiff fibers from the *hackle* (neck feathers) of a rooster. The hackle is what allows the traditional fly to float high and dry — just like a real mayfly.

- ✔ The body is made of fur that is wound around the hook with silk thread.
- ✔ The wing is often made from the soft body feathers of a wood duck.

Not every dry fly is tied to imitate a mayfly, and not every dry-fly mayfly imitation has all of the parts in the picture. For example, I often used the Comparadun on flat clear water. This mayfly imitation has no hackle, but it floats just fine. In most of the world most of the time, however, when people talk about a dry fly, they are talking about the classic mayfly tie illustrated in Figure 4-2.

At the end of the hatch, the spinners fall; and for the next few hours, you may have excellent dry-fly-fishing. In this case, you can use a special kind of dry fly made to imitate the spinner; but this type has a less-bushy hackle and wings that are stretched out rather than upright. More about spinners later in this chapter.

Keeping a dry fly dry (or at least floating)

The whole idea of a dry fly is that is floats on the surface just like a natural fly. But fur and feathers and other fly-making materials have a tendency to get wet in the water (no surprise here). When you consider the weight of the hook, too, you are dealing with something that naturally wants to sink after a while. So you have to do something to help the fly float. You can do three things to give your fly a fighting floating chance:

- ✔ **Use a floatant.** Some floatants (materials designed to waterproof flies) are gloppy and some are liquid, but all floatants are designed to keep the fly on top of the surface film. You don't need to heap floatant on, but you should use it. I find that rubbing the stuff between my thumb and forefinger and then rubbing my fingers on the fly avoids saddling my fly with a large gob of goo on top.

- ✔ **Use a drying substance.** Also useful are commercial powders that work on the same drying-out, or *desiccant,* principle as cat litter. Use a commercial desiccant powder after you catch a fish, when the fly is wet and slimy, or when your fly starts to sink prematurely. Simply take the fly — no need to clip it off the leader — and put it in the desiccant bottle; then close the bottle and shake it. When you take the fly out, it is covered with white power. Blow off the loose powder. Give your fly a few false casts to remove any residual powder and start fishing again.

✔ **Use the air.** Sometimes you run out of floatants and desiccants, or your floatant may have fallen out of your vest or you just plain forgot it. In these cases, swishing the fly in the air with a few crisp false casts usually dries out all but the most waterlogged fly for a reasonable float. In heavy, choppy water, however, you are simply not going to get much of a float without using a floatant or a desiccant.

Wets came first

Wet flies are called *wet flies* because they get wetter than dry flies. (You probably could have figured that out without the aid of this book.) I believe that the original artificial flies were wets. True dry flies aren't mentioned in the literature until many years after Izaak Walton wrote *The Compleat Angler* in the 17th Century. Does that mean that trout anglers didn't fish with duns in the old days? Absolutely not. They just cast their wet flies and allowed them to drift in the same way that today's dry fly angler fishes.

So with the wet fly (shown in Figure 4-3), the question always is, "How does an angler fish it?" The wet-fly-fishing technique is more fully discussed in Chapter 14.

The classic wet fly has the same parts as the dry fly, but the wing is attached differently. Instead of riding high and dry, a wet fly lays down on the water. Also, the hackle is softer *(webby)* so that a wet fly rides in or under the film.

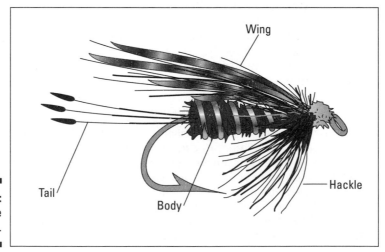

Figure 4-3:
An old-time wet fly.

Good for wine stains, baby barf, and trout flies

Many commercial floatants were designed specifically for trout flies. Scotchguard wasn't designed for flies, but it really works well as a floatant, especially when you forget your regular floatant and are nowhere near a tackle shop.

Nymphs: New kids on the block

Back in the old days, wet flies served for everything: duns, emergers, nymphs, and spinners. Gradually, anglers grew more specialized in their choice of flies. The dry fly came along and spawned a whole school of fishing and fly-tying techniques. Next, anglers looked for a more effective nymph imitation than the traditional wet fly, and the modern artificial nymph was born. An artificial nymph usually looks more like a natural nymph than a wet fly does. The wing is gone and is replaced by a wing case and nubby fur that often imitates the gills that run along the side of a nymph's body (as shown in Figure 4-4). Fished free-floating, or with the purposeful action of a live nymph rising to the surface and hatching into a dry fly, the artificial nymph is a versatile fly that often scores when nothing else does. Remember, even during a blizzardlike hatch, more nymphs are in the water than drys are on the surface, and trout frequently continue to feed on nymphs through the hatch.

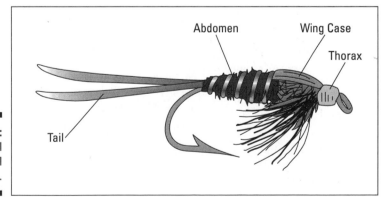

Figure 4-4: A typical artificial nymph.

Of all trout flies, the artificial nymph looks most like the natural product (at least to the human eye). The wing case, thorax, abdomen, and tail all correspond to a stream-borne nymph.

For many years, I preferred the artificial nymph to the dry fly. In part, this preference was because (in those days) I fished on a free-stone Catskill stream with not very much surface feeding. Nymphs seemed to work more. Of course part of the reason they worked more is because I used them more. Which leads to an obvious tip, but one which bears repeating.

Use the flies and methods that you are most comfortable with. In fact, this tip goes for bait fishing and lure fishing, too. If you have no confidence in a certain lure, fly, bait, or a certain technique, you cannot catch many fish. On the other hand, sometimes the "wrong" fly, fished with style and confidence, takes the fish. Or (put another way) it isn't always *what* you fish with, but the *way* that you fish with it that counts.

The opposite point of view

Okay, got that? The "not what you fish with, but how you fish with it" rule *is* a pretty good rule to follow, except when it *isn't* a good rule to follow. I know this statement sounds a little arbitrary, but let me try to explain because I think that your fishing can improve if you understand the exception to this rule. Although many anglers fish the dry fly or nothing, I used to fish with a dry fly only when I saw activity on the water. Back then, my theory was this: "Trout spend a great deal of time eating, so if I do not see them eating on top, they must be eating down below. I'll stick with nymphs or streamers (more on streamer flies later)." Well, that self-advice sounded pretty practical, so I congratulated myself on what a clear-headed angler I was.

Then I started fishing with Ben. Ben is one of those fishermen who can *sense* what the fish want and how to give it to them. Many times we would go out fishing together. Seeing no surface activity, I would put on a nymph or wet fly, and Ben would tie on a little dry fly. Sure enough, Ben would score fish after fish, and I

would flail the water. I learned then and there that my so-called clear-headedness was just an excuse not to try something new. So although the rule that you do best with the methods you know and believe in is true, don't get set in your ways — keep learning new techniques.

Not surprisingly, after I started to fish a dry fly a little more, I became much more attuned to the many subtle ways in which a fish takes a dry fly. In other words, in the old days, I didn't fish drys much because I didn't see any feeding activity on the surface. It turned out that I wasn't seeing that feeding activity because I wasn't looking for the right signs.

And this advice doesn't apply only to fly fishermen. For example, I took the same prejudice to surf casting. If I didn't see any surface action, I fished deep. But only after I saw a veteran surf jockey pull in striper after striper with a topwater plug did I realize that part of what makes a good angler is the ability to *entice* fish, even if you don't see a great deal of feeding activity going on.

Streamers: More than a mouthful

Trout, especially large trout, like to eat small fish. Whether the fish is one of their own kind or just a forage fish, such as a minnow, sculpin, or alewife herring, is not that important. To a trout, a bait fish (compared to a dry fly) provides much more meat on the hoof — make that meat on the fin. Anglers have long known this, and their attempts to imitate this favored food source resulted is the *streamer fly*.

If you take a feather and hold it sideways, it has the rough outline of a fish: for this reason many streamer patterns started out as a pair of feathers tied lengthwise along the shaft of a hook. And many fish were caught, and continue to be caught, with simple streamers. Some more developed streamers have hackle feathers wound around the head of the hook to give the fly more lifelike motion in the water. In addition to feathers, bucktail has long been used as streamer material (although it has always been a mystery to me why the hairs from a deer's rear end attract fish). You never see a trout nibbling at a deer's backside. I think that deer hair (like much of the fur and hair of land-dwelling animals) works so well in flies and other lures because it behaves like *living* material. Marabou feathers also work well when attached to streamers, as do a whole range of synthetic materials that shine, sparkle, and wave seductively.

The Gray Ghost shown in Figure 4-5 is a classic feather-based streamer first tied by Carric Stevens (one of the mothers of American fly-fishing) in the Rangeley Lakes region of Maine at the turn of the century. Decades later, Don Gapen revolutionized streamer fishing with his deer-hair sculpin imitation, The Muddler Minnow.

Figure 4-5:
Streamers
old (top)
and
new(ish)
(bottom).

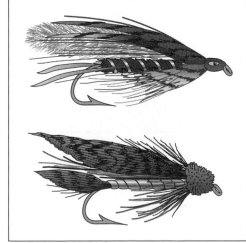

Look at the water

You come down to a stream and see a bunch of rising fish. "Oh, Boy!" you say to yourself as you tie on a mayfly imitation. You float a dry over the trout a dozen times. The trout continues to rise in a very splashy way, sometimes leaping clear out of the water. You are excited, but nothing happens with your fly. "Must be taking emergers," you say. You tie on a wet fly (or maybe you use a special pattern that looks like an emerger). You fish with great concentration, looking for the slightest twitch in your line. The trout keeps rising. You are starting to dislike this trout. It really is thumbing its nose (or maybe "finning its nose") at you. "Hmm, Mr. Trout must be taking a really teeny fly that I can't see," you tell yourself as you give up on that fish and go after another splashy riser.

What went wrong?

Very often a splashy rise means *caddisflies*. As the caddis pupa rockets to the surface, the trout follows it, trying to get up a head of steam that results in an attention-grabbing rise.

Next time you get to the stream, rather than casting blindly to a rise, you must study the water to see what's *really* happening.

Anglers aren't as finicky or precise about caddis imitations as they are about mayfly imitations. A typical artificial caddis with elk hair has a body like a mayfly, but the caddis wing is tied in a down position, and the hackle is often wound through the body (the flytier's term for this winding technique is *palmered*). This kind of hackle breaks up the light pattern on the surface of the water and, from the trout's vantage point, gives the fly a skittering kind of appearance.

Caddisflies

Although a mayfly imitation, fished dry during a hatch, provides first-class trout fishing, using a caddisfly is more like traveling in business class: A caddisfly imitiation can be fished like a dry fly, but somehow the caddis doesn't have the same snob appeal as the mayfly. The *caddis* is a type of insect found in most trout and smallmouth streams. Pick up a rock from the river bottom, turn it over, and chances are you can see some immature mayfly nymphs scurrying for safety. You may also notice a number of little cocoons made of twigs or small pebbles. These little cocoons are *caddis cases.* Inside the cocoons, the caddis larvae grow to their next stage, *the pupa stage,* which is sort of the booster rocket for the mature caddisfly. When the caddis pupa is ready to hatch, it often moves very swiftly to the surface, emerging from the water like a Polaris missile going straight up. Unfortunately, a caddis doesn't usually do as well as a Polaris missile on its first flight attempt. The fly often falls back to the water and tries to take off again. It keeps flapping its wings, bouncing and skittering on the surface. All this activity, both above and below the surface, can excite the trout into feeding. Later, when a swarm of caddis descends on a stream to lay eggs, the trout are on the lookout for these *ovipostitors* (egg-laying insects). You can tell a caddis from a mayfly when they are on the water because caddis wings don't stick up like little sailboats (which is how many anglers traditionally describe the upright wing of mayflies). They lay down flatly.

Stoneflies

The biggest insects in most trout streams are *stoneflies.* You will find stoneflies most commonly in riffles because they seek highly aerated water. A stonefly nymph looks like a big mayfly nymph. When stoneflies hatch and sprout wings, they crawl up on rocks and climb out of their cases while perched on these rocks. That's why you can see many of their dried cases on exposed rocks in midstream. Trout usually take the live stonefly nymphs because they rarely get a shot at a dry fly (examples of which are shown in Figure 4-6). The exception is the salmonfly hatch in the Rockies. This early season hatch was made for duffers. Things like delicate presentation and light leaders, which count for a lot with the hatch of smaller flies on placid water don't matter so much as long as you can plop a really big dry fly on the water and give it a decent float.

The Montana nymph looks like a large mayfly. Its palmered hackle suggests the gills that run along a stone fly's abdomen. Like a mayfly nymph, the artificial Montana nymph has a bulging wing case, a tapering body, and a tail. The salmonfly imitation is big and bushy. If you don't have a fly specifically tied for the salmonfly, anything big and bushy might do the trick.

Figure 4-6:
Two stone-
fly patterns.

Terrestrials

Sometimes, no flies are hatching, no spinners are left over from yesterday's hatch, and no nymphs are getting ready to hatch. Ditto for the caddis. Still, you may see trout feeding, or you may be able to interest them in feeding by using a *terrestrial,* which could be an imitation of an ant, a beetle, a grass-hopper, and the like. They are called terrestrials because their natural environment is on land, not water. When a passing breeze or a sloppy jump deposits one of these landlubbers in a stream, the terrestrial insect is (in a manner of speaking) a fish out of water. And the fish know it. Late in the season, when most of the big hatches are finished, terrestrials can make up a large part of the trout's diet, especially on windy days when many insects are blown out of the bushes and trees. And when the grasshoppers are hopping, a big Muddler or hopper imitation can lure a trout from its lair, even when no natural flies are on the water.

Bass Bugs

Bass sometimes take flies that originated in trout fishing, but there is another whole family of flies that was dreamed up by and for bass anglers. Although the bass is every bit as sporty as the trout, it is not held in the same regard by many flyrodders. Too bad. Bass are terrific on a fly. I have spent countless hours in the freshwater parts of the Everglades and have caught thousands of bass on flies. When bass are keyed into flies, you cannot keep up with the fish. I remember a day out on the Big Cypress Indian Reservation when I took my eight-year-old daughter for her first Everglades trip with the premier bass fly-rod guide in south Florida, the legendary Jack Allen. We caught so many fish that we didn't try to count.

Instead, Jack suggested that we count the fish that he and I caught in a ten-minute period and multiply that result over the course of the day. While Lucy dehooked the bass and kept track, Jack and I caught 32 fish in 10 minutes, which multiplies out to a total of 2,000+ fish in one day's fishing by the two of us. Obviously, we didn't catch that many fish, but we caught hundreds; and I doubt that any worm anglers could have matched the fly rod for action that day.

A few basic types of *bass bugs* constitute the basic arsenal for most fly-rodding:

The popping bug

The popping bug (as shown in Figure 4-7) is usually made out of molded plastic or carved cork. It has a concave face that makes a burbling *pop* as you retrieve it. When fished correctly, you just know that a popping bug is going to catch fish. Of all kinds of bass fishing, this technique is my favorite, and it may be right up there as my favorite overall fishing technique. Popping bugs are not confined to bass fishing. I once caught a six-pound brook trout from under a lily pad in northern Quebec while using a popper, and I have taken both snook and tarpon on poppers.

Figure 4-7: A popping bug.

Deer-hair flies

Because deer hair can be tied and sculpted into so many shapes and because deer hair is highly buoyant, it is a favored material for bassing. The Muddler Minnow works well in many situations, as does a Deer Hair Mouse (shown in Figure 4-8).

Figure 4-8:
The Deer
Hair Mouse
is an old
favorite for
bassing.

Clouser's Minnow

This lead-eyed bucktail streamer may be the most versatile fly to come along in the last 20 years. It was invented by bass angler Bob Clouser for his homewaters on the Susquehanna River. It has proved effective for many freshwater species (as well as such saltwater species as bluefish, redfish, and striped bass). To a fish, a Clouser's Minnow (shown in Figure 4-9) can look like a small bait fish, a large shrimp, a sand eel, and probably many other things. The lead eyes gives the Clouser's Minnow a kind of dipsy-doodle motion that often provokes a game fish.

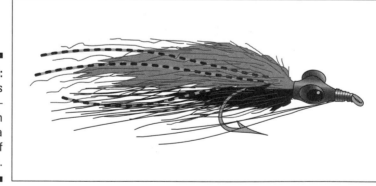

Figure 4-9:
Clouser's
Minnow —
get a bunch
of them in a
bunch of
sizes.

When fishing with weighted flies, such as the Clouser's Minnow, watch your back: Weighted flies have a tendency to whipsaw and move unpredictably. They can really pack a wallop. When casting in windy conditions, be very careful and figure out the path of the fly *before* you cast.

Ten Flies That Work Everywhere

Zillions of pages have been written about flies. Every fly angler has an opinion, a favorite fly, a neat little trick. Although I have no doubt that every situation has a *best* fly, you can spend years learning these situations and *I* would much rather spend my time fishing. If you want to learn a great deal about a great number of flies, don't take this as a warning not to learn. Your continuing study can pay off. Still, as the years go by, I find that I catch more fish with a smaller selection of flies. I really believe that a well-presented fly that gives the *impression* of the real thing is often just as effective as a fly that *duplicates* whatever it is that the fish are eating. And sometimes, the best strategy is to go against the hatch and give the fish something that stands out from the crowd.

So here is a list of ten flies that every flyrodder should have in his or her box. In time, you may make up your own slightly different list; but I guarantee that your list will have a good number of the flies I am recommending here because they are tried-and-true fish catchers.

The Ausable Wulff

This member of the Wulff series of flies is named after the most famous angler of this century, Lee Wulff, who was born in Alaska in 1896. One day in 1934, Lee, who was a commercial artist, was quite upset when a friend of his was fired just a few weeks from retirement. So he told his boss what to do with his job. "I never wanted to compete for money again," Lee later said. He spent that summer camping out on the Esopus Creek in the Catskills. One night, during a hatch of the mayfly known as the Dark Hendriksen, he tied a fly using bushy deer hair for the wing instead of the less-buoyant wood duck feathers of the standard Hendricksen pattern. The new fly, The Gray Wulff, worked well in the high and roily water, and a new style of dry fly was invented. The Ausable Wulff, a variation on the same theme, is lighter in color than the Gray Wulff, and I find it to be an excellent prospecting fly (one you use to search the water when no fish are rising). It works especially well in riffly pocket water. I usually carry an assortment of these Wulffs in sizes 12, 14, and 16.

Salt: Not different, just bigger

As more and more people take up the sport of fly-rodding, many of them discover that instead of driving half the weekend to a stocked trout stream crowded with anglers, the nearby oceans can offer tremendous sport. Saltwater fly-fishing is probably the fastest-growing part of fly-fishing. Saltwater fish are usually bigger than freshwater fish; and many anglers feel that, pound for pound, they are also better fighters. For some reason, this attitude has given ocean-going game fish the reputation of being unselective chowhounds. Consequently, salty flyrodders have contented themselves with just a few flies: perhaps large poppers that make a sound like a hungry German shepherd attacking a lamb chop, or maybe big all-purpose streamers from the Deceiver series, or shrimp imitations that haven't changed much since they were first tied for bonefish in the years following World War II.

The fact of the matter is that saltwater game fish can be as selective as any trout. I have spent many fishless nights casting my poppers and streamers into schools of splashy stripers on a feeding binge. And then someone showed me an imitation of a cinder worm that was in the water. Pow! That very night I caught a half dozen fish, including a gorgeous 20-pound striper that fought as hard and as long as a tarpon.

Now is an exciting time to be a salty flyrodder. As more and more anglers take up the sport, they are devoting the kind of brain power and trial-and-error efforts that, in the past, produced so many effective flies for trout. So, although the old give-'em-anything rule can still produce fish, particularly bluefish, you can do better in the salt if you pay attention to what is in the water and try to imitate it.

Clouser's Minnow

This is another great invention of an observant angler. As I noted earlier in this chapter, the Clouser's Minnow was originally tied for smallmouth bass, but I have caught largemouth bass, stripers, trout, and bluefish on it (and I even used it in a pinch to jig for flounder). Clouser's Minnow is a simple streamer with lead eyes that allow you to give it a jigging retrieve. I carry it in sizes 2, 4, 6, and 8.

The Comparadun

Al Cauicci and Bob Nastas, two buddies who fish the very challenging waters of the West Branch of the Delaware, devised these no-hackle, deer-wing flies so that they would float flush in the surface film. I have found that Comparaduns really score well with highly selective fish. I especially like them when the little yellow mayflies known as Pale Morning Duns are hatching, which they do with great frequency on the blue-ribbon waters of the Rocky Mountains. The Comparaspinners, also no-hackle with *spent deer hair wings* (that is, wings that lie flat and to the side, like outriggers) are the best spinners I know. Size varies depending on what's happening, insect-wise, on the water.

Dave's Hopper

In late summer, in the grass-bordered streams of the Rocky Mountains, a late-afternoon wind can be counted on to deposit a number of big grasshoppers on the streams. You can rarely see a more-explosive strike by a trout than when it attacks a struggling hopper being carried along in the current. There are many hopper flies, but none have worked better for me than the one devised by the great bass-and-trout angler, Dave Whitlock. As for size, catch a hopper in your hand and that's your size.

Elk Hair Caddis

Although elk hair gives this fly extra buoyancy, it still has a sleek and delicate profile. The Elk Hair Caddis is a very good prospecting fly when you see a few splashy caddis rises. I usually carry sizes 14, 16, and 18.

Gold Ribbed Hare's Ear

In a fly survey I did on the Internet, this old, reliable fly, as well as the Wooly Bugger described later in this section, were so far ahead of the rest of the field that they seemed to be running in first and second place with nothing else even on the same racetrack. The Gold Ribbed Hare's Ear is a general impressionistic nymph that picks up flash from gold wire coiled around its body. The fur used to tie this fly comes, as its name suggests, from the ear of a hare. It is gold, brown, white, and black in color, and its texture is stubby and filled with many short hairs that stick out at all kinds of angles. To a hairdresser (no pun intended), these short hairs would be thought of as unsightly split ends. To a fish, this unkempt look is very buglike. In recent years, some anglers have been fishing the Gold Ribbed Hare's Ear with the addition of a shiny metallic bead head that gives it both a jigging action and some more flash. Sizes 8, 12, 12, 14, 16.

Griffith's Gnat

This little all-purpose fly, invented by John Griffith, the founder of Trout Unlimited, is the one I go to when there is small stuff on the water. The hook of the Griffith's Gnat is wrapped with a body of peacock herl (fibers of peacock feather) and a palmered small hackle from a grizzly rooster (which has multicolored feathers of white, black, and gray). To the fish, I think that all those neck fibers sticking out must make Griffith's Gnat look like a buzzing little bug. I've used this fly for gnats, tricos, midges, and ants. It is one of those flies that fish often take even though it may be bigger than the natural insects on the water. Sizes 16–22.

The Muddler Minnow

Many of the great flies are kind of like folk songs or legends: They're really good, but nobody knows where they came from. Quite often, many people had a hand in the fly's creative process. Not the Muddler Minnow. Don Gapen observed that sculpin (a bait fish) make up a large part of the diet of game fish. To imititate this bait, Gapen took some deer hair and tied it in long strips. He spun it into a ball and then gave it a crew cut to create a bulbous head. Voilà! The Muddler Minnow was born. Fished under the surface, it looks like a sculpin. Fished another way, I am sure that it is taken as a crab. Greased, it is often taken as a hopper. And you can fish all three ways on any cast simply by adjusting your retrieve. Carry Muddlers in sizes 2–12.

The Variant

A Variant is a dry fly with no wings. Instead, you rely on the hackle to give the impression of the buzzing appearance of insect wings flapping at great speed and breaking up the light that shines through them. In his later years, Lee Wulff fished for trout almost exclusively with Variants. And the great Art Flick, who wrote *The Streamside Guide* (in my opinion the best and most useful trout-fishing book ever), was a major fan of Variants. When Variants are tied the way that Flick tied them (with oversize hackle and a slim body made from the center quill of a hackle feather), they are the most delicate of dry flies. For some reason, I have always thought of these classic Variants as the fly-fishing version of the simple but beautiful designs of the Shakers who lived just one mountain range over from the Catskill Mountains where Wulff and Flick fished. Sizes 8–18.

The Wooly Bugger

When you can only have one fly, many flyrodders will tell you that the Wooly Bugger is probably the one fly to have. With its simple body and a long supple feather tail, this fly ranked number one on my Internet survey because it catches fish everywhere. Depending on what size of Wooly Bugger you use, it can be taken for a stone fly, a leech, a minnow, or a worm.

I will never forget a day on a slough full of enormous rainbow trout in Argentina. Nothing was hatching, and there was no visible sign of fish. I tied on a Wooly Bugger and stripped it in 6 inches at a time (that is, I retrieved it in short pulls). I caught fish after fish, up to an unbelievable 11 pounds. When one fish struck, I pulled back to set the hook with such violence that the hook pulled out of the trout's mouth, and my momentum carried the fly over my head and into the water about 20 feet in back of me where another 5- or 6-pound rainbow took the Wooly Bugger on my backcast! This was the ultimate case of using the right fly at the right time. Sizes 4, 6, 8, and 10.

Chapter 5

Hooks, Sinkers, Snaps, Swivels, and Bobbers

. . . .

In This Chapter

▶ Picking the right hook

▶ Removing a hook from your finger (without removing the finger)

▶ Rigging your sinkers, snaps, swivels, and bobbers

. . . .

Some people fish with one hook. Others fish with many. Some people hate lead weights, and other people have one for every situation. Taken together, hooks, sinkers, and *bobbers* (the opposite of sinkers) are called *terminal tackle. Terminal* refers to the end of a fishing outfit that begins at your reel and terminates where your hook meets a fish.

Happy Hooking: Use the Right One

A *hook* is a rather simple device — a pointed piece of metal that you attach to your line. Sometimes, the point is buried inside some bait. (That burial requires a special kind of hook.) At other times, the hook is exposed (as it is in a fly or a plug). Different hooks are made for different purposes; and as with everything in fishing, deciding which hook to use for which purpose can get complicated in a hurry. The good thing is, you don't have to absorb all the information about hooks at one time. Some of the information you may never need to memorize, and much of the information is printed on product packages or imprinted on the brains of tackle shop employees.

Figure 5-1 features the different parts of a typical hook's anatomy:

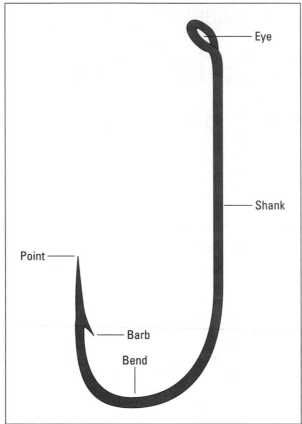

Eye

Shank

Point

Barb

Bend

Figure-5-1:
The
anatomy of
a hook.

Following are the most important parts of a hook:

✔ The *point* is where tackle meets fish. As in many situations in life, the first impression is an important one. If you don't have a good sharp point on your hook, you can have the most expensive rod in the world, but you won't catch fish.

✔ The *barb* is a type of a reverse point that is designed to keep a fish on the hook after the fish bites. Bigger is not better with barbs. Big barbs can make setting a hook difficult when the hook meets up with a tough-mouthed fish like a bonefish. Or big barbs can make too big a tear in the mouth of a soft-mouthed fish like an American shad. Many catch-and-release anglers fish with barbless hooks.

✔ The *bend* is the curved part of the hook, and all those fine-sounding hook names, such as Limerick or Sproat, have something to do with the bend. Actually, such hook names have to do with two parts of the bend: the bite and the gap. I think of the *bite* as the depth that the hook penetrates. I think of the *gap* as the width of the area that your hook is fighting the fish. A relatively wide gap may be necessary to hold certain bait, to get around the snout of a billed fish, or to dig in beyond the width of a thick jawbone. The wider the gap, the easier it is for the fish to bend the hook so that it can escape. Some anglers console themselves if they lose a fish when this happens by saying something like "Gee whiz! Straightened it right out!" The implication is that the fish that straightened the hook must have been one huge fish — a fish that no angler could have held, including the expert who made the comment. The fact of the matter is this: You really shouldn't lose a fish after you hook it. When the hook straightens out, you are using a hook that is either too light or too big in the gap for the amount of pressure that you (not the fish) applied. Losing a fish this way happens to everybody; but still, developing a sense of how much pressure your tackle can take is part of becoming an educated angler.

✔ The *shank* connects the bend to the eye. A shank can be long or short. As with gap, more length means that a hook is easier for a fish to bend. So why aren't all hooks short? The answer has to do with what goes *on* the hook. A short-shanked Salmon Egg hook isn't very effective for Texas-rigging a night crawler (see Chapter 2), but a longer-shanked worm hook is effective. Sometimes the shank has a barb or two to help hold bait more securely. The Eagle Claw, an old favorite of mine, is a bait-holding hook of this type.

✔ The *eye* of the hook (the loop through which line passes) may be turned up, turned down, or straight. The garden variety hook, the kind that most anglers use most of the time, has a turned-down eye. Some exceptions to the rule exist, though. Traditional salmon flies are tied on turned-up hooks, and some anglers prefer turned-up eyes on very tiny flies because small flies have little gap and bite to begin with, and the turned-down eye can interfere.

Bigger number, smaller hook . . . sometimes

The size of the hook is very important in all kinds of fishing (and is especially critical in fly-fishing). The bigger the hook, the more weight it has; and the more weight it has, the more hackle it needs in order to float — and that extra amount of hackle is not a good thing because it just junks up the look of the fly. Whenever one flyrodder asks another what the fish are taking, the answer is often something like, "A size 16 Adams." Flies don't come in sizes. Hooks do. But hook size has become so linked to fly size that everyone thinks in these terms, so here's the deal: When you use the word *size* before you give the number of the hook, you are dealing with smaller hooks. The *higher* the number, the *smaller* the hook. A size 6 hook is much bigger than a size 28 hook. And by the way, hook sizes are counted by twos. No odd numbers until size 1. Actually, the measuring system changes at 1 to the system called the *aughts* (written 1/0, 2/0, and the like) in which the zero is pronounced old style, as *aught*. In the aughts, the higher the number, the bigger the hook. Got that straight? Like getting a wisdom tooth pulled, after you get hook sizes sorted out in your mind, the good part is that you never have to do it again.

Do I snell?

Sometimes you see packages containing hooks that are already attached to leaders, and the package calls them *snelled*. I have always wondered where the word *snell* came from, but I never got around to looking it up until I started this book. (Let me save you a trip to the dictionary: Mine says "origin unknown.") Maybe *snell* is a word that was made up by an imaginative friend of Izaak Walton. *Snelling* is a way of attaching leader directly to a hook's shank (as shown in Figure 5-2) instead of knotting leader to a hook's eye. (Knots, no matter how well tied, have a tendency to break before line does.) I am told that the physics of this type of rigging gives a straighter pull on the hook, making the fight harder for a fish. When a fish is fighting hard, I have never noticed a big difference between a knotted hook and a snelled hook — but snelled hooks do *look* cool.

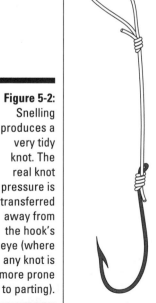

Figure 5-2:
Snelling produces a very tidy knot. The real knot pressure is transferred away from the hook's eye (where any knot is more prone to parting).

Well, if I don't snell, do I sproat?

The hook world has some really cool gear names. You may well go through your whole fishing life without ever giving much thought to different hook types, but knowing a few of the most popular (shown in Figure 5-3) won't hurt.

The *Sproat* hook is, in terms of popularity, the most widely used all-purpose hook. The bend of a Sproat hook — sports car drivers recognize this type of bend as a decreasing radius or sharp turn — is called a parabolic bend, and it provides more strength than a more uniform curve does.

The *Eagle Claw* in its old-fashioned package is probably the hook most often recognized by anglers. The barbs sticking out of the back of the Eagle Claw make it a good bait holder, as hard to escape as the claw of a bird of prey, which is why the manufacturer named this hook after the eagle.

The *Limerick* has a very sharp bend and a great name. This hook is one of the hooks that meet the requirements of both delicate fly-fishing and brawling surf casting.

The *O'Shaugnessy* is a very strong hook. Its strength and penetrating powers make it a top choice for saltwater anglers. When an O'Shaugnessy's eye is bent at a 45-degree angle, it is frequently used for saltwater jigs.

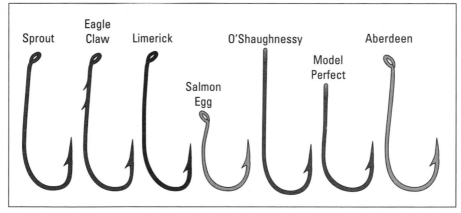

Figure 5-3: Basic hooks.

The *Aberdeen* has a round bend. Largemouth bass fishermen like the Aberdeen very much, and it is also the hook of choice for freshwater jigs. In this case (for jigs) the eye is bent on a 90-degree angle.

The *Model Perfect* is also popular among flytiers. The Model Perfect has a wide bend that gets the point around the jaw of trout and bass. It's not super strong, but proper technique means that you probably shouldn't be bearing down too hard anyway.

The *Salmon Egg* is a weak hook: The shank is too short. The bend is too wide. Its turned-down eye narrows the hooking area. But what else are you going to use to stick into a salmon egg? These hooks are pretty, with a shiny brass finish; and I like the fact that they are so elegant yet they work great for corn, bread balls, cheese, and other unsophisticated bait.

Making sure that your fish gets the point

As I write these words, I have just walked in from the bass pond in back of my parents' house. I used the same popping bug that caught fish on my last visit to that pond. The water had a bit of chop on it — just the kind of conditions that make bass a little less spooky and more eager to hop on a nice slurpy popper. Within ten minutes, I had raised (seriously attracted) and missed six fish. I wrote this disappointing experience off to tentative takes from the bass and slow reflexes on my part.

I was wrong. When I went to change flies, I noticed that all the freshwater hooks in my box were rusty. Then I remembered that, while wading for striped bass in the surf one recent night, my flies had become soaked, and I hadn't bothered to rinse them off. The saltwater hooks showed a little salt staining, but the freshwater hooks (which included my bass bugs) had become rusty and *dull*. Dull hooks never catch fish.

Some anglers think they have a sharp hook as long as the hook's point pricks the skin. But a hook is more than a needle. Even though the point of a hook is relatively small, the point has some area and edge to it. That edge, just like the edge of a knife, needs to be sharpened in order to cut into the fish beyond the end of the barb. Driving the hook home to this depth is called *setting the hook*. How to do this, when to do this, and how hard to do this are all-important elements of angling technique. But you will never get a chance to show off all your mind-blowing techniques with dull hooks.

As I said, a hook has an edge to it, just like a knife has. So you sharpen a hook just as you would sharpen a knife, with a file or sharpening steel. Special hook hones and files are made expressly for this purpose. If your experience is like mine, I know that you will neglect sharpening *until* you lose a good fish. However, before you put on a lure, it is always best to run your file along the edge of your lure's hook to get it good and sharp. And (no matter what anybody tells you to the contrary) you *can* sharpen stainless steel.

Spark plug files (which you can find in any auto parts store) make good hook sharpeners. This makes sense when you consider that spark plug points (like fishhooks) are small, have a narrow gap, and are made of metal. Flyrodders who find themselves out in a stream with a dull hook and no file may want to try using the striker on a matchbook cover to touch up their hooks.

Getting hooked

I've never met you. I don't know how old you are, how big you are, where you come from, or how well you fish. But I do know one thing about you: If you fish, someday, somewhere, you will hook yourself. You may reach up to pull down a tree branch where a fly has snagged. You start to disentangle the fly. Then the branch springs back, and you have a fly right in the meaty part of your finger. Or maybe you have pulled in a nice bass that you caught on a Devil's Horse. You grab the bass by the lower lip (just like the book says to do), and the bass decides to give one last shake that leaves you semi-permanently attached to a still-living bass. In both cases, you have the same reaction: You want to get that hook out of *you!*

You have a number of choices. First, if the lure is still attached to the fish (or anything else for that matter), clip the line to free the lure. Sometimes you can continue to push the hook all the way through the wound and out again. This action is somewhat painful, but it is sometimes doable.

Dehooking yourself

Another method, favored by many anglers, looks as if it shouldn't work, but it does. You need to have some confidence in this method, or you may not do very well. Try practicing this on a piece of raw meat until you understand what you are doing. After you get the idea, it all makes sense.

The following steps, which are illustrated in Figure 5-4, show you how to remove a hook that is embedded in some part of your body.

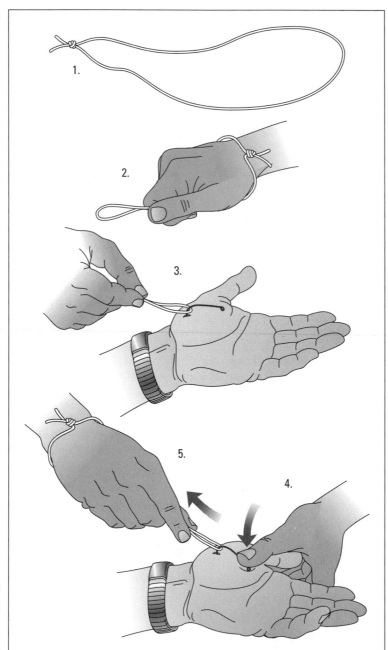

Figure 5-4:
Getting a
hook out.

1. **Take a two foot length of at least 25-pound test line and tie the ends together so that you have a loop.**

   If you do not have 25-pound test line, then double a few strands of 10-pound or 12-pound test line.

2. **Loop the line over your wrist and form a small loop between your thumb and forefinger.**

3. **Take this small loop and put it around the hook in the center of the hook's bend.**

4. **With your other thumb, press down on the eye of the hook.**

   This action should open the wound enough for you to gently back the barb out of your flesh. Getting the barb clear of the flesh is *very* important. If you do not get the barb clear, you should not continue with this procedure.

5. **Finally, pull on the small loop with a sharp jerk.**

   The hook should come free with relatively little pain to you.

Of course, prevention is the best practice, and you can deflect many wandering hooks with a hat and a pair of glasses. Wear them.

Debarbing de hooks

One way to avoid having to go through the whole hook-removal operation is to *debarb* (remove the barbs from) your hooks. Debarbing also helps speed up the releasing process when you are fishing catch-and-release. Simply take a pair of pliers (needlenose work best) and crimp the barb against the hook's tip. Remember that you are not using a wire cutter here, and you are not trying to take the whole point off the hook. On most hooks, a small amount of pressure on the barb does the trick.

Sinkers, Snaps, Swivels, and Bobbers

Sinkers, almost always made of lead, are designed to get your lure or bait in front of the fish. Often, this process involves getting your offering to the bottom of the lake or stream and keeping it there. *Bobbers,* or *floats,* are also designed to get your bait or lure to where the fish are by keeping your bait or lure from sinking.

When using sinkers, sometimes just a split shot or two does the trick. At other times (for example, when fishing in a moving current), you need much more lead. I remember fishing for whiting one February morning off Coney Island. The fish were averaging about a pound. I started off by using eight-ounce sinkers to hold the bait on the bottom in the ebbing tide. As the day wore on, the tide raced more and more, until I was using a pound of lead to catch a one-pound fish. A word of advice: Quit fishing when your sinker weighs as much as your fish. With so little contrast, you probably won't be able to detect a bite; and when you do, the resulting fight to land the fish is about as much fun as reeling in the Manhattan phone book.

Picking the right sinker

Fish are not very particular about which sinker you use. All they care about is the food they think that you are offering them. Your choice of sinker really depends on relatively few factors:

- Is there any current? (The less current, the less weight you need.)
- What type of bottom are you fishing? (Is the bottom covered with rock, sand, weeds, or timber?)
- What do you want your bait or lure to do? (If the bait or lure has to cover a large amount of water, you need one kind of rig. If not, you use another.)

In sinkers, shape is important. As shown in Figure 5-5, a number of sinker choices are available.

Following are the most common types of sinker:

- Pyramid sinkers get to the bottom fast and dig into sand or mud.
- Egg sinkers, or diamond sinkers, move over rocks and rubble a little easier than other shapes.
- Bank sinkers and dipseys work well as *fishfinders,* which are explained in "They call it a fishfinder," later in this chapter.
- Split shot and twist-on sinkers are quick to get on and off and work well when you need a little extra weight.

Snaps and swivels

In rigging up your terminal tackle, you may need to combine a sinker and a bait or lure; but having your sinker right up against your hook is usually not a very good idea: It just doesn't look natural to a fish. I know that a Texas-rigged worm appears to violate this rule, but it really doesn't. To my way of thinking, the bullet shaped head that you use with a Texas rig looks a little bit like a continuation of the silhouette of the worm.

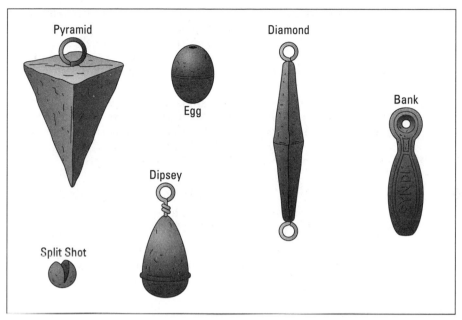

To keep the sinker in one place while the lure or bait swims or floats free, anglers often use an arrangement of snaps and swivels. Many use a combination device called, logically enough, a snap/swivel. The general rule to follow is this: Use only what you need. If a knot works as well as a snap, use a knot. If a simple ring works better than a swivel, use a ring.

A *swivel* is used when the action of the lure, bait, or sinker has a tendency to twist the line. The swivel spins instead of the line, so everything stays tidy. Keeping your swivel six or more inches up the line makes a much prettier presentation.

A *snap* is most useful when you need to change sinkers quickly. Some anglers use snaps for changing lures or baits as well. This technique is a lazy person's way out, and it is definitely *not* the way to get the best action out of your lure. But when you are in a bluefish blitz and the action is furious and you want to change lures in a hurry because the blues have made sawdust out of your plug, you can do fine with a snap.

They call it a fishfinder

Some anglers can tie together enough swivels, sinkers, hooks, and snaps to stock a reasonable tackle department at a major sporting goods store. Some of those anglers even catch fish. Some of them catch a lot of fish. Whether you take the simple route or the Rube Goldberg route, remember that the only thing you ask of any rig is that it puts something interesting in front of the fish.

Many fish feed just off the bottom, so that's where you want your bait to be. The problem with fishing so deep is that the weight you need to get your bait to the bottom may be heavier than the bait itself; so if you tie the hook next to the sinker, your bait has the freedom of movement of a convict with a very heavy ball and chain. This is not a good thing.

The *fishfinder rig,* in all its variations, was designed to give the bait free-floating action while getting it down to the level of the fish, where the big boys are eating. My favorite fishfinder rig is illustrated in Figure 5-6.

To make the rig shown in Figure 5-6, follow these steps:

1. **Tie your line to a swivel or ring.**

2. **Tie a short (9-inch to 10-inch) length of line to the swivel or ring and tie a sinker to the free end of this short length.**

3. **Tie another length of line, about 18 inches, to the swivel or ring and tie a hook to the other end of this leader.**

4. **Attach your bait.**

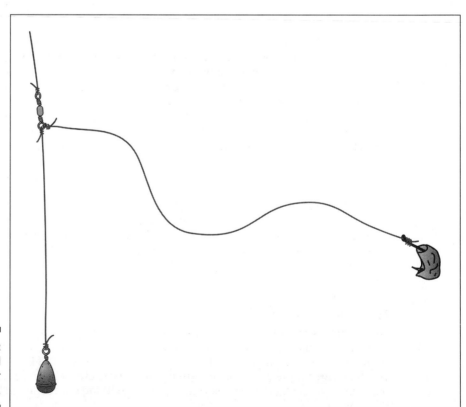

Figure 5-6:
A typical
fishfinder
rig.

Lead is cheap; good fish aren't

They say "If you're not losing a lot of tackle, you're not fishing in the right places." What this means is that if you get your bait down to where the fish are, you are going to hang up on weeds, rocks, deadfalls, old tires, engine blocks, and whatever else nature or man has deposited on the bottom of the ocean, lake, or stream. I am therefore very grateful to the tackle shop owner who showed me a nice fishfinder rig that at least lets me get my fish in, even if it costs me a sinker or two. Figure 5-7 shows this rig. First, you slip on an egg sinker; right under the egg sinker, pinch on a split shot. If you are using this rig and your sinker gets caught in a crevice between two rocks and a fish takes your bait, the split shot pulls off, the sinker falls off (instead of hanging up), and you get to catch a nice fish. Given the choice of losing a couple of sinkers or one good fish, I think you know where I stand.

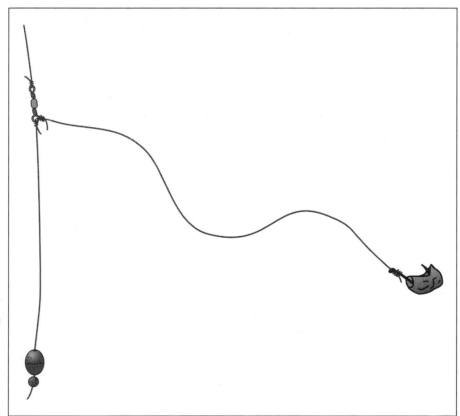

Figure 5-7:
A fishfinder with an expendable sinker.

Bobbers

I think that everybody who ever fished has, at one time or another, fished with a bobber. Bobbers work, and they are fun. Watching the little taps as a fish starts to nibble at your bait and then seeing the bobber go under are two of the most exciting experiences in fishing. Some fishing snobs look down on bobber fishing; but nothing is more pleasant than sitting on a riverbank with a friend or one of your kids and passing the time of day while watching your bobber every now and then. This scenario is a combination of doing nothing and doing something, which, when you get right down to it, is a lot of the fun of fishing.

The most basic float is a red and white plastic globe with a little spring-loaded button on top. To use this type of float, you push in the button and then hook your line around the the hook that protrudes when the button is depressed. I could describe this process step-by-step; but I promise you that my instructions would make the process seem to be much more complicated than it actually is. These floats have two obvious places to thread your line, and that's what you should do. Leave a loose end of line (about a foot or two in length) after the bobber in order to attach your hook. If your loose line is longer, casting gets difficult.

After your hook is on, put some bait on and cast. You cannot cast as far as you did when all you had on was bait and some lead weight, but you don't have to. If you are bobber fishing, you should be near where the fish are to begin with.

Lake bobbing

If you are fishing with live bait, it may start to move around. This movement is good because it can attract game fish. When a minnow gets really agitated because it senses the presence of a predator, fishing can become very exciting. Your bobber gets nervous-looking. (This situation is probably more fun for you than it is for the minnow.)

Wait until the bobber goes under before you strike. Next, drop your rod tip and reel in all the slack line. Then rear back and drive the hook home. Remember, you want that game fish to get the bait well into its mouth before you strike. To complicate things, a bass takes bait differently than does a pike or a crappie; but after you miss a few, you will start to know when and when *not* to strike. If you are fishing with your Dad, your clue for when to strike is when he turns red, starts jumping up and down, and yells "Strike! Strike! Strike!"

Stream bobbing

You can also fish a bobber in moving water. Say you are going for trout or smallmouth in a stream. You may not want your worm or minnow sinking to the bottom. Rig your bobber the same as you did for lake fishing and cast your bait upstream, following its progress downstream with the tip of your rod. Keep the slack out of the line; and when the bobber goes under, strike.

Bobbing and sinking

Sometimes, although it sounds wrong at first, you want to sink and float at the same time (for example, when the fish you want to catch are hanging out at around ten feet of depth). A sinker by itself takes your bait all the way to the bottom, and a float leaves your bait near the surface. A sliding bobber or float rig (as shown in Figure 5-8) works very well at times like these.

To make this rig, follow these steps:

1. **First, pull off about ten feet of line.**

2. **Then create a float stopper by knotting another piece of line around your line at the ten-foot mark.**

   Any knot, such as a simple overhand knot, is okay. (Many tackle shops carry manufactured float stoppers.)

3. **Thread the line through the float and pull it through until the knot stops the line.**

4. **Next, attach bait and weight as you normally would and cast your rig.**

   The weight carries the bait down to the fish, and the bobber keeps the bait in the fish zone.

For Natural-Born Anglers (This Means You!)

If you've read this entire chapter, you've read all about hooks, swivels, sinkers, and floats. Anglers have worked out hundreds of combinations of these four items for different fish and different places. You can have a dozen hooks dangling from a rig. You can fish two bobbers. You can fish two or three baits at different depths. The number of inventions that anglers who came before you have applied to getting their hook in front of a fish is endless. Whenever you come across a new or complicated-looking setup, remember that it was designed to get into that all-important fish-catching zone. When you look at the functions of rigs that way, you begin to see why a flounder rig looks one way and a bluefish rig looks another way. And after you begin to understand those principles, you may even figure out a new and better way to rig tackle. Fishing has come to the point that it has because somebody, somewhere said, "Hmmm. Wonder if *this* would work?"

Most of the time, such new rigs don't work. But every now and again, someone just like you (somebody who may be looking at a given situation for the first time) figures out a great new technique. If you are a novice angler, you don't know as much as a veteran angler does, but you have one advantage over the veteran angler: You are seeing things freshly. Trust your instincts. We are all born with a great aptitude for hunting, gathering, and fishing for food.

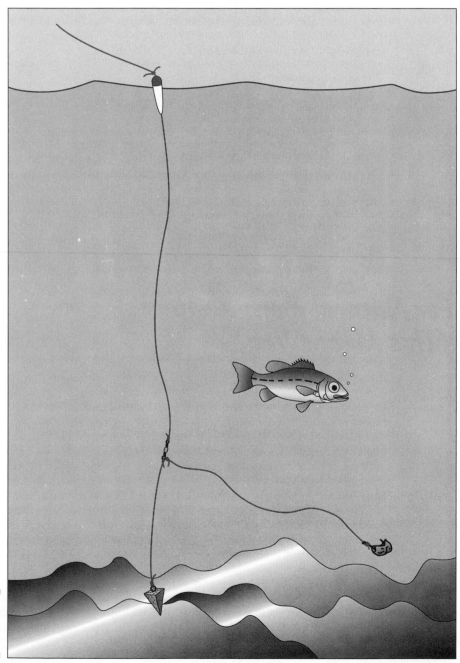

Figure 5-8:
A sliding
bobber rig.

Chapter 6
Lines

Some folks use line strong enough to lift a Ford Windstar and others use line so light that a strong sneeze will break it. Fishing line, whether it's made of nylon, Dacron, Kevlar, or even metal, has two jobs to perform:

- ✔ It should deliver your lure, fly, or bait to the fish.
- ✔ When the fish bites, it should keep the fish on the line without breaking.

The concepts are pretty simple, and although you have choices to make, my guess is that 90 percent of you will be using good-old-fashioned *mono,* which stands for *nylon monofilament* (a ten dollar word that means "a single strand of nylon line").

Fly line is a whole different kettle of fish, but even with fly line, the leader at the end of the line is usually made of nylon monofilament, so much of what I say about the lines you use for spinning and bait casting also holds true for the last few feet of your fly-fishing rig as well.

Test Means They Tested It

If you ever catch a nice fish, there are two questions that your fellow anglers will ask you: The first is usually "What did it take?" And the second often is "What *test* line?"

Test means somebody tested it and that same somebody guarantees that your line won't break if you apply that amount of force to it. In other words, if you apply anything less than 12 pounds of pull to a 12-pound test line, you *should* be fine. A line can be 2-pound test for those of you who use ultra-light gear, or it can be more than a hundred pounds for those of you who are horsing in a marlin.

But line test isn't an absolute measurement. The give or stretch in the line, the kind of knot you use, how many fish you've caught with that line, and other such factors all figure in to the equation, usually to the advantage of the fish, not the angler. On the other hand, most manufacturers play it on the safe side when they list the line test, the same way that the weather people at your local TV station do when they predict a "guaranteed high" for the day: They leave a little wiggle room.

How strong does it need to be?

Once you learn how to play a fish, you might be surprised at how much fish you can subdue with a relatively light line. Notice I said "subdue." Line isn't designed to *lift* fish. You use special tools such as nets, gaffs, tailers, and special leaders for that task (see Chapter 15). Just because the fish weighs six pounds doesn't mean you need 6-pound test line.

Look at it this way: Say you weigh 140 pounds. If I stuck a hook in your lip, I bet you it would take a lot less than 140 pounds of force to lead you around. In fact, we human beings are so wimpy that a pound or two of pressure should have you following along quite nicely. Fish are a little tougher, but still, I've caught hundred-pound tarpon on 20-pound test. (I have also lost 3-pound trout on 6-pound test.)

Thick and thin

In fishing line, as in waist lines, thin is usually better. Thin line cuts through the air with less resistance and likewise sinks more rapidly in the water. You can fit more of it on your spool. It throws less of a shadow in shallow water (a big consideration with spooky fish like trout or bonefish). For any given line material, the thinner product has a lighter line test rating: 6-pound test Stren mono is thinner then 12-pound test Stren mono.

A little quarter-ounce lure has a hard time pulling 20-pound test line off your reel. On the other hand, a 2-ounce lure might snap off or give you a royal backlash if you try to cast it with 6-pound test line. So take this advice: Match the lure weight to the line. Many lure manufacturers recommend a line weight and you can always ask the person at the tackle shop for a recommendation.

Limpness isn't wimpness

Lighter, thinner line is limper than heavier line. Nylon monofilament is generally limper than metal or Kevlar but not as limp as braided line. Limpness is a good thing when you are fishing lures with a delicate action. Heavy or stiff line can interfere with the action of the lure or trolled bait. Sometimes anglers say that heavy line "clotheslines," meaning that it drags the bait or lure through the water with a very unlifelike action.

When action is all-important, go light and limp. On the other hand, when jigging or using a popping bug, you want your rod motion transmitted directly to the jig or bug. A stiffer or heavier line works to your advantage here.

Stretchability

Nylon mono stretches a lot before it breaks. This is a good thing if you have a tendency to set the hook really hard. Many newcomers, as well as a lot of longtime anglers, rear back the minute they feel a bite, sometimes yanking the hook and a few teeth right out of the fish's mouth. Thankfully, most line stretches in these situations. But if you're the kind of person who has really sensitive fingertips and who can feel that tiny bump when a bass picks up a plastic worm, you probably want a little more beef in your line so that you can set the hook with a single, firm stroke. In fighting the fish, mono, which is more stretchy, absorbs more of the shock of any sudden twists or turns.

Erase that bad memory

Line, especially mono, has a habit of coming off the reel in pesky coils. This is doubly true when you pick up your rod and reel for the first time after a winter layoff. Look at it this way: You'd have a hard time straightening out right away after an hour or two nap in your recliner, so it's not surprising that fishing line acts the same way after three months in the closet. Spinning reels are major offenders in the line-curling department.

One way to straighten your line is to let all the line trail behind you as you slowly motor or paddle along in your boat or canoe. Don't tie on any weight or lures. The resistance of the surface tension of the water will lay the line out straight and remove the coils and twists in your line.

If you are not going out in a boat, you can knot one end of your line around a tree and then walk backwards. When you have fed out all the line, pull firmly. ("Firmly" doesn't mean a violent yank: Use steady, medium pressure.) Repeat a few times, pulling and maintaining pressure for ten seconds.

In both cases, when you reel up, keep uniform tension on the line with the thumb and forefinger of your noncranking hand.

Does color count?

It may count to you, but I don't think it means much to the fish. Still, since you are the one doing the fishing, you may get some benefit from more visible line. Fluorescent line shows up nicely in the air but becomes pretty invisible in the water. If you need a little extra help in seeing the above-surface part of your line, then fluorescent line can be worthwhile in detecting those subtle bumps that mean a fish has picked up your bait. As a general rule, you don't want the fish to see the line. So opaque lines, which includes all wire line, put you at somewhat of a disadvantage in clear water. The cloudier or dingier the water, the less this factor comes into play. Bottom line: Color is a non-issue; visibility isn't.

Wear and tear

When you take a spill on the sidewalk and skin your knee, the medical term for your injury is an *abrasion.* When a fish drags your line over rocks, against coral, an overhanging bank, or submerged tree trunk, the line also gets an abrasion. Braided line abrades fairly easily; mono less so. Kevlar, the new super materials such as Spider Wire, and plain old wire are all more sturdy, but *all* line will abrade to some degree.

After catching a fish (and sometimes after losing one) run your fingers along your line, especially that last 20 feet or so. If you feel a nick or rough spot, cut your line at the nick and re-rig your terminal tackle. In fact, after you've caught five or six fish with the same setup, it's not a bad idea to re-rig anyway. Many times, your line will develop invisible fatigue or stress points.

Many of us, after losing a good fish, often say "He just cut me right off. There was nothing I could do about it." Actual meaning: "It was an amazing fish; I'm an amazing fisherman just to have hooked him. I did everything I could do." Wrong! That is a classic example of trying to make a good thing out of a bad thing. Most of the time, when you lose a fish, your line breaks because of a poor knot or structural failure of the line. While it's true that the fish has to win sometimes, it's also true that many anglers (myself included) lose plenty of fish because we just don't take the time to re-rig.

Good wine and good line

Sunlight can affect your fishing line. So can heat. Like wine, fishing line should be stored in a cool, dark place. For most of us, storing means stacking a bunch of rods together in a corner of the basement or closet. It also means you'll probably have a real mess to untangle the next time you go fishing. Stick a couple of nails in the wall in the basement or garage and hang each rod in a horizontal position when not in use.

While you're at it, hold the salt!

If there is one chief enemy in the war against fishing tackle, it is salt, as in saltwater. It rusts and corrodes metal, dissolves synthetics, and in general, does the same number on your tackle as it does on all those pitted out cars you see when you are on the coast. Rinse all your tackle after fishing in saltwater, and that includes your line. You shouldn't let it sit for even a day.

So which line do I want?

Nylon mono is supple. It stretches. It knots well. It doesn't kink, and it's pretty invisible. Still, many people like the strength and punch of braided line and the way it comes easily off a bait-casting spool. It's denser and more visible than comparable mono, but that is not always the most important consideration.

Braided line transmits the feel of a strike better. It's relative lack of stretch makes it a good choice to stick the hook into a fish when trolling. It is not as good at knotting as mono.

Wire line gets down fast, which is important in trolling. It does kink up more than other lines. Knotting isn't easy and it can corrode. Treat it right, however, and it does the job it was designed to do.

The super synthetics like Kevlar and Spider Wire are thin, strong, and very abrasion resistant.

So which one is best? Most anglers would say that nylon mono is the one line to use if you are using only one. Start with mono and then experiment with the others.

Fly Lines and Leaders

A fly line is a totally different animal from all other fishing line. In spinning and bait casting, the weight of your terminal tackle pulls the line off the reel and carries it to the fish. Fly-fishing is just the opposite. The weight of the line carries the relatively weightless fly to the fish.

Way back when, fly line was made from braided horsehair. If you wanted a heavy line you braided more hairs. The modern fly line is a smooth plastic coating around a core of braided nylon or Dacron. Most lines are 70 to 90 feet long and are spliced to another hundred yards or so of thinner backing line (usually braided Dacron). When you buy line or a reel, have the store put the backing on and splice it to your line. You can do this yourself, but why hassle?

Does weight count?

Sure weight counts. It's the weight of the line that bends the rod and it's the bend of the rod as it springs forward that shoots the line towards the fish. Fly lines come with different ratings according to their weight. A One Weight is a very light line that is used with an extremely delicate rod. As the numbers go up, so does the weight. Most trout fishermen prefer something in the Four to Six range. Rods are rated according to the weight of the line they throw. My first fly rod was a Six Weight and I caught trout, bass, an 18-pound pike, many bonefish, and two barracuda on it. (The second barracuda finally broke that rod.)

Although there are no hard and fast rules, Table 6-1 lists my recommendations for line (and rod) weights for some common game fish.

Table 6-1	Fly Line Weights and Common Game Fish
Line Weight	*Type of Fish*
One, Two, and Three Weight	panfish, trout
Four Weight, Five Weight	trout, freshwater bass
Six Weight, Seven Weight	trout, bass, small blues, stripers, bonefish, pike
Eight Weight, Nine Weight	salmon, stripers, bonefish, permit, bluefish, redfish
Ten, Eleven, Twelve Weight	tarpon and other big game

The line weight table gives a bunch of general guidelines. They are not commandments. My favorite bass guide, Jack Allen, feels that with graphite rods, you can usually go up or down one line weight from the recommended number and still be well within the optimum performance range for your rod. And in heavy wind, or when he wants more of a fight on light tackle, Jack has been known to put Eight Weight line on a Five Weight rod.

Taper tips

Most fly lines have a *taper;* that is, they are fatter in one part then another. These days, the most common taper is *weight forward*. It is heavier in the head, which is the first 30 feet or so of line to come through the guides of your rod. The principle behind it is that you want to get a lot of leverage on the rod to develop momentum quickly, and then, when you have developed rapid line speed, the weight of the head will carry the rest of the line. In other words the weight-forward line is ideal for *delivery* of the fly.

You will see some fly lines marked with a saltwater taper or bassbug taper. These, too, are weight-forward lines with a more exaggerated taper. Most fly-rodders, myself included use weight-forward tapers exclusively.

Less common these days than it used to be is the *double taper*. This design is thin in the head, gradually fattens out, and then slims again. The idea is you have a good amount of line in the air to develop momentum, yet the line that lands nearest to the trout does so more delicately than the weight-forward variety. I keep thinking that someday I am going to be a sensitive enough angler to be able to appreciate double taper, but my experience has been that when I want more delicacy of presentation, I go to a lighter rod and line.

Sink or swim

Now that fly-fishing no longer exclusively means dry-fly-fishing for trout in a stream, flyrodders have begun to use different kinds of lines for different fishing situations. Often, this means using some kind of weight to get down to fish that aren't surface feeders, such as stream-borne trout hanging on the bottom, bass three feet down in a pond, or stripers 15 feet down in a bay. In the old days, you used weighted flies or tied some split shot onto your leader. These methods still work in many situations, but then came lead core line (the inner core is literally made of lead), which made for the least pleasant casting imaginable. I once spent a week fishing a Thirteen Weight with a lead core for tarpon in the bocas (river mouths) of Costa Rica. A total bummer!

These day, you have the choice of using *sink tip* lines where the front of the line is weighted and the rest floats for easy casting. I like these lines in rivers and shallow bays. There are a couple of types:

- *Intermediate* line sinks very slowly so that it can be fished as a floater or a sinker. This is far and away my preferred line for saltwater fly-fishing in the northeastern United States. It gets the line below the surface chop and keeps you in contact with your fly.

- *FS,* or *full sinking,* line gets down fast and deep. The best are the *teeny* lines that have come on the market in recent years. They are slim, so they cut through the wind, and they aren't so hellish to pick up and cast as the old lead core.

If you are fishing a sink tip in shallow water, you may not want a long, delicate leader or an unweighted fly. Think about it: Your tip gets down where the fish are and your long leader and weightless fly float to the surface. The sink tip helps get you in the fishing zone. A weighted fly keeps you there.

Leaders

After the fly, the most critical element of the fly-fishing setup is *the leader,* meaning the nylon monofilament line that attaches the fly line to the fly. Remember that a fly line is big and thick, and a fly is delicate and small. The leader must also be light; otherwise, it will overpower the fly, giving it a lifeless action. Add to this situation the fact that a big, fat fly line landing next to a spooky fish is guaranteed to send it straight for cover. A leader that makes as little disturbance as possible increases your chances of connecting with a fish.

As seen in Figure 6-1, the thick section of the leader that joins to the fly line is called *the butt.* What happens between the butt and the fly is a gradual *taper:* as the leader gets progressively thinner and lighter. The result is a smooth and even transfer of force from the rod to the line and down through the leader. The last section of the taper is also known as the *tippet.*

Leaders are usually between 7 and 12 feet in length. You can buy them knotted or knotless. The taper of a knotted leader is made up of progressively lighter lengths of mono knotted together. The knotless type is just a single strand that smoothly tapers.

When you change flies a lot, you end up cutting off and replacing tippet. Using a knotted leader is a handy way to remember what thickness you are fishing. On the other hand, if you are just starting out, knotless is pretty simple, so keep it simple.

Figure 6-1:
For the average dry-fly leader, the butt and taper sections each make up 30 percent of the leader, and the tippet is the remaining 40 percent.

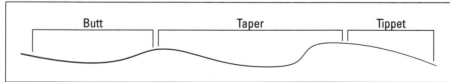

Butt   Taper   Tippet

The X file

If you ever catch a nice trout — make that, *when* you catch a nice trout — you will be asked, "What did you take it on?" This is actually two questions. The first is "What fly?" and the second is "What tippet?" Tippets are rated according to their thickness, which is directly related to their strength. Where the spin fisherman might say "I caught it on 12-pound test," the flyrodder's answer would be "1X."

Why X?

The simple answer, as it is with a lot of fly-fishing, is "The English figured out the system, and you know that if the English are given a

chance to measure anything, they do it differently than the rest of the world."

In the old days, leader tippets used to be made out of silk worm gut. They were sized by being passed through a die that shaved down the thickness of the gut. If you ran it through the die once, it was 1X; twice gave you 2X, and so on. The more shavings it got, the thinner the leader. So the higher numbers represent thinner, lighter leaders.

Beginners usually fish somewhere in the 3X to 5X range.

Match your leader to your fly

A little fly requires a light tippet. If you use a heavy tippet with a little fly, you have a classic case of the tail wagging the dog, or in this case, the line wagging the fly. This setup will never catch a fish.

The rule of thumb for matching fly to leader is to divide the fly size by 4 to figure out the appropriate leader. A big size-8 fly gets a sturdy 2X tippet. Size 16 gets a 4X. Also, if the trout are finicky, you can always go a little lighter. For example, try 5X for that size 16 if you get interest but no takes.

Threading your fly line

As far as fly rods go, the big difference from other fishing rods is the line. Usually, when you thread line through your spinning or bait-casting rod, you pick up the end of the line and thread it through the guides. When you try to do this with heavy fly line, it will find a way to slip back down and make you start all over again. As shown in Figure 6-2, the easy way is to pull off about six feet of line, double it over, and pull the doubled line through the guides. Don't make me explain the physics. It works better.

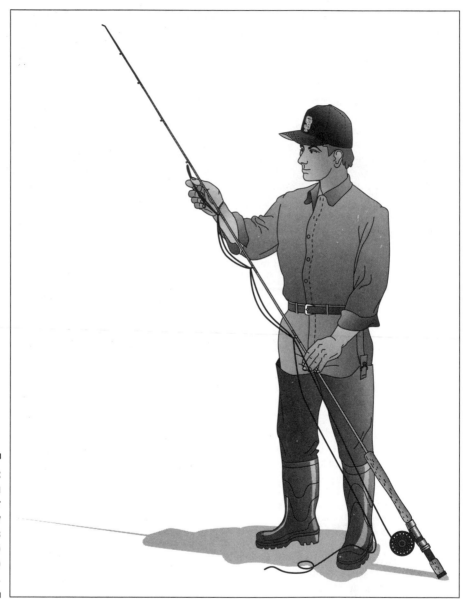

Figure 6-2:
When you
double over
the heavy
fly line, it's
easy to
string up
your rod.

Chapter 7

Rods

• •

In This Chapter

▶ Picking the best rod for you (especially when it's your only rod)

▶ Understanding the importance of rod action rod

▶ Knowing when long is good and when short is better

• •

The rod is the symbol of the angler in the same way that the gun is the symbol of the hunter. Just as you need a bullet or shell to shoot an animal, you need a reel and a line to catch a fish. But the rod, like the gun, is the main ingredient. Rod and gun clubs aren't called reel and gun clubs, are they?

What Rods Are Made Of

In *theory,* a fishing rod can be made of wood, steel, fiberglass, or graphite. In *practice,* however, today's rods are mostly made of some kind of graphite or graphite/fiberglass composite. With the exception of the cane pole, there are very few wooden rods made anymore. You can still buy split-bamboo fly rods, but more people collect them than use them. Likewise, some of the best surf fisherman I know use buttery, one-piece, fiberglass rods, but they are the exception rather than the rule. Most of the time, most of the anglers you see will be fishing with something that has a good amount of graphite in it. The reason? Graphite is light and strong, and it delivers much more power than other materials, yet it is very affordable.

A Rod Is a Rod Is a Rod . . . Is a Rod

All rods (spinning, bait-casting, and fly) share common features, as shown in Figure 7-1.

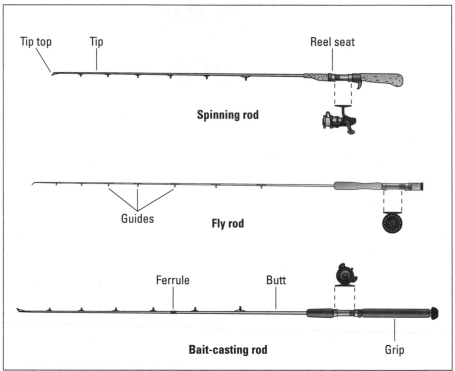

Figure 7-1:
Rod
anatomy.

- ✔ **Tip top:** The point where the line leaves the rod on its way to the fish.

- ✔ **Tip:** The last foot or so of rod. It can bend a little or a great deal and is critical in determining the action and sensitivity of the rod.

- ✔ **Butt:** The bottom half or third of the shaft of the rod. As with the tip, on some rods, the butt really bends, while on others it doesn't.

- ✔ **Guides:** As the name implies, the guides direct the line on its journey from the reel to the tip top. On a spinning rig, the guides get progressively smaller as you go from reel to tip top, channeling the large coils that come off the reel into a straight line to your target.

- ✔ **Reel seat:** Usually a set of screw-tightened washers or rings that fit over the base of the reel and attach it to the rod.

- ✔ **Ferrule:** A male-female connector that joins the pieces of a rod together.

- ✔ **Grip:** What you hold onto. It can be made of cork or synthetic materials. Grips come in many shapes and sizes. The main point is that it has to be comfortable for the way you fish.

The Three Jobs of a Rod

Everybody knows that a rod is for catching fish. To do this, it must be stiff but supple, strong but delicate. If fishing were just a matter of cranking them in, you could use a broom handle. But angling for a fish is a three-part job that requires three different tasks of your rod:

- **Getting the bait, lure, or fly to where the fish is.** That is, delivering the goods.

- **Setting the hook.** Because not every take is a visual one, a rod has to be sensitive enough to let you feel the fish as it takes your worm (or lunges at your jig) and strong enough to set the hook.

- **Fighting the fish.** The rod is a big lever that transmits a great deal of force; and because of its ability to bend, it transmits variable force as required, acting as a shock absorber when the fish suddenly turns or bolts off again.

The way in which a rod accomplishes these three tasks varies. Sometimes the delivery has to be as light as goose down. Sometimes you just heave your bait and hope. To accommodate the different tasks involved and to accommodate the differences in anglers, all kinds of rods are available. In time, if you fish enough, you will discover how to feel the differences in rods. You may like some but not care for others. Your personal fondness for a particular rod doesn't mean that one rod is necessarily better than another (although there are both winners and stinkers out there). It just means that one is better for you and the kind of fishing you want to do at any given time.

Many are classified, but few are remembered

When you apply force to rods, they bend quickly or slowly. Some flex only at the tip, although others bend all the way down to the butt. How fast and how much a rod bends determines its *action*. For the record, tackle manufacturers classify their rods as *ultrafast, fast, moderate,* and *slow.* They also classify rods by how much weight they can optimally throw, using the terms *ultralight, light, medium,* and *heavy.* These classifications are the basis for many tables which list all the actions, all the weights, all the recommended line tests. The end result is a mountain of facts I still can't keep straight after 20 years of writing about this stuff. But I do know something about the principles involved, and that is basically all you need to know as well. Rods often have the optimum lure weight printed right on them. This in turn leads to a general rule of thumb for line weight: *the lighter the lure or the lighter the fish, the lighter the line test required.* The corollary to this is that lighter line (because it slices through the air more easily than heavy line does) also enables you to cast further.

Action: It ain't the meat, it's the motion

As shown in Figure 7-2, a rod can bend a little or a great deal. Fast rods bend in the tip, but slower rods bend through the whole length of the rod. In general, a fast rod casts well when distance is a priority. It is punchier than a slow rod. It is also sensitive in the tip, so that you can feel a strike or even a nibble right away. A slower rod generally allows for a more delicate presentation. Whereas a fast, or *tippy,* rod may have a tendency to tear bait off the hook, a slower action will give a nice even heave. If you are doing a great deal of bottom fishing or jig fishing, the stiffness of a fast rod is desirable. On the other hand, if you are working crankbaits, many anglers prefer a slower rod so that they don't yank the lure out of the fish's mouth the second it shows any interest. Although a fast rod can be more sensitive than a slow rod (with a fast rod, you can feel the tiniest tap-tap of a fish), a slow rod acts as a better shock absorber when you are battling big fish.

You may hear people talk about a rod having *parabolic* bend or action. I can't for the life of me remember exactly what a parabola is, but I do recall that it is a curve of some kind. Here's how this word got into angling language: Some years back, a French manufacturer was among the first to sell a line of rods that were fast in the tip and slow in the butt. This kind of progressive action is called *parabolic* because the French tackle maker called his rods *Parabolique*.

Does tire-kicking do any good?

One of the time-honored ways of testing out a rod in the tackle store is to bend the rod while holding the tip against the ceiling of the store (provided the store has a low ceiling). I don't think that this experiment tells you much. Another favorite pre-purchase ritual is to hold the rod in one hand and wiggle it back and forth to see how much it bends. This experiment does give a little better idea of what to expect from a rod, but it tells you little more than does kicking the tires on a car that you are interested in buying.

You wouldn't buy a car without a test drive. The same thing goes for a rod. Try it out. Cast it with a lure on it. See how it feels and how you handle it. Of course, if this is your first rod and you don't know how to cast yet, you won't have any basis for comparison, so you will be forced to go with the recommendations of others. Get your recommender to try the rod, if possible. Of course, if the recommender is employed at the tackle shop, you are somewhat at his or her mercy. In this case, stick with a name brand. Don't buy a bottom-of-the-line rod if you can afford not to. And (unless you have money to burn) don't buy a top-of-the-line rod because you may not be able to tell the difference between it and a bottom-of-the-line rod at this stage of the game.

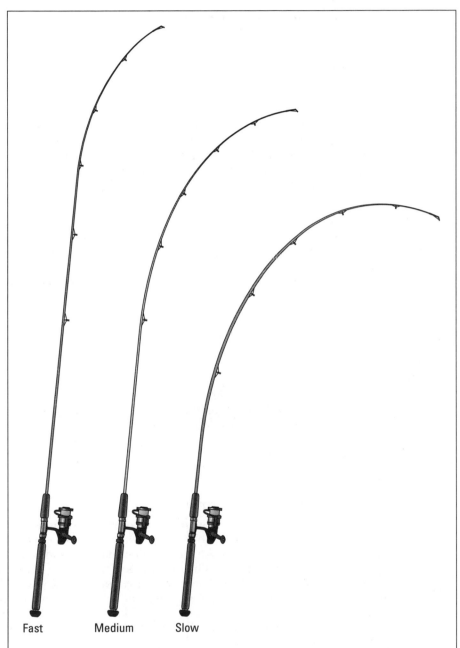

Figure 7-2:
Fast,
medium,
and slow
rod action.

Fast   Medium   Slow

Bait-casting rods

Bait-casting rods are designed to deliver heavier weights than similarly rated spinning and fly rods. They are also more accurate in hitting your target than a comparable spinning setup. Or maybe I should say, in the hands of an accurate caster, they are more accurate. Moreover, the extra heft in casting turns into extra power in setting the hook; and this factor, too, is a plus for the bait caster. The downside to bait casting is that mastering the art of the cast is more difficult than it is with a spinning reel. The upside is that it's fun. Before the advent of the spinning reel, which really happened in this country in the late 1940s, many anglers first learned to fish with bait-casting reels.

If I had only one

My choice for an all-around bait-casting rod would be a medium action rod, six feet long, with a pistol grip (as shown in Figure 7-3). It's light enough to respond to a bass, yet strong enough for northerns (and even muskies). If you are fishing in brushy cover and overhanging boughs, you may want a somewhat shorter rod, but stick with the medium outfit for an all-rounder.

Figure 7-3:
A bait-casting rod with a pistol grip is an easy-to-use rod.

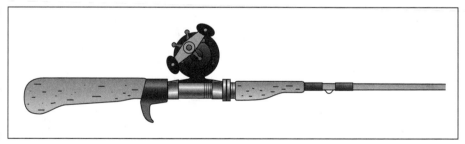

Surf casting is a different story

In surf casting, the basic fact you must confront is that there is only a little surf but a great deal of ocean, so the more water you can cover, the more chance you have of catching fish. I have spent days on end watching schools of feeding fish slashing through bait that was just out of reach of my gear. If I could only get another 20 or 30 feet out of my spinning rig, I would no doubt have been into fish like the guys with the bait-casting surf sticks. Bait-casting surf sticks just flat out cast further. Mastering the technique of using bait-casting surf sticks does take longer, but for delivering the goods, the bait-casting rod is the champ.

If I had only one

Go for a long rod with lots of graphite.

Spinning rods

If I had to name the one thing that revolutionized sport fishing in my life-time, it would have to be the introduction of the spinning reel. Even though matching the explosion in fly-fishing over the last decade would seem to be hard, that phenomenon really is pretty rinky-dink when you consider how many people learned to fish with spinning rods. And after they learned, most of them kept right on using spinning gear. Spinning gear allows you to use all those great lures that were developed for bait-casting rods plus the light lures and bait that were impossible to use with bait-casting equipment. There is an art to casting with a spinning rod, but it is nowhere near as disaster-prone as casting with the whiplash-inducing bait-casting rig.

As with bait-casting rods, a range of actions and weights is available in spinning rods. I have three rods: one ultralight rod for panfish, stream trout, and smallmouth bass; a medium rod for bigger bass, walleye, and pike; and a nine foot stiff action surf stick for the ocean. The rules here are to match the rod to the fish and to use enough rod to catch fish but not so much rod that there is no fight. You could use a heavyweight rod to catch a bluegill, but that wouldn't be much fun. Likewise, a good angler could land a large trout on an ultralight, but do you want to fight one fish all afternoon?

If I had only one

My choice for an all-in-one spinning rod would be a six- or seven-foot, medium-action graphite rod. Such a rod can throw lures in the $1/4$-ounce to $5/8$-ounce range. It is sporty enough to give some pleasure with small fish, but it can also fight bigger freshwater fish (and even the odd bluefish or striped bass).

Surf casting with a spinning rod

Surf-casting rods can be very long, but I find that the real sharpies go for the medium to short rods. Being able to lick a big fish with a light rod has a macho element, but macho only gets you so far. I think that the real reason most fishermen prefer surf rods in the eight- to ten-foot range is that such rods are more *effective* (and that means more *fun*) in the long run. I guess that if you are just bait fishing, a long rod doesn't have much of a downside (except for fitting it in your car or truck). But if you work a lure, you are reminded of the laws of physics as they apply to levers when you fish a very long rod: Even a little weight feels like a big weight when you apply force over a long distance. In other words, using a long rod can be tiring.

If I had only one

As a matter of fact, I do have only one. It is nine feet long and mostly graphite with some fiberglass. A ten-footer would be nice, too, but it wouldn't break down and fit as nicely in the trunk of my car. My own rod has a fairly fast action that works best with 12-pound test line (although it can accommodate 20-pound test if I am more interested in strength than casting distance). If I use line that is lighter than ten pounds, I run the risk of developing so much force in the rod that I literally cast my lure off, breaking the line at the knot. I know that I run this risk because I once did this with my favorite Kastmaster lure.

Take my seat, please

I have hooked *and lost* a couple of nice fish in my day because my reel came out of the screw-tightened rings on the reel seat. I'm sure my problem had something to do with my own carelessness, but it also has something to do with reel seats. The anglers who gets up at 4:30 every morning to fish the striper run in the fall all use duct tape or masking tape to lash their reels to their rods. This way, their reel seats have no chance of coming unscrewed while they are fighting big fish. You can buy rods without reel seats, which means that you are pretty much committed to leaving the reel attached to the rod (but I find that most surfcasters never break down their equipment anyway).

And while you are at it, take my ferrule, too

If I lived out at the beach and had a pickup truck, I would probably have a one-piece fiberglass rod. All the sharpies out my way have this type of rod. And if you know how to handle one, the action that it provides is deliciously slow, and casting is more like relaxing and less like practicing for the Olympic hammer throw.

This leads to the larger question of *ferrules* (the male and female joints by which two pieces of a rod fit together). The old wisdom has it that the more ferrules you have, the more strength and action you give up in your rod. I am not so sure that this wisdom applies to most modern rod designs. Instinctively, I like the look of fewer ferrules; but as a traveling fisherman, I can tell you that you cannot fit a nine-foot rod in the overhead luggage bin on an airplane. Traveling rods that come in four or five pieces are probably a little clunkier — less smooth — than one- or two-piece rods, but I don't think that you really notice that much difference. For most fishing, most of the time, a multipiece rod works perfectly fine (and it has the advantage of being handy anyplace you go).

Fly rods

Although fly-rodding is steeped in tradition, fly rods aren't. In Izaak Walton's day, there were no fancy split-cane bamboo rods — only solid pieces of pliable local woods like willow and ash. Bamboo technology came along only in the last century and only dominated for about a hundred years. Bamboo is fun to cast, and I find something (that I can't quite put my finger on) pleasurable in using material that was once living. No question about it, when fiberglass came along, many more people could afford to get into fly-fishing. And now, the successor to fiberglass — graphite — is the finest casting material so far. Casting is the name of the game in fly-fishing. Much of the pleasure of the sport comes from laying out a good cast; and flyrodders spend much more time casting than other anglers.

You have to cast, not me

Casting a fly is kind of like throwing a baseball: Almost everybody has a different style. I have a kind of three-quarter, sidearm kind of cast that is miles away from the classic English style of straight-up-and-down cast with the elbow held tight against the chest. Some rods that more-traditional casters love give me a problem. Some rods work for me at short distances; but when I really want to lay the line out there, a "dead spot" appears that probably has more to do with my casting motion than it has to do with the rod. So when people ask "What rod is best for me?," I can recommend; but in the end, you are going to have to feel your way into this and get the rod that feels best for you.

If no one had said it before, then I am sure that some flyrodder, somewhere, would have come up with the saying "different strokes for different folks."

Anyway, here are my preferences for different situations.

Small streams, small rods

In general, fishing in small streams with overhanging boughs often leads to a tangle of rod and line. Watching anglers fish in such a setting is almost like watching people in an old slapstick movie: The angler looks in front for obstacles, and then, with equal care, looks in back. Then he or she does it again (so Mother Nature doesn't have a chance to sneak in any trees or shrubs while their backs are turned). Then he or she very carefully casts and — boing! — the line is hung up in a tree in back of Mr. or Ms. Flyrodder. Apart from your being very conscious of where your line is going to go when you cast, a short rod with a fast tip enables you to cast with very little line out of the guides (which is what you have to do when you fish in small streams).

Fast rods for most trout

There is an old saw about dry-fly rods having fast action and wet-fly rods having slow action. I don't agree. A fast tip makes for a tighter casting loop, which is good, especially with small flies. But you need to be careful when setting the hook with a fast rod, especially when using light tippet. If the rod doesn't have much give, you will break right off. To avoid this situation, you need to learn to strike with firm, but not explosive, pressure. As far as wet flies go, when you are fishing a nymph upstream (which is an increasingly popular and effective method of fishing them), you need the same sensitivity that a fast tip affords the dry-fly angler. What my recommendation gets down to is this: I like a fast rod for most trout situations. For starters, an eight-foot six-weight is my pick.

Bass and saltwater: a little-slower rod and a much-slower angler

Fly casting has a great deal to do with *line* speed (which many anglers, unfortunately, confuse with *arm* speed). When you are fishing with big, air-resistant flies (and when you add to them the amount of line you need to carry in the air for distance-casting in saltwater), you don't want to do a great deal of hurry-up casting with a bunch of false casts. Fast trout rods tend to reinforce this tendency to speeding up, and the one thing I tell trout fishermen when they begin saltwater fly-fishing is to slow down. A slower, somewhat softer rod encourages an angler to let the fly line have that extra second or two in the air to load up (flex) the rod fully. The result in your cast is less false casting and longer distances. Ideally, I like a fast tip with slower action through the body of the rod. A nine-foot, nine-weight is a good saltwater all-rounder. (Make that an eight-weight if you want to catch some freshwater bass and pike while you are at it.)

Getting Unstuck

Although one-piece rods are neat, 99 percent of the readers of this book either have (or will have) rods that break down into two or more pieces. Going on the time-honored principle of "If something bad can happen, it will," you can count on a pair of ferrules getting stuck together someday. When this happens, remember the following dos and don'ts.

Don't use pliers. A rod is usually a hollow tube, and pliers are *guaranteed* to break your rod. It may not break right then and there — although it usually does — but take my word for it: You will injure the fibers in the rod, and it will break one day.

The same goes for twisting the stuck ferrule apart like a screw-top soda bottle. First, this technique probably won't work; and second, you could easily snap one of the guides. You do use a gentle twisting motion when you disassemble a rod; but if that technique doesn't work, try one of the following two methods.

It's a good thing

I have broken four fly rods in my career. One of them was on a fish, and the others were while "safely" transporting them in my car. The best way to carry a fly rod around is in its case. But breaking down a rod, unstringing it, reeling up, and storing the reel is a big pain, especially when you are driving around from spot to spot during a day's fishing. Some genius came up with the idea of a breakdown case that allows you to leave your rod strung up — reel and all. Although they are not cheap (the current price is around $50), they are much cheaper than a new rod.

The squat, bend, and push maneuver

As shown in Figure 7-4, put the rod behind your knees and with your arms next to and just outside your knees, grip the rod firmly on either side of the ferrule; then push your knees outward until the ferrule comes unstuck. Don't get violent about it or you may fall down (and probably break the rod in the process). Just a firm, small push should do the trick.

Figure 7-4: Using your knees and hands to unstick ferrules doesn't look pretty, but it works.

Ice is nice

If you have any ice handy, put some in a plastic bag and place it around the ferrule. Leave it for a minute or two. Then remove the ice bag, grab the female (outer) part of the ferrule, and let your hand warm it for half a minute. The part in your hand should expand while the inside remains contracted from the cold. This temperature contrast often frees up the ferrule so that it can be separated easily.

Chapter 8
Reels

● ●

In This Chapter

▶ Discovering the right reel for you

▶ Setting your drag (and when not to)

▶ Maintaining your reels

● ●

*R*eels are one of those things that you think about only when they don't work. Part of the reason for this is that, in general, reels are very well designed and, for the most part, very well made. With a minimum of care, a reel can last a long, long time.

Who Needs a Reel?

Every angler who fishes with a spinning, spin-casting, bait-casting, or fly rod uses a reel. A reel does two things:

✔ It stores line. How else could you possibly fish with 100 or 200 yards of line if it weren't stored on a reel?

✔ It introduces a new level of skill and enjoyment to the sport by giving the fish the option of taking line off the reel. This means you can fish with lighter line than anglers used in the days when there were no reels and just 20 feet of line (or thereabouts) attached to the end of the rod. A reel allows for the give and take of line that tests the skill of the angler.

Bait Casting

The first truly modern reels were developed by the precision German watchmakers of Kentucky. By combining their love of angling for the native black bass with their skill with gears and machinery, they transformed the reel from a thing that conveniently held line to a machine that aided fishing. One turn of the crank or handle, assisted by the gear mechanism of the new reels, produced four turns of the reel.

The principle behind casting with a bait-casting reel is simple: The weight of the lure pulls on the line, causing the spool to spin as it feeds more line. *Backlash* is the bane of the baitcaster and it occurs when the spool gets up a head of steam and moves faster than the line can peel off. Various design advances — like the *level-wind mechanism* that moves back and forth across the spool as it spins, stacking the line evenly, and adjustable *drag* (resistance) — have somewhat lessened the frequency of backlash; but still, this is the most demanding reel to learn how to use properly.

A modern bait-casting reel (shown with a classic reel in Figure 8-1) is not very backlash-prone. In the hands of a great caster, a classic reel, with less built-in backlash control is still the long-distance champ. Note that the reel is mounted on top of the rod. The drag mechanism, in this case known as a star drag because of its shape, adjusts the amount of force needed to pull line off the reel.

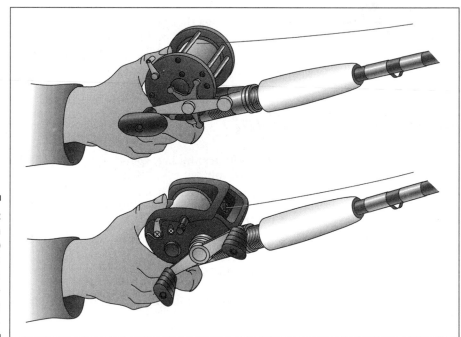

Figure 8-1:
A modern (bottom) and a classic (top) bait-casting reel.

Some preventive medicine

To use a bait-casting reel properly, you need to adjust the drag (resistance) to accommodate and compensate for the weight of the lure or bait. To make your initial setting for casting, hold the rod at a 45-degree angle to the ground. Release the lure or bait by putting the reel into *free-spool mode* — most bait-casting reels have a button that lets the spool spin freely — and letting out line. When the drag is properly adjusted, the lure/bait descends slowly. If it descends too fast, you will get backlash. Too slow, and you won't cast very far.

Spinning

The principle on which the spinning reel works makes it much easier to master and far more popular than the bait-casting reel. In spinning, the spool doesn't move when you cast; instead, the weight of the lure or bait pulls line off the stationary spool. Because the lure only has to move line, you are able to cast lighter lures than you can with a bait-casting reel (which has to move both the spool *and* the line).

Figure 8-2 shows a typical spinning reel. Usually, you can mount the handle on the right or the left side. Customarily, righties mount the handle or crank on the left, leaving their strong arm to assist the rod in fighting the fish.

Although there are many different features available, your garden variety spinning reel has the following characteristics:

- ✔ Most spinning reels are *close faced,* which means they have a *bail,* a device which flips over after you cast so that you can easily wind up line on the retrieve. You can also buy an *open-faced spinning reel* — one that has no bail. In the latter case, you place the line into a little roller that allows you to retrieve line as you wind it in. I do not recommend this type of reel for beginners because it is just one more thing to worry about.

- ✔ There is usually a screw-down mechanism for adjusting the drag located on the bottom of all spinning reels.

- ✔ The *anti-reverse lock,* as its name indicates, keeps the reel from reversing direction. This feature is helpful when fighting a strong fish (especially when netting one) because you can take one hand off the reel to pick up the net while your other hand holds the rod. The lock should be on while trolling and at any time you transport the rod. If you are

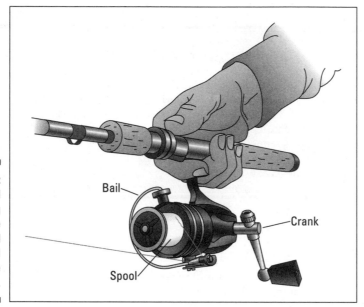

Bail

Crank

Spool

fishing live bait that needs the ability to swim around in order to attract game fish, then leave the reel in free spool, letting line pay out as your bait fish wants to take it. Basically, however, my feeling is, if you don't have a good reason for taking your anti-reverse lock off, leave it on.

Spin casting

Many anglers have their first rod-and-reel experience with a *spin-casting* reel. The Zebco is probably the most famous and widely used brand of spin-caster. For all practical purposes — line weight, lure weight, and the like — a spin-casting rod is a spinning reel with a few different mechanisms to make fishing with it a little more foolproof. Figure 8-3 shows a typical spin-casting reel. The spool is under a cover or housing, and line comes out of a little hole in the top. Monofilament line is really the only kind that works well with this arrangement. (The rougher surface of a braided line does not move through the opening as smoothly as does monofilament line.) Instead of a bail that you flip over for casting on a regular spinning reel, the spin-casting reel has a release button. You push the button to let out line as you cast, and you let up on it to stop more line from going out after you've completed your cast.

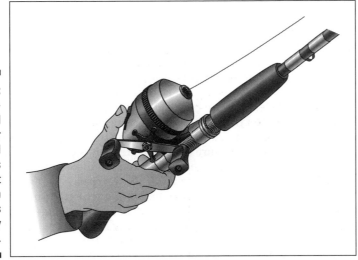

Figure 8-3:
The spin-casting reel is good for kids and beginners because it gives an angler less opportunity to mess up.

MFP (Maximum Fishing Pleasure) and the balanced outfit

As in most everything else in life, the key to fishing enjoyment is the right balance — in this case, a well-balanced outfit. Bigger fish (or fish that have a tendency to run for a long distance) require a great deal of line. In this case, you want to use either lighter-test line and/or a larger spool. (In other words, you want to use line that takes up less space, or you want a bigger spool with space for heavier line.) Spinning, spin casting, and bait-casting outfits all have recommended matchups of rods, reels, and lines. The two guidelines (but not unbreakable commandments) are these: The smaller the fish, the lighter the outfit; and the lighter the lure, the lighter the outfit. As you become a more accomplished angler, you will be able to use lighter equipment to conquer bigger fish.

Your best resource for advice is your tackle dealer. Contrary to many buying experiences these days, I find that clerks at most tackle shops know their subject (which is more than I can say for the people in most computer stores). Anglers are always asking many questions, and clerks are used to answering them. If in doubt, ask. My only strong piece of advice is don't get the cheapest equipment if you can possibly afford to pay a little more. Mid-range fishing equipment is usually pretty serviceable, but as my Grandma used to say, "Cheap is cheap."

Fly Reels

Of all the reels discussed in this chapter, the fly reel has the simplest mechanism. Its first function is for storage of line. Action, gear ratio, drag, and the like are secondary considerations in fly-fishing. The basic fly reel is a *single-action reel,* which means that one turn of the crank handle equals one revolution of the spool. You can buy *multiplier reels* that employ the same kind of gear-driven principle that you find in bait casting: One turn of the crank produces a number of revolutions of the spool. I have never found a need for this kind of reel. Figure 8-4 illustrates a basic reel. It has a spool, a housing for the spool, a crank or handle, and, sometimes, a drag adjustment. The fly reel is mounted below the rod. With most reels, you have a choice of configuring your reel for winding with the left hand or right hand. Because I cast with my right arm, I like to hold the rod in my right hand and reel with my left. This way, I don't have to complicate my life and change hands to fight a fish using the strength of my more powerful arm to assist the rod during the struggle. If you are unsure of how to configure the crank, ask the people in the tackle shop to set it up for you when you buy it.

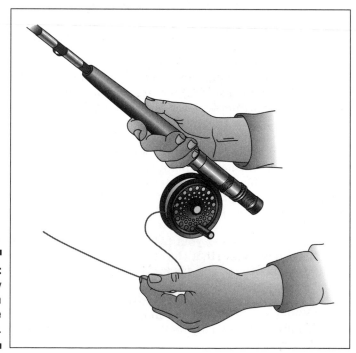

Figure 8-4:
The fly reel — a very simple machine.

The non-importance of drag

In most freshwater fishing situations, setting drag is not a critical issue for flyrodders. Most reels have a simple ratchetlike clicker that keeps the reel from turning too quickly and tangling the line. Within limits, the clicker is somewhat adjustable. When fishing for most trout and bass, you can use a combination of techniques to apply drag:

- ✔ Using the drag from the reel
- ✔ Cupping the revolving spool and using the palm of your hand as a brake pad
- ✔ Raising the rod tip to create an angle that increases line *resistance* (which, insofar as the fish feels it, is the same thing as *drag*)

You should quickly get the hang of the interplay of these forces. The one thing you *do not* want to do is grab the line with your fingers and try to apply drag that way. You will break off any decent fish. At the end of the fight, however, you may secure the line by simply using the forefinger of your rod hand to press the line against the rod, as shown in Figure 8-5. This trick lets you grab or net the fish more easily. If the fish wants to lunge for another run when you are in this position, let it go. That way, you still have a chance of getting the fish in again. When you try to prevent the fish from taking that last run, you will lose it in almost every case.

Saltwater

When playing and landing larger saltwater fish, a more-reliable and adjustable drag is required. When I started fishing, a wonderful American reel called the Pfleuger Medalist, which had a very simple drag, was still made. I caught thousands (well, at least hundreds) of fish, including bonefish, with this reel. I still have the reel. It still works, and the drag has never had to be replaced. But, alas, the day of the classic Medalist is gone for most anglers. Today's Medalist is, in my opinion, a pale imitation of the original. These days, a *good* saltwater fly reel has a more complicated drag than the Medalist's, a drag made especially for saltwater and with more corrosion-resistant materials than were available in the earlier days of salty flyrodding.

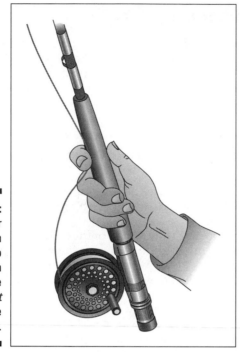

Figure 8-5:
Use your finger on the line to help when landing the fish, *not* during the fight.

As the dentist said, rinse often

Whether or not your reel is designed specifically for saltwater, you need to rinse it after every use in the ocean. No matter what anyone tells you or what any manufacturer promises, there is no fly reel currently made that is 100-percent corrosion-proof in all of its parts. If you rinse your reel in fresh water after every use, your reel will be fine. If you don't, you will become a very familiar and free-spending customer at the tackle shop.

Don't forget to oil

Because reels are made with moving metal parts, they need to be lubricated. Sewing machine oil works well for gears. I like to lubricate spools and spool posts with silicone lubricant, which holds up under a wide temperature range. I use silicone lubricant on everything from my ice fishing gear to the gear stored in the trunk of my car in a Florida parking lot.

Part II
What You're After

The 5th Wave   By Rich Tennant

The fishing lures of Capt. Ahab

RICHTENNANT

In this part . . .

A whole lotta fish. (Actually, a whole lotta fish descriptions and a whole lotta pretty pictures.) Chapter 9 covers freshwater fish, and Chapter 10 covers saltwater fish.

Chapter 9
Freshwater Fish

● ●

In This Chapter

▶ Discovering why rainbows and brookies aren't trout (and why it doesn't matter)

▶ Calming a squirming bass

▶ Revealing the most popular freshwater fish

▶ Picking up a pike without losing one or more fingers

● ●

*W*here you live and the common fish in your local waters have a great deal to do with your choice of a fish that you will fish for. Through the fifty or so generations that people have fished for sport (rather than necessity), they have sought out fish that offer a bit of a challenge to hook. How well the fish fight is another big consideration. Whether or not they taste good also counts. And personal preference also plays a role. Some people find that one fish is more fun to catch than another. I may have left your favorite fish off the following list, and if I did, I apologize. Still, I think that most anglers would agree that the fish that follow are pretty much those at the very top of the anglers' hit parade.

Trout

If the number of words written about a fish is any indication of popularity, then the trouts are the runaway winners. A great deal of what has been written about trout is just a bunch of hot air, but (separating the fish from a bunch of gasbag fishing writers) it is a supreme game fish that is at least the equal of any other sport fish. In the old days, an angler was judged by how many trout he or she brought home; but these days, thanks largely to the influence of American anglers, catch-and-release is more the rule. If you kill the occasional trout, however, don't let anyone make you feel guilty about it. They are delicious fish. On the other hand, if you kill every trout that you catch, you are being more greedy than wise. Trout are the top predator in their environment: They stand at the top of the food chain in many rivers and streams. Top predators are, of necessity, rarer than animals lower down the chain. A little bit of pressure can alter the quality of angling in a stream very quickly. So enjoy yourself, enjoy your meal, but remember that the fish you return to the stream will grow larger and have babies.

The champ: Brown trout

The brown trout is a fish designed for the angler. It often feeds on the surface. It rises to a properly presented fly. It fights like the dickens. The brown didn't acquire a reputation as a "gentleman's fish" because it had particularly good manners and went to the right school. The simple fact of the matter is that rich English gentlemen, with time on their hands, embraced the sport of angling and popularized it everywhere. Because their local fish was the brown trout, it became the fish of choice for sportsmen there and in the New World. If the English sportsmen had started out in Georgia instead of England, the largemouth bass would probably have a lot of flowery literature. If those same anglers had lived in Mississippi, the local Izaak Walton may well have written about the simple virtues and great sporting qualities of the catfish.

The brown trout is a cold-water fish that lives in lakes and streams and is most active when the water temperature is in the 60s. A temperature much above 80°F is liable to kill brown trout. As shown in Figure 9-1, the brown trout is covered with spots everywhere but its tail. The majority of the spots are deep brown, like coffee beans, with a light yellow halo. Sprinkled around its skin, you also find a few red and yellow spots.

The world record brown trout at 40 pounds, 4 ounces was taken by Howard L. "Rip" Collins on the Little Red River in Heber Springs, Arkansas, on May 9, 1992. (Thanks to the IGFA, which maintains an up-to-date archive of world records.)

Figure 9-1:
The brown trout is one of the wiliest and most rewarding fish taken on rod and reel. Its instinct to dash for cover when hooked adds up to a great fight for the angler.

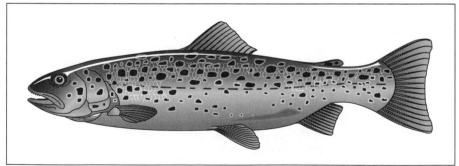

Not quite cricket, but so what?

Brown trout are very wary, and they are also creatures of habit. If you know their habits, and the habits of the anglers who fish for them, you may have an advantage that you can exploit. Case in point: my first visit to the Test, one of the historic English trout streams. I visited during the time of year when a large fly, which the English call The Mayfly, hatches. Whereas Americans called all the up-winged aquatic insects mayflies, the English reserve it for this humongous hatch. It is a big fly and makes a fat target. Trout are supposed to be so easy to catch when this hatch is on, English anglers call this time of year "Duffers Fortnight" because, during that hatching period, *anybody* can catch a trout.

"Anybody" didn't include me. Three or four hours of casting had not yielded even one rise. On a hunch, I cut off my dry fly and tied on a little nymph. I walked upstream and crossed over an old wooden bridge. I walked downstream through thick undergrowth on the unfished side of the river. (With the angler facing upstream, most English trout streams have the left bank cleared so that a right-handed caster can present a fly upstream without hanging up the backcast in pesky branches and grass.) I cast my little nymph about six feet into the current, which was as long a cast as I could manage in those close quarters. I let the fly swing into the bank, and a trout took on my first cast. After an hellacious fight, I landed him. He weighed $6\frac{1}{4}$ pounds and was the big trout of the season on that river.

To catch him, all I had done was present a fly in a novel way. By using the least-favored bank and breaking the English gentlemen's code that requires an angler to cast upstream only, I proved that although the trout of the Test may have been well educated when it came to mayfly imitations presented by a right-handed caster on the left bank, anything that looked like food and that came from a different direction had a much better chance of interesting a good fish.

The moral of the story is this: Try something different if you have a feeling that it may work. (No law says that you have to fish the way that everybody else does.)

Brown trout are long-lived animals and can reach weights up to 40 pounds, but most stream-bred fish average less than a pound each. They say that a few wise browns in every stream usually reach weights of 10 pounds or more. I've never caught one.

High jumpers: Rainbow trout

Guess what? A couple of years ago, scientists decided that the rainbow trout isn't a trout after all. This fish looks like a trout and behaves like a trout. It feeds like a trout and eats flies like a trout. Probably because of those characteristics, those same Englishmen who gave us the lore of the brown trout decided to call the rainbow a trout. (Whenever the English arrived in a new country, they gave the local fish and game the names of similar animals back in Merrie Olde England.)

Who was Izaak Walton anyway?

Without question, the most famous book ever written about angling is *The Compleat Angler* published by Izaak Walton in 1653. Since that time, it has been through over three hundred editions and is probably the most widely read (or at least widely-owned) book after the Bible and the Koran. Because *The Compleat Angler* is an all around handbook for fishing in England, people who are not familiar with Walton have an idea that it is only for purist fly-fishing snobs.

It isn't.

Izaak Walton was primarily a bait fisherman who came late to the fly. He was a self-made businessman who retired in his 50s and wrote the book that would earn him immortality at age 60. His prose is so strong and true that most people today could read his book with much less difficulty than they could read the plays of, for example, Shakespeare.

Much of the best advice in the book was actually written by Charles Cotton, a young man of leisure who was an amazing flyrodder. It was Cotton, not Walton, who wrote "to fish fine and far off, is the first and principle rule for Trout angling." In other words use a light leader and keep your distance from the fish so you don't spook it. This advice is as valuable today as it was three-and-a-half centuries ago when Walton and Cotton filled their days fishing and talking. What a life!

I went through many years confirmed in my belief that the rainbow was a trout; and now that the rainbow has been reclassified as a smaller cousin of the Pacific salmon family, I haven't noticed my angling pleasure diminishing any.

Rainbows coexist nicely with brown trout in many streams. While the brown prefers the slower water and calmer pools, you can depend on finding the rainbow in the more oxygen-rich and swift-running riffles. This scenario is what you would expect from a fish that predominates in the mountain streams of the Rocky Mountains.

If you ask a hundred anglers to name the most memorable thing about the fight of a rainbow, you may well have a hundred answers singling out the rainbow's leaping ability: Although the brown, when hooked, usually *sounds* (dives to the bottom) and makes for cover, the rainbow's instinct is to leap and run and leap some more. These acrobatics are thrilling and, on light tackle, they demand a sensitive touch. As seen in Figure 9-2, the rainbow may have spots over the whole body (although in many rivers and lakes, the larger rainbows are more often an overall silver). A much more reliable sign of "rainbowness" is the pink band or line that runs along the flank of the fish from shoulder to tail. But even this indicator is not always 100-percent foolproof because some stream-borne rainbows have a faded, almost invisible band and many spots, as do the brown and brook trout.

Figure 9-2: The rainbow trout is the leapingest trout and also one of the hardiest fish.

On June 22, 1970, the world record rainbow was caught by David Robert White at Bell Island, Alaska. It weighed 42 pounds and 2 ounces.

Sentimental favorites: Brookies

Like the rainbow, the brook trout, or *brookie,* isn't a trout. It is the animal that fills the trout niche in the cooler streams of the northeastern U.S., east of the Allegheny Mountains. The brook trout is actually a char, which makes it a relative of the lake trout (not a real trout either), the Dolly Varden, and the Arctic char.

I think that because the brookie is found only in wilderness areas explains part of the fondness that anglers have for him. He is a sign of pure water and a healthy ecology. Brookies like cooler water and cannot stand the higher temperatures that the brown and the rainbow can tolerate. Before Europeans cleared the great hardwood forests of the northeastern U.S., most streams had the shade and pure water that brook trout need.

With the clearing of the forests and the coming of brown trout and rainbow trout, the brookie often retreated to the less-accessible headwaters of many streams. As explained by the principle of "smaller fish in smaller water," many people, whose only brook trout experience is on these smaller waters, have assumed that the brook trout is typically smaller than the rainbow or the brown. This is not true. In the old days on Long Island, for example, many brook trout ranged from 4 pounds to 10 pounds.

Steelhead — a salty rainbow

Almost all species of trout, if given the chance, drop downstream to the ocean where they usually grow to much greater size then trout that are confined to streams and lakes. Sea-run brookies and browns (those that forage in the ocean and return to spawn in fresh water) also appear in North America, but the main target for anglers of sea-run trout is the steelhead, which is nothing more than a rainbow that has gone to sea. Steelhead have usually lost the distinctive coloration of the freshwater rainbow (although they still have the pink lateral line). As their name suggests, steelheads have a bright, metallic coloration.

Although it is much praised for its great beauty, many anglers regard the brookie as an empty-headed glamour-puss. I have to say that I agree in most cases. This isn't to say that very wary, hard-to-catch brookies aren't out there, but by and large, most of them are prettier than they are smart.

The brook trout has many red spots that are surrounded by a blue halo. The fins have a telltale black and white tip. The belly and fins have an orange cast that can be quite brilliant and almost crimson in spawning season. The tail of the brook trout is more squared off than that of the brown and rainbow (see Figure 9-3), hence the nickname *squaretail*.

The world record brook trout (a 14-pound, 8-ounce fish) was caught by Dr. W. J. Cook in the Nipigon River, Ontario, Canada, on July 8, 1916. Before that, the record fish was attributed to none other than Daniel Webster, the great United States senator who is widely thought of as the greatest orator in the history of the United States. Daniel Webster's fish story is a great one, and I have gone through local church records and ancient sporting magazines trying to get some hard evidence of its basis in fact. I never did find any, but it still makes a nice tale.

Figure 9-3:
The brook trout, originally a native of the east coast of North America, is universally admired for its gorgeous coloring.

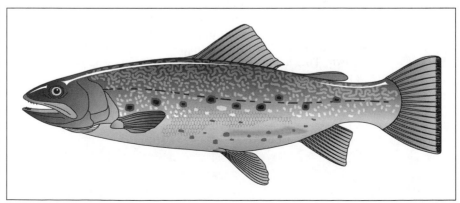

The trout and Dan'l Webster

Years ago, in 1828 to be precise, Long Island had a number of gin-clear trout streams full of big beautiful brookies, many of them fat from their summer diet of bait fish out in the Great South Bay. Daniel Webster and his fishing buddy, Martin Van Buren, often fished the Connetquot River, being particularly fond of the spot below the mill pond of local innkeeper Sam Carmans. A local rumor told of a great trout feeding in the mill race, and Webster, Van Buren, and Van Buren's slave, Apaius Enos, spent the better part of a day trying to entice the brookie (who could be seen feeding steadily), but they couldn't interest the fish. The next morning, somewhat the worse for a night dipping into Sam Carmans' rum barrel, Webster and Van Buren went to church, having left instructions with the slave to come and get them if that trout began to feed.

The trout appeared and Apaius carried out his orders. Webster and Van Buren tiptoed out of church as inconspicuously as they could; but everyone knew what was up, so pretty soon the preacher was left preaching to an empty church. At the pond, Webster took up his rod — which was nicknamed "Killall" and after two casts, hooked the fish. A memorable battle took place until, finally, Webster led the brookie to the slave's net. Screaming "We have you now, Sir!" Apaius scooped up the fish. It was weighed on Carmans' scale (which, if anything, gave short weight), and a figure of 9 pounds, 4 ounces was recorded. It was packed on ice, and the next morning, Webster caught the first stagecoach for Delmonico's, the great restaurant of old New York. There, the chef, Charlie Ranhofer, served it poached in white wine and showered with slivered almonds. Webster was awarded the world record and held the title for nearly a century.

The cutthroat

You may think of the cutthroat — which is really a cousin to the rainbow — as the Rocky Mountain version of the brook trout because in many undisturbed waters, just like the brookie, the cutthroat is the native fish. After ranching, logging, and the introduction of other game fish takes place, the cutthroat often retreats to unpressured headwaters. As with the brook trout, the cutthroat has the reputation of having less intelligence than the brown trout. Apart from the fact that I don't know how one can administer an intelligence test to a brown or a cutthroat, I don't agree. Cutthroats (sometimes called *cuts*) can be extremely selective. They do not have the bulldog, head-shaking determination of the brown nor the leaping instinct of the rainbow, but in all of Troutdom, there is nothing like the surface take of the cutthroat: He comes up, sips the fly, and shows you his whole body before descending with the fly. All you need to do is come tight to the fish and you're on.

The cutthroat is the native trout in the drainage of the Yellowstone River, where it is protected by a complete no-kill policy in all of the flowing water in Yellowstone Park. To fish them at the outlet of Yellowstone Lake is one of the great angling experiences in North America.

As you can't really see in Figure 9-4, cuts get their name from the slash of red or orange on the jaw and gills. The world record, a 41-pound behemoth, was taken at Pyramid Lake, Nevada, in December 1925, by John Skimmerhorn.

Figure 9-4: The cutthroat trout is most easily identified by the red and orange slashes around the lower jaw and gills.

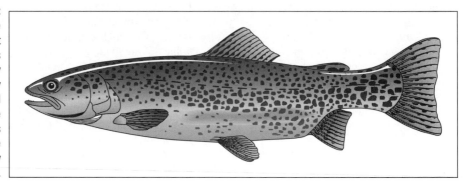

Lakers: Big macks

Widely known as Mackinaws or gray trout, the lake trout (or *laker*) is the largest char. The Mackinaw requires colder water than any other freshwater game fish, optimally about 50°F, and it will die at 65°F.

Right after ice-out in the spring and right before spawning in the autumn, lakers may be taken in shallow water. But during the rest of the season, anglers have to fish deeper, often trolling with wire line or lead core.

Unlike all the other trout (true trout as well as rainbows and chars), the laker spawns in lakes, not streams. This fact is much on the minds of biologists in Yellowstone Park, where some lame-brains dumped a few lakers in Yellowstone Lake a few years ago. Prior to that, this lake held the last pure strain of cutthroats in the Rockies. The lakers began to prey on young cutthroat fry. This situation was bad enough. But because lakers don't run up the rivers as the cuts do, about 20 percent of the food supply of the grizzly bear, osprey, and eagle have been removed from the ecosystem. This is a prime case of messing with Mother Nature. I don't blame the fish, however. In fact, I like lakers. I do blame the fishermen who dumped the lakers in Yellowstone Lake, though.

As shown in Figure 9-5, the laker, like the brookie, is heavily spotted. It has a forked tail (in contrast to the square tail of the brookie). The largest one ever taken on rod and reel weighed 66 pounds and 8 ounces and was caught in Canada's Great Bear Lake on July 10, 1991. A 102-pound laker was netted in Lake Athabasca in Saskatchewan.

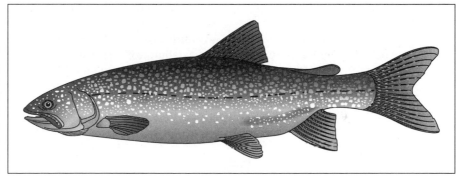

Figure 9-5:
The lake trout looks like a giant brookie with a forked tail.

The Basses

The trout may win the number-of-pages-written-about-them contest, but if the number of anglers counts for anything, then the basses (largemouth and smallmouth) are certainly the most popular game fish in America. The largemouth and smallmouth are not, however, true basses. That distinction belongs to the bass of Europe who had first dibs on the name. The American basses belong to the sunfish family. When you stop to consider this situation, though, the largemouth and smallmouth don't know or care what they are called; and the American basses, also known as the black basses, are pretty amazing game fish.

Largemouth

To my mind, no experience in angling is as thrilling as the moment that a largemouth bass takes a topwater plug. There you are, on a still summer day. Things couldn't be quieter. A few dragonflies buzz around a lily pad. A frog or two basks in the heat. You cast a topwater plug to the lily pad. You let it rest for a few seconds, and then you twitch it. You twitch it again. A fierce ripple knocks into your plug followed by the cause of the onrushing water, a ferocious largemouth that engulfs the plug. The instant it feels the hook, it begins to shake its head and jump or dive or both. An experience like this never ceases to thrill me, and it never ceases to take me by surprise.

The largemouth bass, originally a native of the Mississippi drainage and the southeastern U.S., was early recognized as a prime game fish and has since been transplanted all over. Lakes, rivers, streams, and brackish coastal water all have populations of largemouth.

They take lures, plugs, flies, plastic worms, real worms, crayfish, and crickets. In short, they are opportunistic feeders and are most catchable when the water is in the 65°F to 75°F range.

As shown in Figure 9-6, the jaw of the largemouth extends further back than the eye (which is not true of the smallmouth). The largemouth is usually dark gray to dark green in color with a dark band along the lateral line. The dorsal fin is divided into two distinct portions: hard spines in front and softer ones in the rear. The largemouth is also known as the bucketmouth because of his large mouth, which appears even larger when it attacks your lure, fly, or bait.

Figure 9-6:
The largemouth bass, the most sought-after game fish in America.

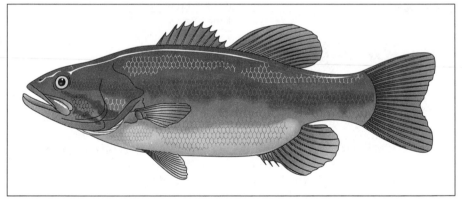

Smallmouth: The gamest fish

In what is perhaps the most-quoted phrase in angling literature, retired Civil War surgeon James Alexander Henshall called the smallmouth bass, "Inch for inch and pound for pound, the gamest fish that swims." This opinion set off a century of debates. Some said trout were the gamest fish; others awarded that honor to salmon. Bonefish, permit, snook, and tarpon all had their partisans, but no one ever said that Henshall was out to lunch for the high opinion in which he held the smallmouth, known affectionately as the *bronzeback*.

A true fish tale

It was rainy and windy on June 2, 1932, and nineteen-year-old George Perry was out before dawn with his fishing buddy Jack Page.

"My father died the year before," Perry later recalled. "I had my mother, two sisters, and two brothers. We lived three creeks further back than anybody else, and in those days it was a good deal of a problem just to make a living. I took money we should have eaten with and bought myself a cheap rod and reel and one plug."

Perry remembers that he wasn't feeling very lucky that morning on Montgomery Lake near Helena, Georgia. He tied on an imitation of the local bait fish, the creek-chub. A bass took the lure. Perry struck but couldn't budge it. Then the fish moved, and Perry knew he was into a major bass. When it finally surrendered, even though it was enormous, Perry later said, "The first thing I thought of was what a nice chunk of meat to take home to the family."

Thankfully, Perry had the presence of mind to make a detour at the general store in Helena, Georgia, where the bass that he had pulled out of Montgomery Lake tipped the scales at 22 pounds and 3 ounces, duly notarized and witnessed. It is a world record that stands to this day.

With his place firmly enshrined in the history books, young Perry went home and prepared a very large largemouth meal for the family.

Like his largemouth cousin, the smallmouth is a native of the Mississippi drainage, which makes him a true heartland (or maybe "heartwater") fish. Where the largemouth likes slow or still water with lots of food-holding weeds, the smallmouth prefers clean, rocky bottoms and swifter water, ideally in the 65°F to 68°F range. Any warmer than 73°F and you can forget about finding a smallmouth. Lake dwelling smallmouth often school up, which means that if you catch one, you can catch a bunch. In rivers and streams, they are more solitary.

Like the largemouth, the smallmouth is a pretty opportunistic feeder; but if you give smallmouth a choice, both crayfish and hellgrammites score well.

As shown in Figure 9-7, the smallmouth has a series of dark vertical bands along its flanks. The dorsal fin is one continuous fin (as opposed to the separate spiny and soft parts on a largemouth's fin). Another difference is that the smallmouth's upper jaw does *not* extend backward beyond the eye.

David L Hayes caught the world record smallmouth in Dale Hollow Lake, Kentucky, on July 9, 1955. It weighed 11 pounds and 15 ounces.

Figure 9-7:
The mouth of the smallmouth isn't *that* small, but its upper jaw is shorter than the largemouth's. It's all relative.

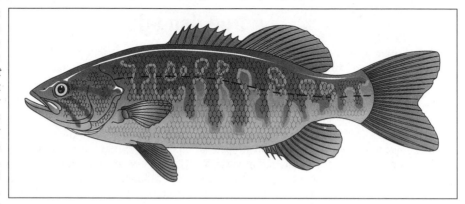

How to pick up a bass

If you try to pick up a bass by grabbing its body, it is about as easy as trying to diaper an angry baby. The little suckers can *really* squirm. Even worse than babies, bass have spiny fins that can deliver nasty pricks. With a bass (and with many other soft-mouthed fish), however, you can nearly immobilize it if you grab it by the lower lip, holding it between thumb and forefinger as shown in the adjacent figure. Be very careful of hooks, especially of lures that have multiple treble hooks. While picking up your catch by grasping the lower lip between thumb and forefinger works very well with bass, it has been reported that this technique doesn't work as well in singles

Double dip

Question: How many people have both an element and a fish named after them?

Answer: One. His name was Deodat Dolomieu, and it happened in 1802. Dolomieu was a famous man-about-town in Paris as well as a mineralogist. The mineral dolomite was named after him. Dolomite is a favorite rock of anglers because its high limestone content makes for streams rich in food (which means *big fish*).

A naturalist named Lacepede also lived in Paris at that time. Someone had sent him a strange-looking 12-inch fish for classification. It was a smallmouth from Louisiana, which was still ruled by France in those days. This smallmouth had a gap in its dorsal fin, probably from a run-in with a pike or a beaver. Lacepede had never seen a smallmouth before, leading to his assumption that all smallmouth had teeny fins. So he called the new fish *Micropterus* which means "small fin" in Latin. Then he needed a second half for its Latin name, but nothing came to mind. Because Dolomieu was coming to dinner that night, Lacepede, at a loss for anything better to call the newly classified fish, decided to name it after his friend, which is why the smallmouth bass is known to scientists as *Micropterus dolomieu*.

Good Eats: Walleye

On a number of trips to the state of Minnesota, more than one angler has said to me, "You can have your bass, and you can have your trout, but the walleye is the best eatin' fish there is, bar none!" Having tasted the flesh of this largest member of the perch family, I would have to agree that it ranks right up there with the best. Their excellent flavor may explain why walleye are often the preferred fish when they are available. In addition to being delicious, they are found in schools, hang out around underwater structures, and usually locate themselves near a drop-off. In other words, they behave just as a textbook game fish should behave — not a pushover, but not impossible to catch either. In many places, you can hear people talk about a walleyed pike, which is a local name for walleye but not an accurate one. The pike is a completely different animal.

The walleye requires a great deal of water and is rarely found in smaller lakes or ponds. Clear water and a rocky bottom are also high on its list of environmental preferences with water temperatures in the mid 60s (and never higher than the mid 70s) being optimum. It eats any bait fish that is available; and when they aren't, leeches are a terrific bait (as are worms).

The take of the walleye is subtle, not unlike the way a bass plays with a worm and then swims away with it before it finally decides to eat. The angler must give the walleye time to accomplish this maneuver before striking.

The walleye is a very light-sensitive fish, so although you may take one in shallow water, chances are that you will do this only in low-light conditions.

Mabry Harper holds the record for a 25-pound walleye caught on Tennessee's Old Hickory Lake on April Fool's Day, 1960.

As shown in Figure 9-8, the walleye is a torpedo-shaped fish with big eyes (hence wall-eye), a brownish-greenish color, and a white tip on the tail and dorsal fin.

Figure 9-8:
The walleye looks like another member of the perch family, the sauger, but you can always tell a walleye by the white tip on its tail.

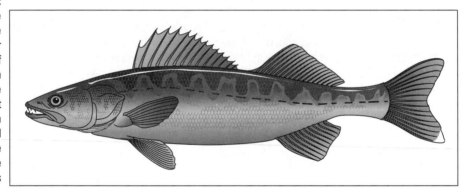

Pike

For flat-out mean looks, nothing in freshwater rivals the looks of a pike, pickerel, or muskellunge. A long fish with big eyes, a pointed snout, and rows of stiletto teeth, the average pike looks like what you might get if you crossed a snake, a bird, and a shark.

Northern pike

The most popular member of the pike family is usually known simply as *the* pike. It is also called a *northern* and is a native of the Great Lakes and its cooler tributaries.

Pike are clearly designed to attack and devour. One observer called them "Mere machines for the assimilation of other organisms." All forms of bait fish and game fish, birds, muskrats, frogs, snakes, snails, leeches, and anything else it finds within striking distance can (at one time or another) find its way into a pike's belly.

You are liable to find pike in weedy shallows where they wait for prey to ambush. As stealthy as a lion in wait or as swift as a springing panther, pike stalk and pursue their prey most actively at water temperatures in the mid 60s.

When fishing live bait, the angler must give the pike time. Sometimes it will snare a fish crosswise and take some time to maneuver it into swallowing position. Usually, a pike pauses right before it swallows any bait. When the pike pauses, strike.

When fishing with artificials, strike when the pike does. You will be rewarded by the sight of the writhing form of the pike rocketing from the water. Don't be fooled when the pike seems to surrender after a fierce, but short, initial run. As soon as it sees you or your boat, you usually get a very satisfying second (and even third) run. The Daredevle is an amazingly effective pike lure.

The world record belongs to Lothar Louis who took a 55-pound, 1-ounce pike on October 16, 1986 in the Lake of Grefeern, Germany.

As shown in Figure 9-9, the pike is a sleek and ferocious-looking predator.

Figure 9-9: The northern pike, a well-designed killing machine.

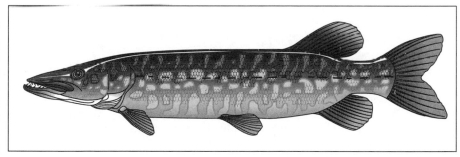

Talk about sharp!

When landing a pike, be extremely careful of its sharp teeth. They are about the nastiest thing in freshwater fishing. (This advice goes for the pike's cousins, the muskie and pickerel.) As shown in Figure 9-10, the safest way to land a pike is to grab the fish by the eye sockets (the socket, *not* the eye!).

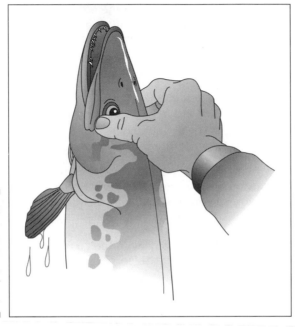

Figure 9-10:
The finger-preserving way to land a pike, muskie, or pickerel.

Muskellunge

If you are the kind of person who likes the odds in the state lottery, you should enjoy fishing for muskellunge. Your chances of winning the lottery and catching a muskie are roughly equal. (Actually, that is a bit of an exaggeration, but not by much.) The old-timers say that when fishing for muskellunge, it takes 10,000 casts for every strike. And then when you do get a muskie on, its teeth are so sharp, it can be so big, and its fight can be so dogged, that it takes brawn and skill to land one. If you manage to land a muskie, you have a real trophy.

Like the pike, the muskie hangs out in likely ambush spots: weed beds, deep holes, drop-offs, and over sunken islands. Although it spends most of its time in the depths, it appears to do most of its feeding in shallower water (at less than 15 feet). Optimum water temperature for muskies is in the low 60s.

The muskie is an opportunistic predator that strikes any number of baits or lures in any number of ways. Sometimes, a muskie strikes far from your boat, but sometimes it follows a lure right up to the gunwales. The muskie is completely unpredictable, and my advice to the beginning muskie fisherman is to get a guide or a local expert to take you until you get the hang of it.

The muskie is a northern fish, found in the upper parts of the Mississippi drainage, the St. Lawrence River, all over New England, and through most of Canada.

The world record, a 65-pound fish, was caught by Kenneth J. O'Brien at Blackstone Harbor, Ontario, on October 16, 1988.

Figure 9-11 shows that a muskellunge's appearance is quite similar to that of a pike. You can't always be sure which is which unless you get pretty close to the fish, in which case you can see that the muskie, in contrast to the pike, has no scales on its lower cheek and gill covers. Its markings tend to look like dark bars or spots, but northern pike usually have lighter-colored spots that are shaped like beans.

Figure 9-11:
Muskies are typically bigger than northern pikes, but they both have the same murderous mouth.

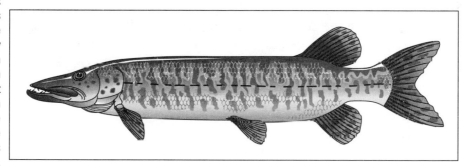

Pickerel

Though smaller than the pike and the muskie, the pickerel is (in every other way) as pugnacious and predatory as its larger cousins. When fishing a shallow bass pond on a day when nothing is happening, look for the arrowhead-shaped wake of a feeding pickerel. Whether the pickerel is cruising or sprinting from its lair in a weed bed, I think you will agree that it is exciting to watch a well-equipped predator going about its deadly work.

If you are working a spoon or spinner, you have a better chance if you retrieve your lure parallel to a weed bed, because you never know where a pickerel may be hanging out. Fishing for pickerel in water in the upper 60s is optimum.

The pickerel is to angling what the toy is to a box of Cracker Jack. The toy isn't the reason you buy Cracker Jacks, but it's a nice surprise when you get a good one, and many a bassless day has been saved by the voracious appetite of the pickerel.

The world record weighed 9 pounds and 6 ounces and was caught by Baxley McQuaig, Jr. on February 17, 1961 in Homerville, Georgia.

Figure 9-12 illustrates a chain pickerel, whose dark green side markings appear to line up like the links in a chain.

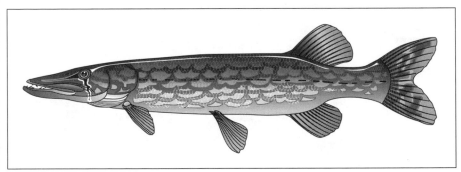

Figure 9-12: The chain pickerel looks like a miniature pike, but these two predators do not commonly coexist in the same waters.

Pacific Salmon

Pacific salmon come upstream to spawn just as Atlantic salmon do. The Pacific salmon's flesh is pink, just like the flesh of an Atlantic. They even taste the same. But the six species of Pacific salmon are completely different animals than the Atlantic salmon, which is the only *true* salmon. The Pacifics are the much larger, mostly ocean-going cousins of the rainbow trout.

Some years ago, Pacific salmon were introduced into the Great Lakes to help control the spread of the alewife herring. The alewives were so plentiful and the salmon fed so well on them that the Great Lakes now hold the greatest fishery for both the coho and chinook sport-fisherman. This situation, though good for angling, shouldn't allow us to forget the alarming depopulation of these great game fish in their home range. Overfishing in their natural range has dangerously depleted them, as has the construction of dams.

In the Great Lakes, Pacific salmon are a big favorite among trollers. This method of taking fish, of course, requires a hefty boat and expensive gear, both of which are beyond the means (either financial or technical) of most beginning anglers, so I will just leave the fine points of trolling to the guides or your rich uncle.

Shallow-water and stream anglers have the most luck when the fish gather at stream mouths just before spawning. Fishing when the salmon are still *bright,* or fresh from the ocean or lake, can be great sport with these brawny, athletic fish. After they have been in the stream for any length of time, I find that landing even a 30-pound fish is about as much fun as lugging a duffel bag full of books up a steep staircase.

Pacific salmon like cold water, about 55°F. They move with currents and tides to maintain themselves in that *thermocline,* which is a big word meaning a region in a body of water with a specific temperature. A cold front may bring salmon close to shore. A wind may drive the cold water and the fish further offshore. When looking for them in a lake, using a thermometer to check water temperature is absolutely necessary.

As with many saltwater fish or as with fish that spend a good amount of time in saltwater (the term for fish that live in both fresh and saltwater is *anadromous*), the chinook and coho like flashy, bright-colored lures.

For bait, you may be hard pressed to find better than smelt or alewives. Salmon eggs are a fine choice as well. (Which always makes me wonder: Why would a fish want to eat its next generation?)

The world record chinook is 97 pounds and 4 ounces and was caught on May 17, 1985, on Alaska's Kenai River by Les Anderson. The record for the smaller coho is 33 pounds and 4 ounces; it was caught by Jerry Lifton on the Salmon River in Pulaski, New York, on Sept 27, 1989.

Figure 9-13 shows the coho and chinook salmon. The usually smaller coho has black spots only on the upper part of its tail, although the chinook's tail is spotted on both top and bottom. The chinook's dorsal fin is spotted; the coho's isn't. The gum in the lower jaw of the coho is grayish, but the same gum in the chinook is black.

Few fish are as delicious as the Pacific salmon (which is one of the reasons they are so heavily harvested by commercial fishermen). In many areas, particularly in the Great Lakes, fish can pick up toxic pollutants. The presence of pollutants doesn't make Pacific salmon less fun to catch, but eating fish from these waters is not a good idea. Always check the local health advisories before you take a fish for a meal.

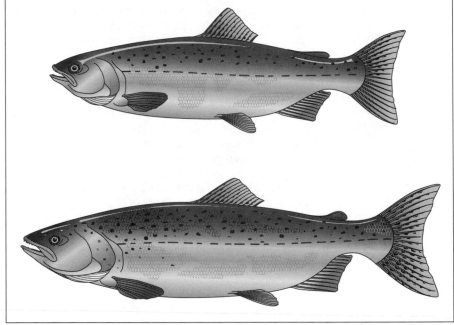

Figure 9-13:
For many
freshwater
anglers, the
coho (top)
and chinook
(bottom)
salmon are
by far their
largest
quarry.

Panfish

"Panfish" is really a catchall category that includes a whole range of fish, including most of the sunfish (except the largemouth and smallmouth bass) as well as crappie. Panfish are called panfish because they fit in a frying pan. This fact tells you something — namely, that panfish are good to eat.

In addition to edibility, another good thing about panfish is their "catchability." Whether caught with a cane pole, fly rod, or light spinning rig, panfish are extremely sporty. Worms, grubs, crickets, little spinners, popping bugs, dry flies, small jigs, bread balls, and corn are all effective panfish catchers. Since they are often the runts of the pond or stream, panfish will pretty much attack anything that looks remotely edible.

Figure 9-14 shows some of the more popular panfish.

✔ **Bluegill:** Sometimes known as the *bream*. It has a blue edge to the breast area and a dark ear flap and is probably the most-caught sport fish in America. The world record bluegill weighed 4 pounds and 12 ounces and was caught by T. S Hudson at Ketona Lake, Alabama, on April 9, 1950.

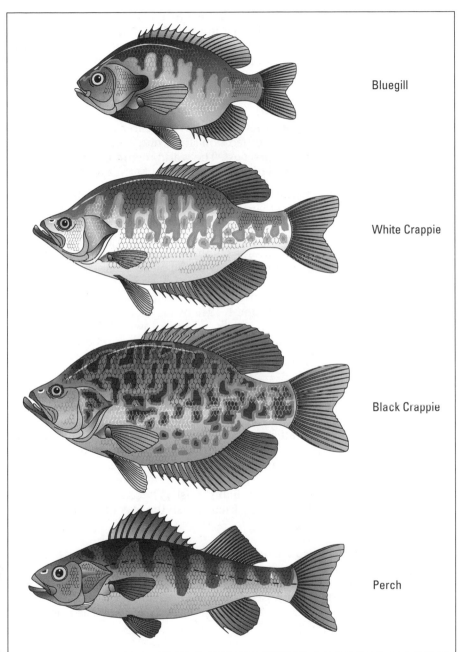

Bluegill

White Crappie

Black Crappie

Perch

Figure 9-14:
Four
popular
panfish.

✔ **White crappie:** A very widespread fish all over North America. It is a terrific fish on a jig, but it, too, takes all kinds of bait and small lures. It thrives in silty and slow-moving water and has flourished in the impoundments that have been created in the south since World War II. The white crappie is the only sunfish with six spines on the dorsal fin. The world record white crappie weighed 5 pounds and 3 ounces and was taken at Enid Dam, Mississippi, on July 31, 1957 by Fred L. Bright.

✔ **Black crappie:** Prefers somewhat clearer water than the white crappie. Because of its mottled skin (the white crappie is more barred), a local name is also *calico bass*. The world record belongs to L. Carl Herring, Jr., for a 4-pound, 8-ounce fish caught at Kerr Lake, Virginia, on March 1, 1981.

✔ **Perch:** Both white and yellow perch are completely delicious fish. French chefs steam them in parchment and call the process *en papillote*. In Door County, Wisconsin, the old-time commercial fishermen would get the same effect by wrapping their perch in wet newspapers along with some onions, salt, and pepper and throwing them on the housing of their overworked diesel engines. Because these fishermen cooked on the domes of their engines, their meals were called "domers." The world record white perch was caught at Messalonskee Lake, Maine, on June 4, 1949 by Mrs. Earl Small. The world record yellow perch was caught in Bordentown, New Jersey, by Dr. C. C. Abbot in May of 1865. Now that's a long-standing record!

Catfish

Because most catfish feed at night, I suppose that their looks don't prove much of a drawback. Counting bullheads, there are more than 20 species of catfish in the U.S., and they are very popular because of their catchability, their accessibility, the relatively low cost of the tackle required to catch them, and lastly (but probably mostly) because of their wonderful taste. People usually eat crispy fried catfish the way they eat potato chips — until the last one is gone.

Because catfish are nocturnal feeders, they rely on touch, taste, and smell to identify food. So the general point I made in Chapter 2 — that taste and smell of potential foods don't matter to fish — doesn't apply to the catfish. Some of the most nose-plug-requiring baits — called, appropriately, *stinkbaits* — attract catfish even though they smell as ripe as a marathoner's sweat socks.

When bait fishing, keep your bait on the bottom. That's where the catfish are. Lures are not that productive except with the channel cat, which is found in somwhat clearer moving water and often takes a deep-running plug, spoon, or jig.

Catfish are active in warm water and may be taken with water temperatures in the high 80s.

The world record blue catfish weighed in at 109 pounds and 4 ounces; it was caught by George A. Lijewski, March 14, 1991, on the Cooper River in South Carolina. The record channel cat, at 58 pounds, was caught in South Carolina's Santee-Cooper Reservoir on July 7, 1964, by W. B. Whaley.

Figure 9-15 clearly shows the difference between proper catfish and bull-heads. Notice that both have long whiskers or *barbels*.

When you handle a catfish, it will "lock" together its pectoral and dorsal fins. The projecting spines are very sharp and carry a toxin. Though not fatal, a wound from these spines can be nasty and painful. If you are pricked while handling a catfish, treat the wound immediately with a disinfectant, as swift action often nullifies the poison. Apply a bandage. Your revenge on the catfish is that you get to eat him.

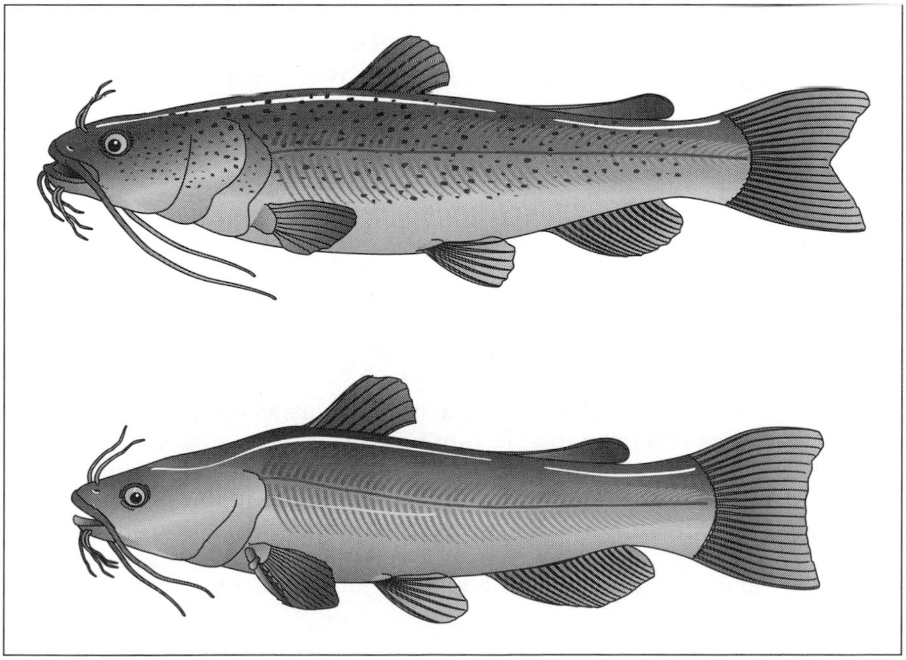

Figure 9-15: The channel cat (top), a true catfish, has a deeply forked tail, but bullheads (bottom) have a more rounded tail.

Shad

The shad, which is a large member of the herring family, lives most of its life at sea and returns to the river of its birth to spawn and die. This anadromous trait is not its only similarity to the more aristocratic salmon. The shad does not feed after it enters a river, but again, like the salmon, it can be induced to strike a brightly colored fly or lure. Nobody knows why they do this. I have read that they do it out of anger, or perhaps because they are reminded of food that they ate in the stream as a baby. Because most shad lures, which are called *darts,* look like really cheesy costume jewelry, you have to wonder about a shad's food memory.

I have fished for the smaller hickory shad in Florida in March. When hickory shad are in the rivers, thousands of white pelicans come in from the Atlantic to feast on their carcasses. In the northern part of the United States, the main river systems for shad anglers are the Delaware, Susquehanna, and Connecticut, where you can take them from a boat or while wading.

When playing a shad, remember that its mouth is very soft. Give it room to run. If you try to *horse* the fish (muscle it in), you will surely pull your lure or fly out. If you let it run, it will reward you with a number of beautiful leaps, just like a salmon.

The only type of shad for which world records are kept, the American shad, weighed 11 pounds, 4 ounces and was caught in the Connecticut River in South Hadley, Massachusetts, on May 19, 1986 by Bob Thibodo.

Both the American and the hickory shad have the large scales and deeply forked tails characteristic of the herring family, as shown in Figure 9-16. The hickory shad is generally smaller, and its lower lip extends out past the upper lip.

Atlantic Salmon

The Atlantic salmon is regarded by many as the aristocrat of fishes. Perhaps it has this reputation because you have to be an aristocrat to be able to afford a few days on one of the choice salmon rivers. Not surprisingly, with something that has become the sporting property of upper-class gentlemen, one is required to fish for Atlantic salmon with a fly rod; and on many rivers, one also has to rent a guide. Don't hold any of this against the salmon. He had very little to do with all the tradition surrounding him.

Figure 9-16:
American shad (top) and hickory shad (bottom).

The salmon is a cousin to the brown trout but spends most of its time at sea (although a salmon's infancy is passed in a river, and it is to that river that it returns to spawn). The Atlantic salmon (shown in Figure 9-17) does not die after spawning once, so you may return a salmon to the stream after catching it and be confident that it may well return to create even more fish the following year. This practice is good because the Atlantic salmon is a very pressured animal. Perhaps if we conserve our salmon harvest now, they will return to the numbers they had back in George Washington's day, when they were so plentiful that farmers used them for fertilizer!

If plenty of action is what you crave, salmon fishing is not for you: Just one fish a day is a very good average on most streams.

Henrik Henriksen caught the 79-pound, 2-ounce world-record Atlantic salmon in 1928 on Norway's Tana River.

Figure 9-17:
The Atlantic
salmon.
Despite the
efforts of
fishery
biologists,
transplanting
this
magnificent
game fish
to the
Pacific has
proved
impossible.

Chapter 10

Saltwater Fish

. . . .

In This Chapter

▶ Staying uncut, unbitten, and in one piece around saltwater fish

▶ The best fish to cure the winter blues

▶ Why the striped bass is the trout of the ocean

. . . .

*T*rout are gorgeous. Bass are exciting. Salmon are awe-inspiring. But pound for pound, the fight of a fish in the ocean is, in the opinion of most anglers, a great deal more fierce than the battle put up by any freshwater fish. Ocean fish are big and strong, and when they feel danger, they need to run far and fast. For all of these reasons, ocean fishing is a tremendously popular form of angling and one that is currently experiencing a tremendous growth spurt. To walk along the shore with the surf crashing, flights of ducks cruising overhead on their way to winter quarters, pods of gulls wheeling and diving over acres of bait fish, with big schools of game fish showing in the breakers — that's one of angling's great feelings!

Bluefish — Good and Tough

The bluefish is Fishdom's version of that guy in the bar who asks every newcomer, "Hey, buddy, are you looking at me?" and then, without waiting for an answer, throws a punch. The guy can be big or little, can win or lose a fight, but he keeps coming back for more. Fighting is in his nature.

When blues are around, they hit anything — live bait or cut bait, plug, jig, or fly. Bluefish are excellent fish for newcomers because:

✔ They are very catchable — not real finicky about what you offer them.

✔ They are strong fighters, so even the novice can begin to learn how it feels to handle equipment in a tough fight.

✔ If you catch one, you will probably catch more because they usually travel in groups.

✔ They are delicious when eaten fresh. In fact, if you want a good lesson in the difference between fresh fish and funky fish, eat a fillet of bluefish on the day that you catch it and then leave one in the fridge for a few days. The fresh fish will taste light like a flounder. The refrigerated fish will have that oily taste that reminds me of last week's tuna salad.

Bluefish inhabit all of the world's oceans, spending a good half of the year in deep water. In the warmer months, when surf temperatures are between 55°F and 75°F, the blues follow bait fish into shallow coastal waters. When they do, they can be taken on all kinds of tackle with all sorts of bait, lures, and flies.

Bluefish have very sharp teeth, so whatever method of angling you use, you often find that you lose fewer fish if you use a wire leader. To avoid the chance of a bite, pick up a blue as you would a pike, by squeezing it behind the eye sockets. Use pliers to unhook a blue.

The world-record bluefish weighed 31 pounds and 12 ounces and was caught off Cape Hatteras, North Carolina, on January 30, 1972, by James M. Hussey.

Figure 10-1 shows a typical bluefish that, sure enough, looks kind of blueish on top when out of the water; but when you see them in the surf, they appear more coppery-green.

Figure 10-1:
The bluefish has extremely sharp teeth, a white belly, and usually a black blotch at the base of the pectoral fin.

Flounder, Fluke, and Halibut — Flat and Fun

In addition to being highly catchable and delicious, the flounder is one of the great early-season fish. When the first warm days of spring make it harder and harder to think about work, nothing is more pleasant than giving winter the kiss-off by catching a bucketful of flounder. A small boat and a simple fish-finding rig (see Chapter 2) with a piece of clam on the hook are all you need to explore the protected bays and sandy coves where early-season flounder rest on sandy, muddy bottoms. They will strike your bait with a persistent tap-tap, your signal to rear back and strike. The type of rod you use isn't important. I have even caught flounder with a fly rod. Although tying a bait hook with a piece of bloodworm onto your expensive fly-rod outfit doesn't look very tweedy, it is fun.

The summer flounder is also known as the fluke. Its mouth and eyes are located on the left side of the fish. (The winter flounder is right-eyed and right-mouthed.) The fluke is a little more spunky than its cold-weather cousins; and although fluke, too, are found mainly on the bottom, they sometimes surprise you by chasing your bait when you are after blues or weakfish.

The halibut (shown with the fluke and flounder in Figure 10-2) is also a member of this family; and in contrast to the flounder, it will often use its broad, flat body to put up a terrific fight that may have you thinking that you are into a nice striped bass.

The world record fluke weighed 22 pounds and 7 ounces and was caught by Charles Nappi at Montauk, Long Island, on September 15, 1975. The record winter flounder, caught on Fire Island, Long Island, on May 8, 1986, by Einar F. Grell, weighed 7 pounds. The largest line-caught California halibut weighed 53 pounds and 4 ounces and was caught off Santa Rosa Island, California, on July 7, 1988, by Russell J. Harmon

Weakfish and Sea Trout

These are two different but closely related fish. Neither of them is a trout, but their torpedo shape and spotted skin (as shown in Figure 10-3) are similar to a trout's. The weakfish is exclusively an Atlantic Seaboard fish, but the sea trout (or *speckled trout*) can be found from New England through the Gulf of Mexico. Weakfish and sea trout live side by side in the mid-Atlantic states.

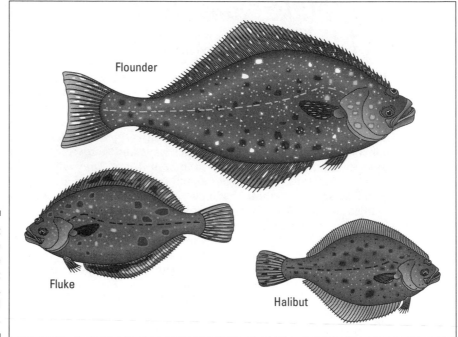

Figure 10-2:
Three
favorite
flatties:
flounder,
fluke, and
halibut.

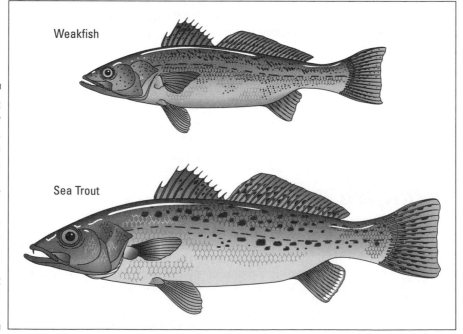

Figure 10-3:
Two closely
related fish,
the
weakfish
and the sea
trout (or
speckled
trout) have
telltale
coffee-
bean-like
spots just
like brown
trout have.

Although no one has ever been able to explain why, weakfish, like many other game animals, experience sudden upticks and declines in population. Some scientists think that the weakfish/sea trout population fluctuation has to do with the availability of food in the deep-water wintering grounds somewhere off the Continental Shelf.

Bait fishermen do well with sandworms in the early season, switching to crabs and shrimp as the warm weather progresses. In the grass beds of Florida and the Gulf of Mexico, shrimp are far and away the preferred food; and the trick for the angler is to get a shrimp (or an imitation shrimp) to ride just above the top of the grass beds to avoid getting hung up if a fish strikes. Weakfish cruise these beds like white-tailed deer grazing in a pasture.

When fishing the bottom, a fishfinder rig with one or two hooks (as described in Chapter 2) scores well for many anglers.

In the absence of any grass beds to hold shrimp, you need to fish tidal structures (rocks, inlets, drop-offs) just as you would with any other fish, looking for areas that are likely to carry bait fish in the moving tide. Surfcasters do well with spoons. Fly-rodding with shrimp imitations or poppers can be productive. No matter how you angle for weakfish, remember its name and how it got it: The mouth is soft; so even though it requires steady pressure to keep the fish out of the weeds, you also need a light touch so that you don't pull the hook out.

Two anglers are tied for the record weakfish at 19 pounds and 2 ounces. On October 11, 1984, Dennis Roger caught his in Jones Beach Inlet, Long Island, and five years later, on May 20, 1989, William Thomas caught his in Delaware Bay.

Striped Bass: A Silver Treasure

For the surf fisherman or fisherwoman, the striped bass (shown in Figure 10-4) is *the real thing,* the serious fish that makes your day. The striper, like the trout in freshwater, offers a special challenge and a special satisfaction. Like the trout, the striper can sometimes be caught without a great deal of thought on the part of the angler; but more often, stripers can be maddeningly selective. You can hear them slashing all around; but no matter what you throw them, they will not take because they are keyed in on one particular bait that is all-but-invisible to the angler.

Figure 10-4:
The striped
bass, as its
name
suggests, is
easily
identified by
the thin
black
stripes that
run the
length of its
body.

Figure 10-4: The striped bass, as its name suggests, is easily identified by the thin black stripes that run the length of its body.

Found from the Carolinas to Maine, and having been transplanted to the west coast and a number of reservoirs all over America, stripers are a favorite game fish. *Shoolie* (small) stripers can be caught on any form of light tackle. But the little guys aren't the only ones that run in schools. During the great migrations of spring and fall, stripers tend to travel in packs in which all the fish are of uniform size. (I have had days in early December off Montauk when they were all 30 inches long and gorging on herrings.)

Stripers take a variety of baits. Bait fish such as the bunker (also known as menhadden) produce well, as do herrings and bloodworms. Live eels can yield enormous fish. (While fishing with his dad in the autumn of 1995, Keith Meyer, *The New York Times* photographer who shoots the pictures for my fishing column, took a 64-pound striper on a live eel while fishing under the Triboro Bridge that connects Manhattan, Queens, and the Bronx.)

Plugs and spoons (the latter often fished with the hook buried in wiggly surgical tubes) both work well for stripers. You will do better fishing deep during the daylight. But surface lures are usually more effective in low-light conditions.

Fly-rodding for stripers is a fast-growing sport and one that has revolution-ized fly-fishing in the northeastern U.S. Now, instead of making the long drive to crowded trout streams in the mountains, flyrodders are finding great sport close to home with stripers, often with major league fish in the 20- to 30-pound range.

Even though you may score on subsurface flies, nothing is more thrilling than watching a striper rush to engulf a popper. Even if surface fishing sometimes means catching fewer fish, the thrill is well worth the price.

Little fly, big fish

I became a believer in flies for stripers about ten years ago, around Thanksgiving time, when Jim Clark, a retired high school teacher in East Hampton, Long Island, called to tell me that the big ones were in right by his house near Georgica Beach. When I got there, the ocean looked anything but fly-fishable. The surf was high and roily and a strong in-your-face wind made casting very difficult.

"Ain't gonna happen, Jim," I said.

"Tie on a streamer and get out on that jetty quick, before the spinning guys beat you to it," he ordered.

Halfheartedly, more to please Jim than because of any faith in the fishing, I did as I was told and cast my small streamer into the heaving surf.

Pow! I was into a fish. After a beautiful fight, I beached a 36-inch bass. Jim, our buddy Peter, and I went on to catch nine fish in the next hour, all on two-inch-long Clouser's Minnows. Meanwhile, the conventional-tackle guys with the big surf sticks and the huge plugs were fishless, which speaks volumes about the importance of having the particular bait that the fish are taking (or at least something that looks like the right bait). In fairness to conventional-tackle anglers, I have noticed that many of them fish a bucktail dropper fly that looks just like a streamer; and often, on days when I do well on the fly, I have noticed that the dropper anglers do equally well.

My main advice for fishing stripers is this: When there is no visible surface activity, fish them with the same strategy that you would use for freshwater trout or bass. Like the trout, the striper hangs on the edge of the current and looks for feeding opportunities. For that reason, tidal rips are often the first place to look. And like the freshwater bass, the striper likes to hang around sheltering structures, picking off similarly-minded bait. In this case, jetties and rocky shorelines can produce good striper action. This affinity for a rocky habitat no doubt accounts in part for the name *rockfish,* by which the striper is known in the waters south of New Jersey.

The world record is held by Albert R. McReynolds, who caught a 78-pound, 8-ounce striped bass off Atlantic City, New Jersey, on May 7, 1992.

Redfish: A Cook's Tale

Thanks in part to the success of Louisiana Chef Paul Proudhomme's wildly popular recipe for blackened redfish, more people experience redfish on the plate rather than with rod and reel. In fact, Proudhomme's recipe caught on so well that the redfish were nearly fished out on the Gulf Coast.

TIP

Puffing for reds

With redfish and sea trout, I have found that if you don't *see* them on the grassy flats, that doesn't mean that they are not there. They could be following in the wake of a ray and picking up shell fish that the ray has stirred up as it cruises. Look for tight puffs of turbid water that indicate a recently-made cloud of mud. Cast into the trailing edge of the cloud and begin to retrieve line. I have caught many fish by this kind of blind casting. (Actually, it's not so much blind casting as it is blind hope!)

Also known as the *channel bass* or *red drum,* this crustacean-loving game fish is caught from New Jersey to Houston, Texas; but it is on the grass beds of Florida and the Gulf of Mexico that the redfish (shown in Figure 10-5) becomes a super-challenging opponent. And the shallower the water, the more thrilling the fight.

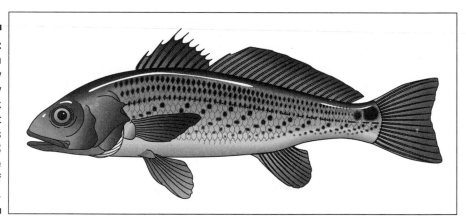

Figure 10-5:
The redfish is easily identified by the black spot that resembles the CBS logo on the base of its tail.

New Orleans redfish guide Bubby Rodriguez has taken me out to the shallow salt marshes where the Barataria Bayou eases into the Gulf of Mexico and has put me on 10-pound fish in less than a foot of water. This is hold-your-breath, one-cast fishing. It is also very demanding. You need to put the fly right in front of the fish's nose (within two inches). And you have to avoid spooking him with your line at the same time.

Actually, you don't so much *spook* as you *turn off* the fish. Often, a bad cast gets a look from the fish, after which it stays within casting distance but ignores you after you have been "made," to use a term that cops use for having blown your cover.

The best fly for a red in Louisiana is a crab imitation. Shrimp also score consistently.

The world-record redfish weighed 94 pounds and 2 ounces and was caught off Avon, North Carolina, on November 7, 1984, by David G. Deuel.

Cod

The cod, a delicious fish, is probably the most important commercial fish in history. Ever since Europeans arrived in the western hemisphere, commercial fishermen have made the long voyage from Europe to the fertile fishing ground of the St. Georges Banks. Their catch could be sold fresh or salted and dried. And cod, which prefer water temperatures in the mid 40s, can be taken through the winter when other fish desert the Continental Shelf for mid-ocean depths or southern waters.

Because you can catch cod in the cold months, they are a lifesaver for anglers on the Atlantic Seaboard. Party boat captains know where to find the wrecks that concentrate forage (bait) fish and the cod that feed upon them.

Cod angling is pretty much of the meat-and-potatoes variety: simple bait fishing or jigging just off the bottom. A sturdy boat rod with a bait-casting reel or a surf stick with heavy spinning tackle are the preferred instruments of most cod anglers. Because cod can often tip the scale at greater than 30 pounds, you want heavy line (at least 30-pound test).

The world-record Atlantic cod weighed 98 pounds and 12 ounces and was caught off the Isle of Shoals, New Hampshire, by Donald Vaughn on July 7, 1984.

Figure 10-6 shows an Atlantic cod with the telltale single *barbel* (whisker) hanging from its lower jaw.

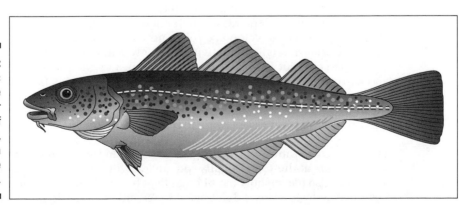

Figure 10-6: An Atlantic cod. Like other members of this family, it has a goatee-like whisker.

Bottom Fish: Reef Fish

If you fish for blackfish (also called *tautogs*), groupers, snappers, or any one of the scores of delicious fish that fill buckets and bellies of anglers everywhere, you know that each species has its pleasures and subtleties. But they are all alike in that they are almost always fished with bait on or near the bottom, and the angling technique requires nothing more than positioning yourself over a fish, dropping your bait, and waiting for a bite. The trick is knowing where to fish and when. For this reason, my advice is this: Go out on a party boat (also known as a *head boat*) where, for a modest fee, you get tackle, bait, a ride to the fishing, and a boatload of experts who are more than ready to give you free advice. This is a great way to take the kids fishing with at least a reasonable expectation that they will catch fish.

Inshore Grand Slam: Especially with a Fly Rod

People have been fly-rodding in the salt for more than a hundred years, but not until just after World War II did it begin to catch on with a wider public. For the next 20 years, it was something that rich guys or pampered outdoor writers did to fill the time between the close of one year's trout season and next year's opening day. In the last ten years or so, with The Great Fly-Rod Boom that followed in the wake of Robert Redford's film, *A River Runs Through It,* a number of flyrodders have discovered that there is terrific sport in the saltwater close to home. This is true whether your home is in New York, Boston, Savannah, Miami, New Orleans, Houston, San Francisco, Seattle, and on up into British Columbia.

This tremendous upsurge in interest gave birth to the first generation of full-time fly-rod guides in many of these waters. Because their work takes them on the water so many more days than the average angler spends, and because their living depends on their clients catching fish, the successful guides have had to develop and refine new flies and techniques in a nation-wide flowering of angling creativity. The only parallel I can think of is the work done on trout fishing flies and techniques by the great Catskill guides and fly-tiers from the 1870s up through the 1970s (roughly from the time railroad brakeman Roy Steenrod tied the first Hendricksen dry fly, through the innovations of Lee Wulff, and up to the Comparadun series of Al Caucci and Bob Nastasi on the Delaware River).

These are good times in which to live and fish. In the same way that salmon and trout are at the top of the fly-rod angler's hit parade, the saltwater flyrodder also has a short list of great fish: bonefish, permit, snook, and tarpon. And by the way, I don't mean to exclude conventional-tackle fishermen. All of these fish can be taken on lures and baits as well.

Bonefish: gray lightning

If one fish is responsible for kicking off the saltwater fly-fishing craze, it is this silver-gray denizen of sandy and coral flats in the world's warm-water oceans. From the west coast of Africa to the Caribbean to the paradise of the South Pacific, the bonefish is among the wariest shallow-water fish and, like the trout, responds well to the right fly, properly presented. A sloppy presentation, on the other hand, will cause the bone to turn tail and run for deep water with the speed of a cheetah.

The conventional angler can do well with live shrimp or an imitation-shrimp jig. The preferred fly-rod fly is a little shrimp imitation. The first trick to learn in fishing for bones is to see them. Initially, if you go with a guide (which is the *only* way for a newcomer to start bonefishing), you may feel that your guide is a liar or that you are close to blind because the guide may constantly call out, "Bonefish at 10 o'clock — 40 feet out."

You will see *nothing*. You will continue to see nothing for a long time, but trust me: Sooner or later, the bones will materialize. Eventually, you will be able to see the telltale black tip of their tails (and then their silver-yellow-green outlines) as they cruise. When you do, the trick is to cast four or five feet in front on the same line on which the fish is moving. In other words, lead the bonefish as a shotgunner would lead a duck or goose.

When the bonefish are feeding in shallow water, their tails will often stick up in the air. This activity is known as *tailing,* and it is to the bonefish angler what a rising trout is to the freshwater fisherman. I remember one Christmas, shortly after I was married, my wife and I went to check out Christmas Island, an atoll about 1,500 miles due south of Honolulu. The fishing was spectacular, and on Christmas Day, we were invited to the feast and singing contest at the main longhouse in the village called Banana (honest, that was its name). Because we were two of the only six non-Micronesians on the atoll, we were highly honored guests. The food was great; the singing was great. After lunch, as they smoked hand-rolled cigarettes of highly prized tobacco, the village elders began to tell tales of courage and adventure on the high seas. Just as they were getting to the classic legends, my guide showed up and said, "The tide is moving out, and there are five miles of tailing fish on the flat."

Right about there, I lost my interest in Tall Tales of the South Seas. We hightailed to the flat. As promised, the shallow water held ten thousand (or maybe ten million) bonefish, each with its tail waving in the pink-gold sun of the late afternoon. For the next three hours of the tide, we cast and caught, cast and caught. After you have been in and among tailing fish, catching one after another, you will understand the almost mystical awe that long-time bonefishers have for this fish in shallow water. One wrong move and you will spook hundreds of fish. But if you take your time and fish carefully, you can catch them until you decide to give up, which is one of the most rarely satisfying feelings in all of fishing.

With its big eye and downturned mouth, as shown in Figure 10-7, the bonefish is well designed to find food on the flats. I can't get it out of my mind, though, that despite its valor as a game fish, the eye and mouth give the bone a goofy look (as in Goofy, the cartoon character).

The world record bonefish was caught in deep water off the coast of South Africa on May 26, 1962, by Brian W. Batchelor. It weighed 19 pounds. Because he wasn't fishing for bonefish and it wasn't taken on the flats, I have always had a problem with this record, but my having a problem ain't gonna change things until you or I take a bigger one the "right" way.

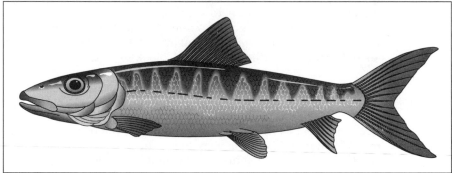

Figure 10-7:
The bonefish: gray wolf of the flats.

Permit: wishful thinking

Only one fish may be harder to interest in a bait, lure, or fly than a permit — a dead fish. Although permit eat (otherwise how would they grow?), this broad-sided pompano is the most finicky fish when it comes to taking a fly. I have tried and tried and have never even *turned* one.

You should have more luck with bait or lures. Shrimp and crabs both produce well. In addition to being highly spookable, a feeding permit usually has its head down in the sand, looking for crabs. It concentrates on an area of just a few square feet. An angler's success in getting one to look up from feeding is like a parent's success when trying to get the attention of a teenager reading an Archie comic book: unlikely.

Permit are found in the same kinds of water and under the same condition as bonefish. Blistering as the bonefish may be in its initial run, the permit is its equal and then some. Add to this the fact that when a permit turns its body broadside to you, it can really put up some resistance. The result is a fish that many anglers classify as the hardest fight for its size.

I caught two permit on jigs at the mouth of the Boca Paila lagoons in Mexico. I was fishing with 12-pound test and a medium-action rod. The first fish took a good 25 minutes to land and had me running up and down the beach the whole time. I must have jogged three miles as the permit took me in and out of the surf. From the fight, I figured for sure that I had a 20-pound fish. But when the permit finally surrendered, it was a 5- or 6-pounder. I can only imagine what the feeling must be to catch a permit on a fly.

The world record permit weighed 53 pounds and 4 ounces and was caught in Lake Worth, Florida, on March 25, 1994, by Roy Brooker.

Often, the first thing you see on a permit, as shown in Figure 10-8, is the black tips of its fins as it cruises in shallow water. When permit flash by in large schools, their subtle gray-green coloration is very visible.

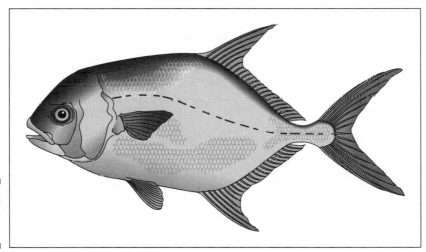

Figure 10-8:
The Atlantic permit.

Snook: no schnook

A snook is a funny looking fish. Come to think of it, the word snook itself is pretty silly, too. A snook looks like a baby striped bass with shoulder pads. Perhaps this extra heft in the shoulders is what gives this resident of Florida and Central America such pugnacity when it fights, an experience that I can compare best to the struggle of a great largemouth bass. Although snook present a fair challenge to the angler, the commercial fisherman has little trouble in harvesting this delicious, white-fleshed fish, which is why it is relatively scarce in places where it was once abundant. I can recall fishing a river on the Atlantic side of Costa Rica and coming upon two Indians in a canoe piled high with snook — maybe 200 fish. These same Indians were out there every day, harvesting snook, so you can imagine how depleted the coastal creeks were becoming.

Killer gills

Dehooking a snook by holding it by the lower lip — just like you would dehook a bass — is best. You should not put your fingers in gill covers which are super-sharp.

Thankfully, snook have been protected in recent years in the U.S. and have begun to make a comeback. They are like savage bass when they hit a plug, and I have also had great luck catching them with a fly rod and bass bugs. At night, when they congregrate under the lights of bayside docks, the fishing can be unbelievable. When the tide is running, the snook hang around the lights, picking off bait fish. By casting a streamer, first at the outside of the group and then further into it, you can take a half-dozen nice fish before you have exhausted the possibilities in any one *pod* (small group of fish).

Though snook make great eating, they are under so much pressure that I would advise you to keep them rarely, and only as a special treat. By returning them to the water alive, you can do your part to help bring back a classic sport fishery.

The snook shown in Figure 10-9 has the bright silver sides and clearly defined lateral line that are typical of this fish.

Figure 10-9:
The snook,
built like
a bass
designed by
John
Madden.

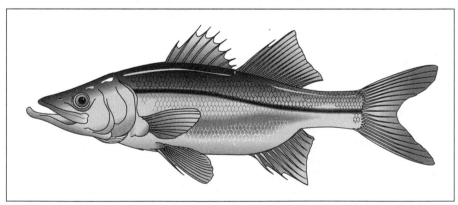

Tarpon: the silver king

The tarpon is a big fish — a very big fish — that can be taken on light tackle in shallow water. It can run forever and leap ten feet in the air, writhing as it does so. I can't imagine what more anyone could want out of an angling encounter.

Tarpon, which are very large herrings, have been taken on rod and reel for about a hundred years. Claims for having caught the first tarpon pop up in turn-of-the-century sporting literature with the frequency (and "checkup-ableness") of Elvis sightings. I am partial to the claim of Anthony Dimock, a tireless explorer of fishing opportunities in early Florida who reportedly subdued the first tarpon with sportfishing tackle in the 1880s. But then I am a fan of any guy who made and lost a couple of fortunes while maintaining his angling passion: Each time he was in the pink, he completely gave up Wall Street to become a full-time fisherman. His *Book of the Tarpon* has a remarkable series of photos of his fight with a huge fish, a fight that occurred nearly a hundred years ago.

Tarpon take squid, shrimp, or bait fish as well as plugs. I prefer them on flies, although I caught my first two tarpon (both better than 80 pounds each) with a Zebco spin-casting outfit, which goes to show that you don't need megabucks worth of tackle to enjoy catching this biggest of game fish encountered on the flats.

Whatever way you choose to fish for tarpon, heavy tackle is preferred because this fish requires all the force you can muster if you want to land one in less than half an hour. A long fight, in fact *any* fight, with a big tarpon can be very tiring; and the longer you have one on, the greater the chance you have of losing your fish to a shark. This has happened to me, and though exciting, it is also kind of a bummer. A strong rod quickens the fight in favor of the angler and also lets the angler strike hard and repeatedly in order to drive the hook home.

The great thing about a tarpon in shallow water is that it has nowhere to go but up, and this lack of room leads to a fight marked by thrilling acrobatic leaps. Many experienced anglers are happy just to hook and *jump* a tarpon and then to have it spit out the hook so that they can hook and jump another one.

With tarpon and other really big game fish, there is no question in my mind that you should hire a guide until you are a real veteran. In addition to everything else (like knowing where the fish are and having the right heavy-duty gear), the experienced guide knows how to tie a super-heavy shock leader with the Bimini Twist knot, a complicated knot that, as far as I can tell, requires the knotter to be able to execute a series of ten consecutive somersaults and a double axle from a sitting position.

Using your head

Sometimes the experience you gain in one kind of fishing pays off in a completely different angling situation. This point was driven home to me when I was fishing for tarpon during the hatch of the palolo worm in the Florida Keys. We were literally 5 minutes from Key West Harbor when the little red worms hatched and 50 acres of water erupted with feeding tarpon. The scene looked like a trout pool filled with fish during a mayfly hatch — the only difference was, these "trout" weighed one hundred pounds each.

I was fishing with Keys guide Dave Kesar and John Cole, an ex-commercial fisherman on Long Island who also wrote a number of great fishing books, among them *Striper* and *Tarpon Quest*. Residents of Maine may remember him as the editor of *The Maine Times*.

It was my turn to wield the rod when the hatch started. I cast and stripped, cast and stripped, getting into a rhythm. It crossed my mind that my little artificial might go unnoticed by the feeding fish, but I kept casting. After ten minutes, John took a turn, and then Dave did. The rod came around to me again. I cast and talked. Dave remarked on a nice boat that was going by. I turned my head to look back, leaving my fly to hang in the current. That was the time, of course, that the tarpon chose to slam my fly. I tried to set the hook. The tarpon took to the air and broke off.

"Hmm," John said softly (which, in a Down-Easter, passes for hysterical excitement).

I rose to the bait. "Hmm what, John?" I asked.

"The tarpon took your fly at the end of the swing, just the way a salmon would roll and take. I think if we treat this current like a salmon stream and fish it that way, we might be on to something. Anyway, it couldn't hurt," he replied.

I gave John the rod. He cast across the current, *quartering down tide* (that is, casting diagonally across the tide and in the same direction in which it was flowing).

"Right . . . about . . . there," John said (more to himself than to us). "Whomp — tarpon on!" The fish jumped and broke off. Dave tried next, then me. We hooked a dozen fish — one of them within ten feet of the boat. When he took to the air, he sprayed us like a Labrador retriever shaking the water off his wet coat.

Though we did not land a single tarpon, I felt privileged to have seen an observant angler at the moment he "invented" a new way to fish for tarpon. (I also liked connecting with the fish.)

The world record for tarpon belongs to two anglers. On April 16, 1991, Yvon Victor Sebag caught a 283-pound, 4-ounce fish off Sierra Leone. Thirty-five years earlier, an M. Salazar caught a tarpon of the same weight in Lake Maracaibo, Venezuela.

As shown in Figure 10-10, the tarpon is easily recognizable because of its protruding lower jaw and huge eye. In fact, its Latin name, *Megalops,* means *very big eye*.

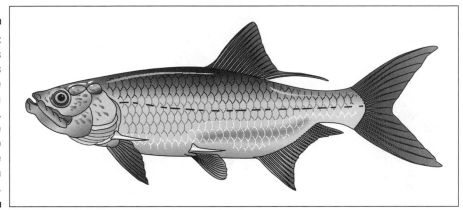

Figure 10-10:
The tarpon's large scales look like those of a herring, which is the family to which the tarpon belongs.

Really Big Game

Chances are, you will not be going for monster game fish by yourself, especially if you are a newcomer. Big game fish are serious animals. They can be dangerous, and they require special, costly equipment. As I advised with tarpon, get a guide.

Sharks: Underwater Hell's Angels

Because sharks (shown in Figure 10-11) have such a well-deserved reputation as ruthlessly efficient predators, they appeal to many anglers' macho instincts (fisherwomen can have macho instincts as well as men). To be locked in combat with a deadly killing machine is sure to get your juices running; in fact, such combat is probably the reason why we evolved juices in the first place. Add to this the big buildup that shark fishing got as a result of the movie *Jaws,* and you have the explanation for the boom in shark fishing of the last 20 years.

In that time, charter captains have become more savvy, and equipment has evolved so that more anglers are taking more sharks than ever before. The consequence is that there are fewer sharks to be had. My strong recommendation is that you keep no more than one shark a year and return the rest after tagging.

Your captain wil set you up with tackle — usually pretty hefty stuff. The captain will also have a good idea about how to play wind, tide, and underwater structures to give you the best shot at a shark. Still, *you* have to do the catching.

Figure 10-11:
The mako
shark, like
all members
of the shark
family, is
highly
streamlined,
with rough
skin and
super-sharp
teeth.

The most critical maneuver is the strike. *Don't* strike the instant that your bait is taken. Give the shark time to swim with it, play with it, and take it deep. Reel down as you would with a freshwater bass (in other words, lower the rod as you reel in). Point your rod tip at the fish; and when you *come tight* (that is, you have recovered all the slack), rear back and really slam that hook home. Then hold on. The shark will give you a tenacious and long fight. If you are lucky enough to hook a mako, you will be rewarded with a series of dazzling leaps — often 10 or 15 feet in the air! The fight can last a half hour or three hours. Either way, you will be tested to the limits of your endurance. And when you want to give up and cry uncle, remember that you are the one who wanted to go fishing in the first place; so, when you finally have a fish, don't weenie out.

Sharks come in many species and sizes. You can catch a 1-pound blackmouth or a 1-ton great white. Anything in the 100-pound class is a bona fide big game animal.

They're only dead after you cook them

After you catch a shark and bring it on board, you may want to get an up-close look of your prize catch (or even a photo of yourself holding the fish). Don't do it! Plenty of supposedly dead sharks have taken a nasty chunk out of anglers trying to handle them. And even if the teeth don't get you, a hook may, or a thrashing tail could give you a good knock. Leave the shark handling to the pros.

Tuna

If striped bass are like white-tailed deer — a fair-sized quarry, with the occasional trophy-sized one thrown in — then tuna are like elk. Tuna are big — truly one of the world's great big game animals. Because you can catch them within a few hours of New York City, people tend to discount what rare prized game they are. But to someone in Nairobi or Berlin, a giant tuna is as much an exotic trophy as a water buffalo or a red stag is to a New Yorker. Furthermore, like the elk and other large herd animals, the tuna undertakes a semi-annual migration: In autumn, it travels from its summer grounds off the northeastern coast of North America to its winter quarters in the depths of tropical seas. In the spring, it returns northward.

The ultimate in tuna fishing is getting out to deep, blue water, 70 to 100 miles from shore, where whales and dolphins and sharks are also found. You may just as well be 1,000 miles from shore. It feels like a whole other world out there.

Like sharks, tuna (shown in Figure 10-12) come in all sizes. All of them fight beautifully. When it comes to pure fight, my favorite fly-rod fish is the false albacore at about 8 or 9 pounds. The much larger yellowfin and bluefin are definitely heavy-tackle, charter-boat-type fish. These fish range from 30 pounds up to 1,000 pounds plus.

Figure 10-12:
Both the yellowfin (top) and the much larger bluefin tuna (bottom) have the classic tuna shape of big shoulders and a tapered body. They're designed for a great contest with the angler.

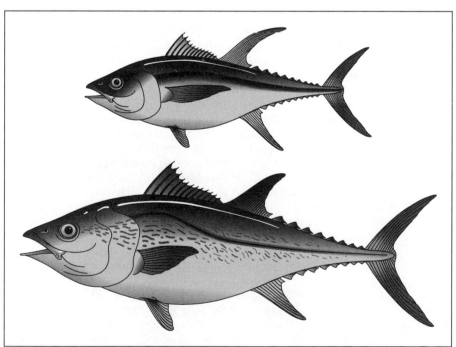

Giant tuna have been taken on rod and reel for only a little more than half a century. The legendary Lee Wulff told me that he once entered a rod-and-reel tournament held by the government of Labrador in the late 1930s. When he won the contest with two giant bluefins, the provincial governor noticed Lee's picture in *The New York Times* and offered him a plane and financial backing to explore angling opportunities in Labrador. Wulff learned to fly, got his pilot's licence, and in the following few years went on one of the great fishing exploration trips of this or any century, opening many new lakes and rivers for anglers seeking giant brook trout, huge pike, and Atlantic salmon.

Overfishing and the huge upsurge in popularity of sushi (a Japanese delicacy made from raw tuna) have made tuna so scarce that a big fish can fetch $10,000 to $20,000 at the dock. Here, as with all big game, only strict regulations and a catch-and-release conservation ethic can preserve the thrill of tying into one of the giants of the ocean.

The world record bluefin tuna was caught at Aulds Cove, Nova Scotia, by Ken Fraser on October 26, 1979. It weighed 1,496 pounds. The record yellowfin, at 388 pounds and 12 ounces, was caught at Isla San Benedicto, Mexico, on April 1, 1977, by Curt Wiesenhutter.

Marlin

The marlin is *it* — The Big One. It leaps like a tarpon, runs line like a bonefish, and dives like the stubbornest brown trout. The only difference is that a *small* black or blue marlin is the size of a defensive tackle on the Dallas Cowboys, and a big one is the size of a pickup truck. If you want to take your measure against a fish, the marlin can test all of your angling skills (and your strength and endurance, too).

The white marlin, the smallest of the group, is an Atlantic fish. The blue marlin is both an Atlantic and Pacific fish, and the black is a Pacific fish. Bait fishing is the most effective angling method. Bonito and wahoo are the baits I have used the most. Trolled lures can be very effective, and marlin have even been caught on flies. This last method involves a very intricate angling method. The fish is *teased up* (induced to strike) with a hookless lure that makes a great deal of commotion. When the marlin is within casting distance, the teaser is cranked in, and the fly is presented to the fish. This same teasing technique is also used with conventional tackle.

If and when you do catch a marlin, bear in mind that they must have evolved that big sword (shown in Figure 10-13) for something. It packs a wallop, so my advice is this: Don't touch it if the marlin is alive and assume that the marlin is alive until somebody tells you otherwise.

Figure 10-13:
The distinguishing feature of all marlin is their sword, a dangerous weapon to other fish and anglers.

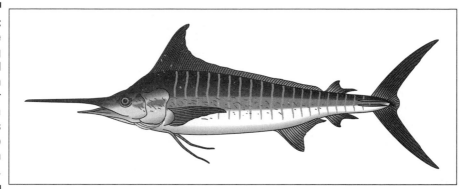

The world-record black was 1,560 pounds and was caught off Cabo Blanco, Peru, on August 4, 1953, by Alfred C. Glassell, Jr. The record blue was a leap year fish at 1,402 pounds and 2 ounces, caught by Robert A. Amorim on February 29, 1992, in Victoria, Brazil. The record white was 181 pounds and 14 ounces and was caught on December 8, 1979, by Evandro Luiz Coser, also in Vitorio, Brazil.

TIP

Pumping iron water

Ernest Hemingway was a marlin fanatic. In fact, the main reason he moved from Key West, Florida, to Cuba was to be closer to accessible marlin fishing. In the Florida Keys, the run to the marlin grounds out in the Gulf Stream is a long one. In Cuba, "The Stream" runs right into the island, and you can be on marlin in minutes.

I once visited Hemingway's Cuban house along with his eldest son, Jack. We walked up to the old swimming pool, and Jack recalled how his father would train for marlin fishing. Whenever Papa returned from a trip abroad — which always involved a great deal

of drinking and carousing — he ended up very out of shape. So each morning, for two or three weeks after his return, he would take a bucket, a broomstick, and a chair up to the swimming pool. He'd sit in the chair and slip the broomstick through the handle of the bucket. Then he would lower the bucket in the water and fill it, after which he would rock backward, lifting the bucket out of the water. He did this for 20 minutes each morning and afternoon, exactly mimicking the motion of fighting a marlin. In this way, he built up his stamina for the toughest contest in all of fishing: angler versus marlin.

Part III
Now You're Fishing

In this part . . .

You'll find tons of diverse and helpful information. This part is the real meat of the book. In just about every chapter, I provide tons of how-to advice and present easy-to-follow, step-by-step instructions. The chapters themselves cover everything from tying knots to spincasting to landing fish and even dressing properly.

Chapter 11

Just a Few Knots

In This Chapter

▶ The three most important knots

▶ A couple of other pretty important knots

Knots are a compromise. They always weaken your line, but you need them to attach lures, hooks, sinkers, and all kinds of other stuff to your line. You couldn't very well go fishing without tying on a hook. People have opinions about knots in the way they have opinions about politics. Often, people express them just for the sake of argument and "Mine is better than yours." But where your political opinions may not affect your day-to-day life that much, your ability to tie knots well is the the difference between catching big fish and catching no fish. Learning how to tie proper knots takes time, but, once mastered, they are not forgotten.

So Many Knots, So Little Time

At last count, the experts in knotology say there are about 3,000 different knots. I do 90 percent of my fishing with three knots. These three knots are not the prettiest knots, but they are the easiest, and they are as strong as any knot you can name.

In this chapter, I have tried to describe some knots (including my three favorites) and illustrate them. (Actually, I didn't really illustrate them myself. I can't even draw a smile button. The figures in this chapter, like all the other figures in this book, are the creations of Ron Hildebrand, who gets a big vote of thanks from me!) But great illustrations and the clearest descriptions are, at best, just a guide. Whenever I read angling books and attempt to learn the knots shown in them, I find myself trying to look upside down or doing almost-impossible contortions. The long and the short of knot-tying is that you just gotta do it (and do it again and again and again).

I will say this: Every knot has a logic to it, and every time you learn a new knot, there comes a point in the learning process when you will understand *why* the knot works and *what* it does.

Some knot-tying words

Most knot-tying instructions use a few standard terms. These terms are pretty self-descriptive, but just to make sure that we are all on the same page, here they are:

✔ **Tag end:** The end of your line. This is the part that does the knot-tying. When you are finished tying, the tag end is the sticking-out part that you clip.

✔ **Standing end:** The rest of your line. You tie the tag end around this.

✔ **Turn:** Sometimes called a *wrap*. A turn is created when you pass the tag end through one complete turn around the standing end.

The Fisherman's knot

The real name of this knot is the *Improved Clinch knot.* But back when I started fishing, many people called it the Fisherman's knot because every angler knew how to tie this knot, and it was often the first knot they learned. Use the Improved Clinch knot to attach your line to your hook.

If a knot ever fails on you, 99 times out of 100, the place where it fails is right next to the hook, so the knot you use at this critical place should be the most reliable one that you can tie. Since I began fishing, I have read many claims for many other knots; some of the claims were quite learned and passionate. But guess what? The Fisherman's knot still gets the nod from me. Here's why:

A few summers back, my oldest daughter, Lucy, went to The Catskill Fly-fishing Center. This organization's wonderful two-day introduction is held on the Willowemoc River, which is about as close as you can get to holy water in fly-fishing. You may think that the folks at the center taught Lucy some knot that could only be learned by people who had a reading knowledge of Latin. Wrong. They taught her the Improved Clinch knot, and they called it the Fisherman's knot.

To tie the Improved Clinch knot, as shown in Figure 11-1, follow these steps:

1. **Run the tag end of the line through the eye of the hook and pull 8–10 inches of line through the hook eye.**

2. **Wrap the tag end around the standing end for five wraps or turns.**

3. **Now pass the tag end through the loop next to the hook eye.**

   You will have formed another loop that includes your wraps.

4. **Pass the tag end through that loop.**

5. **Wet the loops with some saliva to lubricate the knot.**

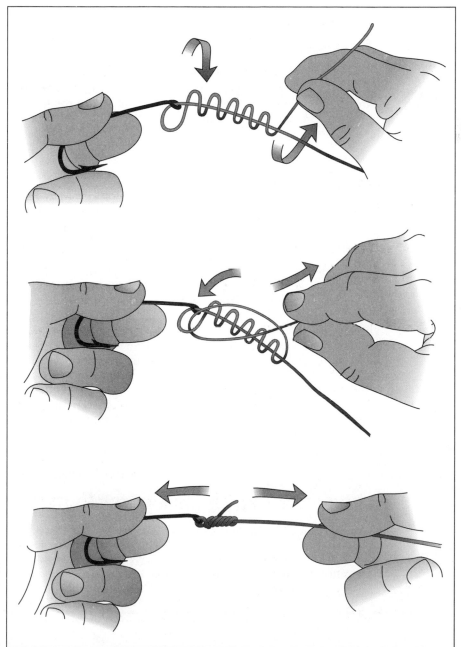

Figure 11-1:
The
Improved
Clinch knot.

6. **Hold the tag end and standing end in one hand and the bend of the hook in the other; then** *pull with steady pressure.*

   If you are not sure about safely holding the hook, grip it firmly but not super firmly with needle-nose pliers.

7. **Tighten slowly.**

8. **Clip the tag end so that only** $^1/_8$ **inch is left.**

 A standard fingernail clipper is a great tool for making a clean final cut on the tag end. Here's another tip: Leave the remaining tag end about $^1/_4$-inch to $^3/_8$-inch long; then touch the very tip of the tag end to the hot end of a lit cigarette (or a just-blown-out match) in order to create a ball on the end of the line, which prevents the tag end from pulling out under stress.

The Surgeon's knot

Twenty-five years ago, I was on the Beaverkill River in the Catskills. No one was catching fish except for this one silver-haired guy. He laid out line like he was shooting a laser. He caught fish after fish. After a while, he left the stream. When he passed me on the bridge, I complimented him on his fishing prowess, and I offered him a pull of bourbon that I had in a flask to ward off the early spring chill. As we talked, I learned that he was the well-known fly-fishing author, Doug Swisher.

While looking at his fly, I noticed the ugly knot joining the last length of tippet to his leader. (See Chapter 14 if you're unfamiliar with the terminology of fly-fishing gear.) I asked about the knot, and, by way of reply, Doug demonstrated the Surgeon's knot. This knot got its name because it's the same one that surgeons use to close up their handiwork. I use it to join two pieces of line that are close to each other in diameter. The Surgeon's knot takes the place of the more-complicated Blood knot (which is not described in this book), but it is not as pretty.

You have *two* hands and *ten* fingers

When tying knots, remember that there is no law against changing hands while you are tying. Sometimes you can hold the standing end in one hand, and sometimes you can hold it in the other. If you try to tie a knot by starting with the standing end in one hand and keeping it there until the end, you will end up in a pretzel position. Again, try to understand how the knot functions; then use whichever hand works best at the moment.

More than one fly-fishing buddy has turned his nose up at my scraggly looking Surgeon's knot. Hey, it may not *look* great, but it *works* great. And if a surgeon feels that this knot is dependable enough to close up a wound, I am willing to trust it to haul in a catfish.

To tie the Surgeon's knot, just follow these steps:

1. **Lay about 10 inches of tag end on top of your standing line, as shown in Figure 11-2.**

2. **In one hand, hold about four inches of standing line and the tag end and make a loop.**

3. **Pinch the loop together between thumb and forefinger.**

4. **Take the other end of the tag end and the end of the standing line and, passing it through the open loop, wrap them twice around the two strands of your loop.**

5. **Using both hands, pull evenly on all four strands.**

6. **Wet the knot with saliva when you are just about ready to finish pulling the knot tight.**

7. **Clip the tag ends.**

After a little practice, you will see that the Surgeon's knot is easy to tie. After you know how to tie this very well, practice tying it in a dark room or step into a closet and tie it. Knowing how to tie a simple knot in the dark can be a handy skill. (I leave it up to you to explain things when someone opens the closet door and finds you standing there with two lengths of fishing line in your hands.)

A perfect match

If you use the Surgeon's knot to create a tapered fly leader, you want to make sure that you have an *even* taper. If one piece of line is much thicker than the piece to which it is joined, you will wind up making a sloppy, fish-scaring cast.

Here's the easy way to see if one piece of leader overpowers the other in any connection you make. When you have two pieces of mono that are matched (close, but not quite the same, in diameter), they make a nice even curve (a smooth oxbow loop) when you push them together. When the thicknesses are unmatched, the weaker of the two lengths of leader collapses or pushes in against the stronger length. If your fly leader isn't turning over (unrolling completely) then you are probably connecting lengths of line that are unmatched.

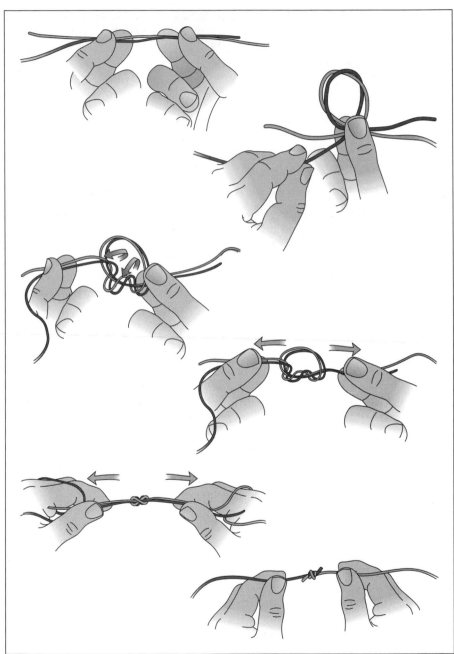

Figure 11-2:
The
Surgeon's
knot.

The Perfection Loop

The Perfection Loop is another of those less-than-gorgeous-looking knots. I use it to connect my leader to the butt of the fly line. I also use this loop to make droppers for 8-ounce sinkers when I am fishing live eels for stripers 80 feet down in the currents of Hell Gate on the East River in New York. In other words, the Perfection Loop is a versatile knot. It is very fast to tie, and (like the Surgeon's knot) you can do it all by feel in almost total darkness.

Check out Figure 11-3 and follow these steps to tie a Perfection Loop:

1. **Create a 1^1/$_2$-inch loop and pinch between thumb and forefinger.**

2. **Repeat the action, creating another smaller loop around the first loop and pinch again.**

3. **Run the tag end between the two loops and continue to hold everything pinched together.**

4. **Pull the second loop through the first loop and start to tighten the knot, providing the final tightening with a pair of pliers.**

A Few More Knots

The three basic knots that I have discussed in this chapter can get you through most fishing situations. Not *all* situations, but *most* situations. You won't be able to lift a tarpon into your boat with these knots, and they are not designed to be tied with metallic materials. But in terms of getting a hook on the line, splicing line, and having enough loops to suspend weights and other hooks off your main line, you are covered. Now, here are a few more knots that can take you even further on the road to fishing success.

It helps if the line is tied to the reel

There you are — casting away into a pod of feeding fish. Thwack! Your rod bends double, and you feel the pull of the biggest fish you have ever felt in your life. It keeps pulling and pulling. You are getting more and more excited. You are down to the last couple of feet of line on the reel. You decide to chance it and apply a little extra pressure, hoping to turn the fish and recover just a few feet of line. You lean into the rod, it bends more, the fish starts to turn and then, disaster strikes. The rod springs back as you watch the end of your line pass through the guides, and away goes Mr. World Record Fish with 200 yards of your line and a nice $6 lure in his mouth. It's times like these that make me feel like Wile E. Coyote feels when he runs off a cliff and his legs keep going until he looks down and sees where he is, at which point he plummets like a stone.

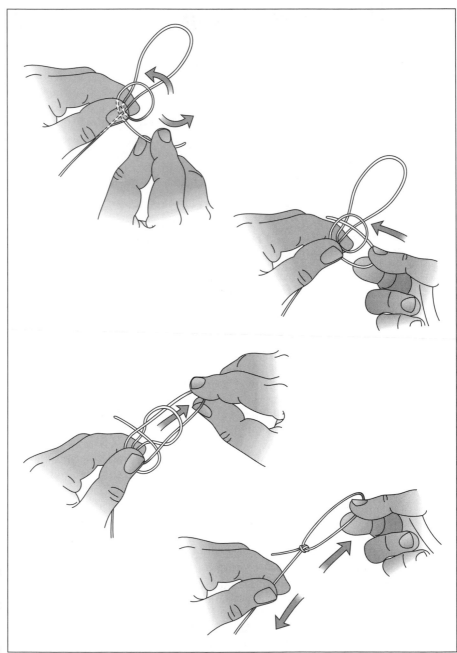

Actually, you should finish fighting your fish (or the fish should finish with you) a long time before you get to the knot that connects your line to your reel. But even if you never get into this extreme predicament, you need to tie the line to your reel. (For more info on putting new line on a reel, see Chapter 6.) I suggest that you use the Arbor knot, which is shown in Figure 11-4.

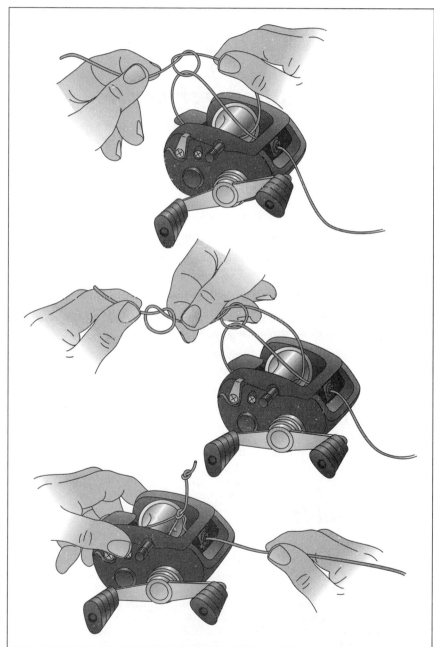

Figure 11-4:
The Arbor knot is one of the best and easiest ways to attach line to a reel.

Here's how you tie one:

1. **Pass the tag end around the center post of the reel spool and tie a simple Overhand knot, passing the tag end around the standing end.**

2. **Take the tag end and tie another Overhand knot with it.**

3. **Pull on the standing line until both Overhand knots come tight against each other and against the center post.**

Joining fat line to skinny line

When joining wire to leader or backing to fly line, I use the Albright knot. This knot works well even if the two pieces being joined are very far apart in diameter.

Here's how you tie an Albright:

1. **Make a three-inch loop in the heavier piece, as shown in Figure 11-5.**

2. **Pass the tag end of the lighter line through the loop for 7 to 8 inches.**

3. **Pinch the loop and the light line together and take the tag end and wrap it six times.**

   As you do this, try to include the new wraps in your pinch.

4. **Pass the end of the line you have been using for wraps back through the loop on the same side that it entered.**

5. **Pull gently on both ends of the lighter line so that the wraps slide up against the end of the loop.**

6. **When everything is lined up and fairly snug, give a good firm pull (not a yank) to finish the knot.**

The Albright knot is one of those knots that sounds and looks a little complicated; but as you tie it, you see that there is a logic to it. It really isn't hard to make.

A final loop

I often use the Uni-Knot (also known as the *Duncan Loop*) for such things as bass bugs or Rapala's, both of which need unrestricted movement. (See Chapter 3.) The reason I like the Uni-Knot is because it is so much like an Improved Clinch knot, and like most anglers (and fish as well), I am a creature of habit. This knot also works in place of the Arbor knot for attaching line to your reel.

Figure 11-5:
The
Albright
knot.

The Uni-Knot is illustrated in Figure 11-6. Follow these steps to tie one:

1. **Thread the tag end through the hook eye and run it parallel and right next to the standing line.**

2. **Form a loop with the tag end and wrap the tag end around this new loop four or five times.**

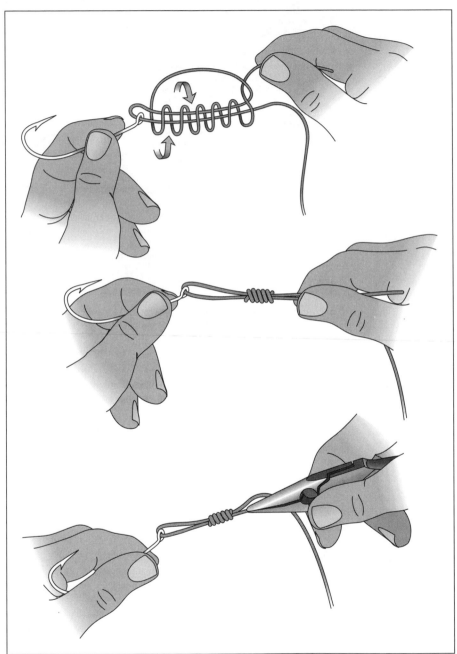

Figure 11-6:
The
Uni-Knot.

3. **Pull on the tag end to tighten the loop until the wraps are fairly snug against each other.**

4. **Pull on the standing end until the loop is the size you want it to be (just enough to give the lure room to swing freely).**

5. **Pull on the tag end with a pliers to make the knot good and tight.**

When a fish strikes, the knot slides up against the hook eye, closing the loop. Because the loop closes, you must retie this knot after you have unhooked your fish. A minor pain, but at least you caught a fish.

Don't trust your knots

No matter how well you tie your knot, it will weaken the line to some degree. The more fish you catch with one knot, the weaker that knot, or the line just next to it, becomes.

After every fish you catch, you should check your line for abrasions and nicks. And after catching a few fish, clip your knot and retie the hook or lure. After you lose an expensive eel or a nice lure, you may come to agree with me that retying is better than losing a lure and a fish.

Chapter 12

Bait Casting

· ·

In This Chapter

▶ Casting without backlashing (most of the time)

▶ Underhanding, sidearming, and other contortions

▶ Why I love my thumb

· ·

*1*f you want to know if a person can fish, watch how he or she casts. Good casting form is a sure sign that someone has put in serious practice time while learning to use a delicate, yet powerful tool. No one is born knowing how to cast. In fact, no one achieves the proper technique the first time out. After all, you didn't learn to walk all at once, and you didn't learn to throw all at once.

Think of a fishing rod as a new part of your body. To become proficient at any new skill, you have to educate your body. Of course, when you learn to walk and everyone laughs at you because your walking style looks really cute, that's kind of fun (if you are one year old). When you are older and are learning how to cast, you don't want to be laughed at and told that you're cute. You want to catch fish.

The Purpose of the Cast

If you could walk up to a fish and drop a lure and line in front of its mouth, you wouldn't need to cast. But you can't do that because fish are not that suicidal. They head for cover long before you can get within arm's length of them. The *cast* is the long-distance method you use in order to deliver the fly, lure, or bait to a spot where a fish may be enticed, rather than alarmed, by your offering. So in addition to *delivery* (which is concerned with *where* your hook lands), casting also involves *presentation* (which is *how* the bait, lure, or fly lands).

Only Three Factors

Casting involves three elements: the rod, the reel, and the line.

The rod

All casting — bait, spin, and fly — requires the ability to handle a rod and to get it to flex and release your offering in a controlled way.

The reel

In addition to proper handling of a rod, bait casting (and spinning) require proper handling of the reel and the line as it comes off the reel.

Bait casting is difficult to master initially. Everybody has a natural tendency to produce depressing backlashes, but proper casting technique isn't rocket science. With a little persistence and a healthy dose of caution, you can actually be up and running pretty quickly. After that, it's a matter of finesse, and that comes with practice.

The line

Line handling, while critical to the flyrodder, is less so to the baitcaster. Once the lure or bait is cast, there isn't a whole lot of line handling involved.

Casting and Hitting a Baseball

There is a fourth element in the casting equation — *you*. The closer you get to making your cast into one seamless motion — from body to rod to line to lure — the more effective you can be. The one big concept I can give you is this: Think of what's going on at the end of the line. This notion is something I learned while writing a magazine story about Charley Lau, the great batting coach who has had such an influence on modern hitting technique. Lau used to tell his hitters to "think the ball straight up the middle, over second base." His theory was that if a batter did that, he would be more likely to make proper contact with the ball. And by making proper contact, he would get more hits (and even the occasional home run).

Charley was also a great fisherman. In fact, in the years between retiring as a major league catcher and starting as a batting coach, he spent some time as a fishing guide in the Florida Keys. He applied the same spirit of analysis to casting. Every angler tends to think about what is happening right next to his or her hands, he said, where the rod and reel are. But the critical point is farther away — way out there at the end of the line. If you think about where your bait, lure, or fly is and *what it is doing* in the water, you can affect your cast in a positive way.

If you don't think the body mechanics of baseball and fishing are related, you should look at a video of the casting technique of baseball great Ted Williams. The way that The Splendid Splinter handles a fly rod and line is the same as the way that he handled a bat — smoothly, fluidly, powerfully, and accurately.

Bait Casting: It's All (Well, Almost All) Thumbs

Each type of casting has its own techniques. Bait casting is often very frustrating at first, but, as they say, "No pain, no gain."

The overhand cast

This is the cast that you will use in most situations. Before you move on to the more specialized casts, really try to get this one down pat.

1. **As seen in Figure 12-1, the overhead cast begins as you grasp the rod with the crank facing *up*. The shoulder of your casting arm is pointed toward the target.**

2. **Put the reel into *free spool* by disengaging the *clicker*.**

   You should have anywhere from two to six inches of line hanging out of your *tip top* (the top line guide on the rod). Keep your thumb on the spool so that it doesn't move.

3. **Point the rod at your target.**

   Your body is aligned so that, if you are a right-handed caster, your left foot is forward. (If you are left-handed, your right foot is forward.)

Figure 12-1:
The
overhand
cast.

4. *Before* you start the lifting or *backstroke* of your cast, position the rod at about a 35-degree to 45-degree angle.

    This action will put some flex into the rod as you begin your cast. Keep your thumb on the reel and keep the reel locked all through the backstroke.

5. Crisply lift the rod, applying power until the rod is pointed at the 12:00 position.

    The momentum of the cast will bend the rod farther backward, putting flex into the rod. The rod is designed to do this. You don't need to apply any more power on the backstroke. If you do, you will *overload* (develop too much torque on) the rod.

6. As soon as you stop the backstroke, begin the forward *power stroke*, releasing thumb pressure as you do (so that the lure can pull line off the reel as it travels to the target).

    The power stroke ends when the rod returns to the original 35-degree to 45-degree position.

7. Continue to allow the line to unspool.

    This is the key part of the cast and the part that is most prone to backlashing unless you successfully complete Step 8.

8. As the lure nears the target, apply more and more thumb pressure so that the reel gradually slows down and comes to a complete stop just as the lure hits the water.

    If you don't do this, the reel will keep spinning as the lure hits the water, a sure recipe for a backlash.

The way to learn bait casting with minimum heartbreak is to try it a little bit at a time:

1. Before you make your first cast, get yourself up to Step 4.

2. Next, while holding the thumb on the spool, lift the rod another 15 degrees or so.

3. Release some thumb pressure so that the lure descends pretty freely; then, as it does, put more pressure on the spool to slow it down so that it stops completely by the time the lure hits the ground.

After you have accomplished this smoothly, you will have at least an idea of the thumb control technique needed for real casts. Try short casts at first, using the thumb as a brake (better to use too much braking rather than too little when you start out). Your casts may be short of the mark this way, but you will not have a backlash. As with all the casts discussed in this chapter, I recommend that you practice on a lawn before you try it out under combat conditions. The more you continue practicing your technique on a lawn in between fishing sessions, the better you will become.

The sidearm cast

When Joyce Kilmer wrote "I think that I shall never see / A poem as lovely as a tree," he wasn't thinking about fishing. Trees and tree limbs are the enemy of the caster. They are immovable obstacles that have been the graveyards of more lures than any other feature of the natural world. I would say avoid fishing around them if it weren't for the fact that fish like to live under tree limbs. Think about it: It is very hard for a hawk or an eagle to dive around a tree limb to snatch a fish. For similar reasons, it is hard for a bear or raccoon to reach in and around underwater tree roots. Fish know this, so you can always find them in the shade of trees or nestled in roots that project underwater. Face it: You are going to *have* to deal with trees if you don't want to pass up many great fishing spots.

One trick you can try is to cast upstream from the tree and then allow your lure to drift under it (or, if there's no current, cast beyond the branch and reel your bait or lure under the tree). While this does the job in many cases, sometime, somewhere, you are going to have to get *under* that limb in order to have a prayer of catching a completely tantalizing fish.

In that case, having a few different casts at your command is helpful. After you have mastered the overhead cast, you can proceed to the sidearm cast (shown in Figure 12-2). But make sure that you have truly got the overhead cast at your command first; otherwise, you are just kidding yourself. Making two lame casts is rarely better than making no casts at all, and it certainly is worse than making a good overhand cast consistently.

1. **The right-handed caster faces the target with left foot slightly forward. (The reverse is true for the left-handed caster in this and the following steps.)**

   Note that the spool is facing up. The amount of line coming through the tip top is the same as in the overhead cast.

2. **Using a short casting stroke, crisply move the rod to the right no more than 90 degrees.**

3. **Stop the backstroke and begin the forward stroke. As the rod approaches 45 degrees, release thumb pressure.**

4. **Stop the forward stroke when the rod is in front of you, pointing at the target.**

5. **As with the overhead cast, begin to apply pressure as the lure nears its target.**

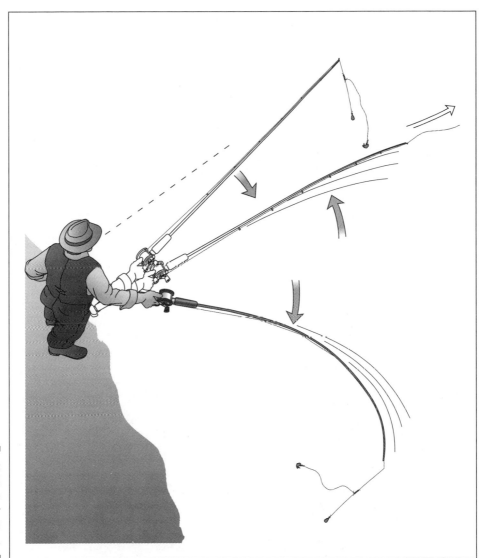

Figure 12-2:
Finesse and
touch are
required for
a good
sidearm.

Remember to stop the forward stroke when the rod points at the target. If you continue the stroke past this point, your cast will veer way to the left.

Don't try the sidearm cast in a boat with another angler. One day, you may flex too much going forward or backward and drill your companion with some fast-moving treble hooks: not a great way to lay the foundation for a long-term fishing relationship.

The underhand cast

This is another good cast for getting under obstacles. It is usually more accurate though less powerful than the sidearm cast. I have to confess that when I first saw this cast diagrammed in Al MacClane's *New Standard Fishing Encyclopedia,* it looked wrong. Years later, when I had the chance to spend some time with "The Master" (I mean it; MacClane was *the greatest* writer and angler), I asked him about this. He demonstrated the cast, and he was right. Again, I urge you to become a good overhead caster before you start to mess with the underhand cast (shown in Figure 12-3). In all casting, remembering to let the rod do the work is important. With this cast, it is critical. If you try "to muscle" or try "to put too much arm" into the cast, it won't work.

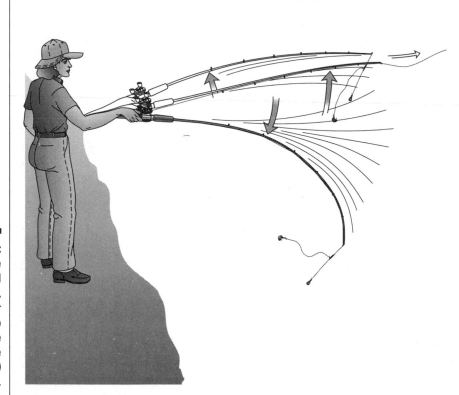

Figure 12-3:
The underhand cast, another way to reach the hard (make that fishy) spots.

Just like the old-fashioned foul shot in basketball, the underhand technique is sweet and accurate.

1. **Aim the rod at the target.**

   For the right-handed caster, the right shoulder points at the target as well (lefties point the other shoulder, etc). Note that the crank handle is pointing upward.

2. **Crisply, but not overpoweringly, lift the rod tip to shoulder height.**

   The weight of the lure flexes the rod tip down.

3. **Start the rod's downward stroke, stopping the stroke when your wrist returns to the starting position.**

   Momentum carries the rod tip downward again, adding even more flex.

   The rod tip naturally returns to the starting position.

4. **Release the spool and point the rod at target in a straight line.**

   The bend in the rod sends the lure toward the target.

5. **Apply thumb pressure to slow down the spool as the lure approaches the target.**

After the Cast

As soon as the lure hits the water, it is time to transfer the rod from your *casting hand* to your *fighting hand*. As shown in Figure 12-4, when a fish strikes, you reel with your right hand and work the rod with your left hand (if you're right-handed).

Your cast may wind up with some slack in the line. You need to retrieve this slack line so that you can strike effectively when a fish hits. If you leave the slack in, a fish may go for your plug, decide it is a phony, and spit it out before you have a chance to drive the hook home. Get rid of the slack. To do this, point your rod tip at your lure or bait. Then grab the line and press it against the shaft of the rod so that some tension is on the line as you reel up, as shown in Figure 12-5. If you don't keep tension on the line, it will coil loosely onto the reel, and you will get a backlash. Actually, I don't know if this is technically a backlash, a frontlash, or just a plain old-fashioned mess. The result, however, is the same: You won't be able to fish until you straighten it out.

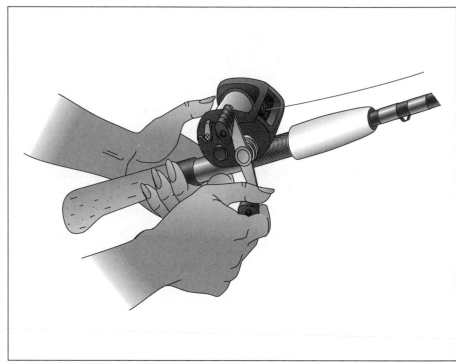

Figure 12-4:
After
casting, the
reel is
in a ready-
to-fight
position.

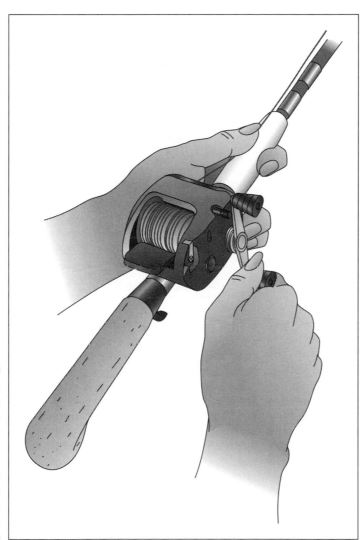

Figure 12-5:
Reeling in is one of the few things in modern life where more tension is better than less.

Chapter 13

Spinning and Spin Casting

· ·

In This Chapter

▶ Holding a spinning rod the right way

▶ Doing the right thing when you hang up in a tree

▶ Doing the wrong thing when you hang up in a tree

▶ Casting far and casting near

· ·

Spinning is the easist way to cast. Spin casting, which is a form of spinning, is even easier. Why? Because spinning doesn't mess up so much as bait casting and fly casting. In other words, it's easier. This statement doesn't mean it's a no-brainer, but it is much less accident-prone than bait casting and much less demanding of technique than fly casting. The only downside to spinning is the tendency to *line twist*, but this comes with the territory, so you can't totally avoid it. The best remedy for line twist is periodic straightening (as discussed in Chapter 6).

But First a Word about Getting Started

I have shown many people how to fish on the mistaken assumption that they know how to *begin* a cast. Most teachers make this same assumption. But if no one ever showed you how to open the bail on your spinning reel and get the line ready for casting, you probably won't figure it out for yourself. It reminds me of the time that I bought my first computer, a big clunky Kaypro that looked like a large lunch box. It came with all kinds of instruction about plugging it in, turning it on, and beginning computing. It also came with a little thing called a *floppy disk* that held the program, but the floppy disk had no diagram to tell me which end of the disk went into the computer first. I guess the Kaypro folks thought that it was self-evident; but I had never seen a floppy disk before and found nothing self-evident about it. So I sat there with a two thousand dollar computer that I couldn't use because I didn't know where to put my $1.98 disk.

So if you are one of those first-timers with a spinning rod, here is how to begin. When you prepare to cast, the reel is on the bottom and the crank (or *handle*) is pointed *away* from your casting arm (as shown in Figure 13-1). To begin the cast, follow these steps:

1. **Move the reel's metal arm (or *bail*) over until it clicks into the open position.**

   Use your free hand to do this.

2. **Now, with your casting hand, grip the line with your index finger, holding it against the rod handle under the fleshy party of the first joint.**

   If you don't hold the line, the weight of the lure will pull too much line off the reel. Also, note that your middle finger should be on the same side of the reel seat as your index finger. You are now ready to cast.

Don't worry if you do forget to open the bail. (We all do it.) The only problem is, the lure isn't going to travel very far if all it has to work with is the few inches of line you've pulled through the tip top.

The Overhead Cast

Ninety out of a hundred times, the overhand cast (as shown in Figure 13-2) is the only cast you will use. But even with the more specialized casts, the preparation is pretty much the same.

Follow these steps to complete an overhand cast:

1. **Pass enough line through the guides so that the rod is slightly flexed by the weight of your bait or lure.**

   Usually, use no more than six inches of line for normal freshwater rods and somewhat more line with a surf-casting setup.

2. **If you are right-handed, face the target and position yourself so that your right shoulder points to the target. Lefties point the left shoulder at target.**

3. **Point the rod at the target, open the bail, and secure the line with your index.**

4. **To begin the cast, position your rod at about 50 degrees.**

5. **Your backstroke should be a crisp (but not overpowering) flick until the rod handle is pointed at 12:00 (that is, directly upright).**

6. **As soon as you reach the 12:00 position, *stop* your backstroke.**

   The rod will continue to flex behind you.

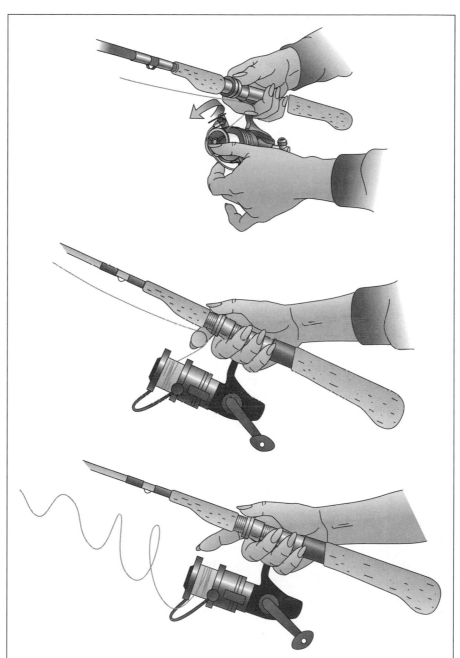

Figure 13-1:
Getting
ready to
cast (top
and
middle).
You release
your line as
you cast
(bottom).

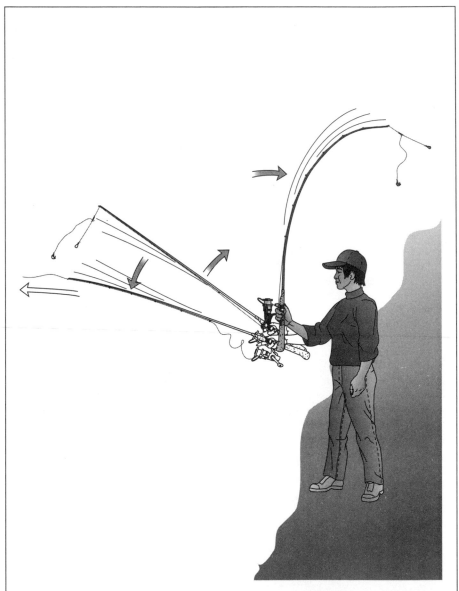

Figure 13-2:
An
overhead
cast.

7. As soon as you stop your backstroke, *begin* the forward stroke.

8. Release the line, completing your power stroke, when your rod tip is at about 40 degrees (or at about 2:00).

9. When the cast reaches the target, press your forefinger against the line on the spool, which stops more line from paying out.

Most beginners (and quite a few veterans) neglect to use their finger as a brake on the spool. Try this and you will see how much slack develops, all of which you will need to retrieve before you are able to begin fishing. If a strong wind is blowing, you will have a great deal of line to recover if you don't use your forefinger. As you develop a feel for this technique, you can actually slow down the rate at which line pays out (in much the same way that thumbing will slow down a cast with a bait-casting reel). This technique is called *feathering your cast*. Feathers are light, and mastering this method, therefore, requires a light touch.

The Underhand Cast

The underhand cast (shown in Figure 13-3) is helpful when you need to sneak that bait or lure under an overhanging limb, beneath a low bridge, and the like. It is for *close-in* work. If you need distance *and* you have to get under something, my advice is to get a boat or to try angling someplace else. However, if you are close to where you want the cast to wind up, then this cast (which has to be executed delicately) will catch you some nice fish that you would otherwise have to pass up.

Follow these steps for the underhand cast:

1. **With bail closed, strip line off the reel until the rod is flexed slightly (3 to 6 inches).**

2. **Face the target, point your casting shoulder at the target, and aim the rod tip straight at the target.**

3. **Open the bail and secure the line against the rod shaft with your forefinger.**

4. **Flex your rod by lifting the tip.**

   This action doesn't require very much power at all.

5. **Continue lifting until the rod tip reaches eye level.**

6. **With just a little more force, push downward; stop your motion when the butt of the rod is back at the starting position.**

   The tip will continue to flex downward.

7. **As the tip begins to return to the starting position, release the line.**

8. **To stop the line when it reaches the target, press your forefinger against the line paying out of the spool.**

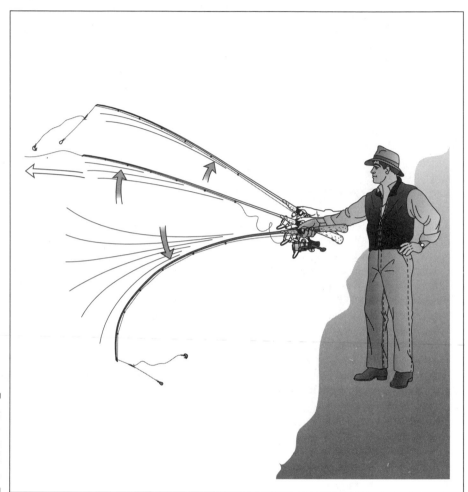

Figure 13-3:
Never over-
muscle the
underhand
cast.

The Sidearm Cast

Sometimes you see a nice fish, and the only possible way to cast to it is with a sidearm motion (shown in Figure 13-4). Maybe the day is too windy, or an overhang prevents an overhead cast. Maybe some underbrush prevents an underhand cast. As with the underarm cast, this maneuver is one that you will only perfect when you truly understand that the rod has to do the work for you. Muscle this cast, and you will end up casting way off target.

Follow these steps for the sidearm cast:

1. **Strip off just enough line to flex the rod slightly (3 to 6 inches).**

2. **Face the target. Righties, put your left foot slightly forward. (Lefties, put the right foot forward.)**

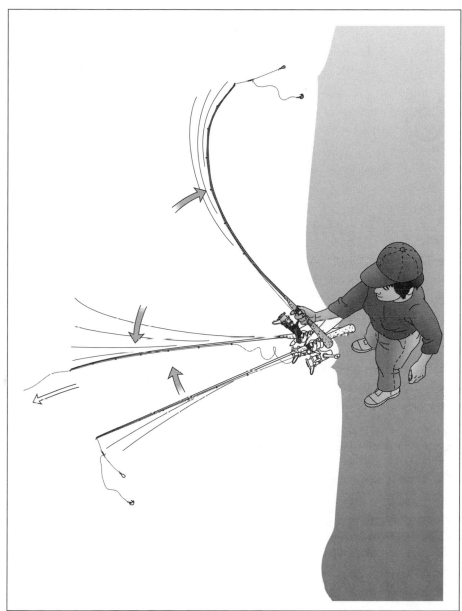

Figure 13-4:
The sidearm cast is all a matter of touch and finesse.

3. **At belt level, point your rod at the target, open the bail, and secure the line with your forefinger.**

4. **Righties should move the rod with an easy stroke to the right about 45 degrees. (Lefties should move the rod left 45 degrees.)**

5. **Snap the rod back crisply to the starting position.**

6. **As the rod tip begins to point more to the front than it does to the side, release the line (which was held down by your forefinger).**

7. **Point the rod straight at the target and stop the line with your forefinger as the lure or bait reaches the target.**

 As you did with the underhand cast, strive for an easy motion, and just let the flexing of the rod do the work. Understatement (or *undercastment,* if that's a word) is what you want here. This cast is a good one to have in your arsenal, but it is not one you want to perfect in an actual fishing situation. Do it on the lawn until you have it down. And beginners, don't do this in a boat with a friend (even if you don't like the friend very much).

Spin Casting

Spin casting is the least "mess-up-able" method of casting with a rod and reel. The main heartbreak that it avoids is backlash. Still, you do have to cast. The actual cast is executed like the casts with the spinning reel. The difference is that the reel is positioned on top of the rod, as with bait casting. This is to accommodate your thumb on the push button at the bottom of the spin-casting reel. Otherwise, the physics of the cast is the same as spinning: Where you are instructed to release line in a classic spinning cast, you simply depress the button on a spin-casting outfit. When you want to stop the line from paying out, release the button (as shown in Figure 13-5).

Oops! It Went Too Far and Wrapped around a Branch!

Successful fishing is often a game of inches. Come to think of it, what sport isn't? A curve ball on the outside corner, a forward pass between two defenders, a drive over a bunker — these skills require accuracy, too. The same goes with fishing. So if you want to get your cast in there where the fish are, you are going to miss by inches and hang up from time to time. Everybody does. With care, you will do it less, but you are still going to do it. Sometimes you can also undo it.

The most common hang-up involves wrapping your line around a branch. The natural reaction here is usually a three-act play:

ACT I: You realize your mistake as the lure starts to overshoot the target.

ACT II: You say "Oh, shoot!" and instinctively recoil.

ACT III: The lure snugs up against the branch, often adding a knot to your troubles.

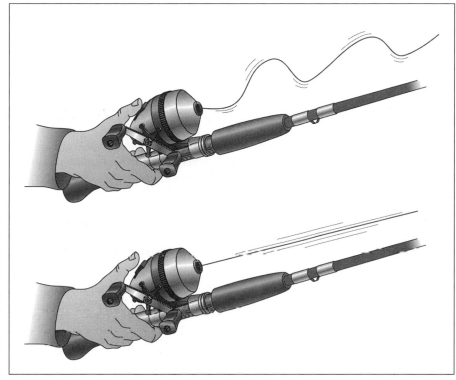

Figure 13-5:
Thumb in to cast and thumb out to stop the cast with a spin-casting outfit.

Restrain yourself. Don't pull back on the rod. When your lure wraps around a branch, the damage is done, and pulling is not going to undo it. (It will only make the situation worse.) Sometimes, if you do nothing, the line will wrap, and then, as it comes to a sudden halt, the momentum of the cast causes the lure to recoil and unwind all by itself. (This happens more times than it doesn't when fishing a plastic worm with the hook embedded in it.) If you have come this far and you are lucky, you now have a hook and line draped over a tree limb. Here's what to do next:

1. **Point your rod at the hook.**

2. **Very gently, reel up any slack until you come tight.**

3. **By reeling slowly and gently and just nudging the rod tip, you can often coax the hook over the limb, thereby freeing it.**

4. **Retrieve your lure normally.**

   Sometimes, the resulting *kerplunk* of the lure on the water makes for a more natural landing than a well-executed cast, and the reward can be a fish.

I wouldn't be doing my job if I left you thinking that every bad cast can be undone by keeping a cool head and using an unsnagging trick like this. While it *may* work, it doesn't always work. Face it: You are going to lose line and gear at least some of the time.

While I'm on the Subject of Hang-ups

Tree branches aren't the only lure-and-line stealers. You can hang up on underwater rocks (or *any* submerged obstacle). And as with catching fish, a number of techniques and strategies (including a couple of important *don'ts*) apply:

✔ Don't rear back with your rod and put a lot of pressure on it, and don't jerk it either. You will break a rod one of these days (which is a big price to pay, even if the alternative is losing an expensive lure).

✔ If firm (but not overpowering) pressure won't free a snagged line, I often put the rod down and strip some more line off. Then I wrap the line around my hands a couple of times and pull straight on the line, being careful that I don't let the line cut into my hands. Usually, if the hook has any chance of breaking free, this does the trick.

This wrap-and-pull technique is good for underwater obstacles, particularly the kind you run into off the beach. Don't try this method if the hang-up is in a tree. You can slingshot a lure out of a tree with tremendous force, and chances are you will be looking straight down the line at your lure. Guess what path that lure is going to take as it hurtles out of the brush — right at your face!

✔ If you are in a stream, sometimes walking downstream to see if changing the angle of pressure will free the hook is helpful. If you can't get downstream (if the stream is too deep, or if the current is too swift), I have seen anglers put a bobber on the line and then let the bobber float downstream. This trick can have the effect of exerting some downstream pressure as you reel in.

✔ The final decision is to "fish or cut bait," as the saying goes. In this case, it can also mean cutting line, lures, flies, and the like. After trying to rescue your equipment for a while, you need to consider the following: You wait all week to try and get in a little fishing. When you get right down to it, you don't spend all that much time actually fishing, even when you do get the time. Getting rigged up, in and out of waders, in and out of boats, and the like eats up a great deal of time. How much time do you want to spend trying to save a lure or bait? Sometimes the answer is "give up and get back to fishing!" You will be amazed at how good you will feel as soon as you catch a fish.

Chapter 14

Fly Casting

. . . .

. . . .

*O*ne of the great pleasures of the sport of angling is casting a fly well. There is something in our nature that almost hypnotizes us when a cast is well executed. As in most things in angling, I would strongly recommend that you have someone who knows how to fly cast work with you in the beginning. I can tell you from experience (mine) that if you apply yourself, you can master every cast in this chapter in two days. You won't be perfect at these casts, but you will be fly-fishing.

Momma Didn't Lie

Remember how your Mom used to tell you, "It's not what you say, it's the way that you say it?" She may well have been speaking for all the millions of uncaught trout who have ever rejected a fly because it was delivered short of the mark or because it landed with a clunk. Presentation of the fly is the single most important skill in fly-fishing. To do it well and to do it with all kinds of wind conditions requires a few more casts than conventional bait casting or spinning gear. But if you master the casts, you will be able to catch fish in almost any situation. In the words of famous fly-fisherwoman Martha Stewart, "It's a good thing."

Strive for the Oneness of Rod and Line

Apologies for sounding like a wise and ancient kung-fu master, but I would like to plant an idea in your head that may help as you approach fly casting. When flexed, the rod bends into a curve. If you are moving line at the right speed as you cast, your line will shoot off that curve in a straight path.

If you hesitate too long at any point and if the arc that your rod moves through is too big, your line will no longer be able to continue the curve, and your cast will lose shape and power. Figure 14-1 shows a rod flexed properly. Note how the line smoothly continues the bend in the rod. Also note how the line curls back. This segment of line, shaped like the crook in a candy cane, is called a *loop*.

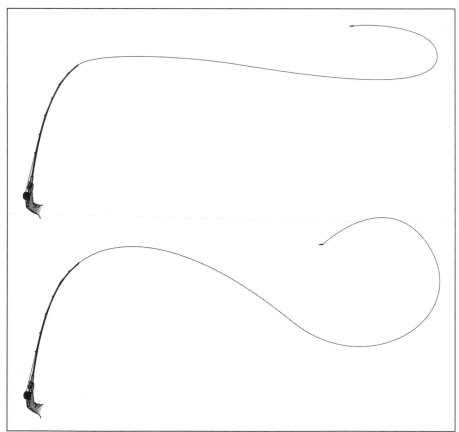

Figure 14-1:
A flyrodder with a nice tight loop and one with a sloppy backcast and a wide loop.

How Tight Is Your Loop?

Think of the loop on your rod as the prow of a boat. In the same way that a boat's prow cuts through water, the loop cuts through the air. A nice, slim v-shaped boat will move through the water with little resistance. On the other hand, if you hook up an outboard to a bathtub, you will meet a great deal more resistance to your forward motion. The same is true of the cast. A tight loop will slice through the wind. A wide loop will just hang there like a — the phrase that comes to mind in describing how it hangs there is *limp noodle*.

Get a Grip on Yourself (Or at Least on Your Rod)

There is basically one right way to hold a fly rod. I say *basically* because I use a different grip for close-in dry fly work. Many people have criticized me for it, but I was happy to see, on the few times that I fished with him, that Lee Wulff did the same thing. Still, I suppose there is something to be said for keeping it simple.

1. **Grasp the rod as if you meant to shake hands with it.**

2. **Now "shake hands" with it.**

3. **Close your fist around the cork grip of the fly rod and keep your thumb extended.**

Figure 14-2 illustrates this classic grip.

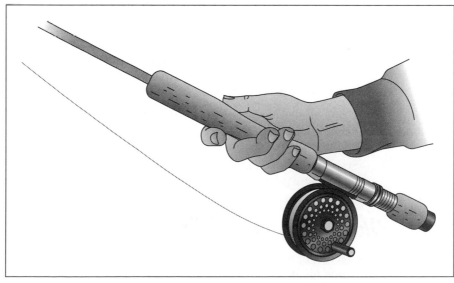

Figure 14-2:
The proper way to hold your fly rod to deliver the most power, most efficiently, is with the thumb up.

The Forward (And Sometimes Sidearm) Cast

I would estimate that 75 percent of all your fly-fishing casts will be a version of this basic forward cast. If you are a saltwater fisherman, make that 95 percent.

Figure 14-3 illustrates this fundamental cast.

To complete a forward cast, follow these steps:

1. **Pull about ten feet of line off the reel and pass it through the top guide.**

   Pulling line off the reel is called *stripping*.

2. **Stand sideways, or mostly sideways with your left shoulder in front if you are a rightie. (Lefties, point the right shoulder.)**

3. **Strip another two feet of line off the reel and hold it in your left hand, as shown in Figure 14-3.**

4. **With the rod held at a 45-degree angle, crisply lift the line in the air, snapping your wrist upward as you do. Your backstroke should stop when your wrist is at 12:00 (vertical). Momentum will carry your rod and wrist along the arc you have started.**

   The momentum of the line in the air should flex the rod backward.

5. **As the line straightens out behind you, let your arm drift with it and then move the rod sharply forward. Again, stop your power stroke dead on 12:00; as you do so, continue to drive forward with your wrist as if you were pushing in a thumbtack.**

6. **When your rod reaches the 45-degree angle, drop the rod tip.**

   If you have executed this cast well, you will feel a tug on your left hand, which is holding the extra two feet of line that you stripped out in Step 3, before you started the cast. Let go of the line and it will shoot out of your top guide, giving you an extra couple of feet to your cast.

Okay, what did I do wrong?

With ten feet of line out of the guides, you probably performed a reasonable approximation of a cast. Now, do the same thing with 15 feet of line. This will probably begin to show some of the problems in your beginning cast. Try to keep the line in the air as you execute a few false casts. (A *false cast* is the name given to what you do when you flick the line backward and forward before finally delivering the fly.)

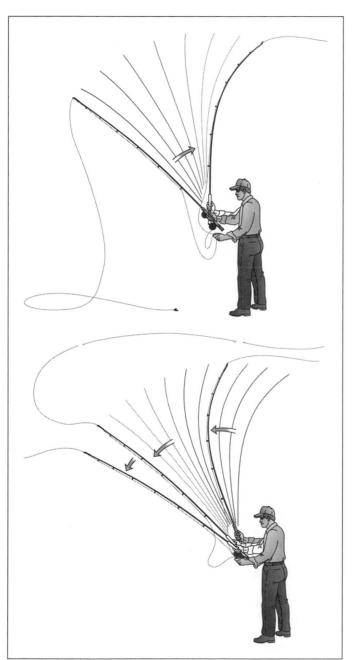

Figure 14-3:
Master the forward cast and you can fly-fish right away.

A false cast serves two purposes:

- It lines up your cast with your target.

- It develops *line speed,* which allows you to work more and more line through the guides so that you can hold it in the air, get up speed, and shoot a longer cast to your target. With good use of line speed, you can easily shoot line to double the distance of your cast.

But before you worry about distance, concentrate on casting mechanics. You need to get out on the lawn with your 15 feet of line and (standing sideways) watch your line in the air as you cast. This will require you to drop your arm for more of a sidearm delivery, but don't worry about that. Sometimes a fishing situation calls for precisely that maneuver.

What am I looking for?

As you watch your line, your goal is to keep it moving in the air and parallel to the ground. If the line drops below the horizontal, you are moving through too wide an arc. You are forgetting to stop your power stroke at 12:00. I can't emphasize this enough. Stop the rod tip high, and the rod will do the work for you.

Another common error is hurrying the cast. Casting a fly is not like shooting a bullet out of a rifle. It's not just one flick of the finger followed by delivery of the fly. In casting a fly, four things have to happen:

- You transfer muscle power to your rod.

- Your rod bends and multiplies that force over distance.

- Your line is set in motion by the action of the rod.

- The bullwhip action of the fly line develops even more speed as you finish the casting motion.

All of this action takes time. You back cast. The line straightens out and pulls on the rod. You move through the forward cast (or *power stroke*), and the line buggy-whips forward. You shoot line and drop the rod tip.

A beginner's cast often falls apart at a point between the end of the backcast and the beginning of the forward cast (power stroke). You need to pause at this part of the cast until you feel a little tug or, if you are not a great tug feeler, pause until you see the line straighten out.

If you are teaching someone to fly cast for the first time, let your student try a few casts. If he or she just doesn't seem to get the hang of it, you can demonstrate what a good cast feels like. While your student is still gripping the rod, stand behind the student, put your arms around the student's arms, and grasp the rod. Tell your eager fishing pupil to relax and see if he or she can feel how a proper casting stroke should feel. Then execute a series of false casts. Many times, getting the actual feel of a reasonable cast will fill in the gaps that a verbal explanation leaves out.

Now What? Preparing to Catch an Actual Fish!

After the fly is out there, it might interest a fish. In order for you to catch that fish, which is the point of all this, you need to make the transition from casting the fly to fishing the fly. You wrap the thumb around the rod and extend your index finger so that it holds the fly line against the rod shaft. This trick ensures that anytime a fish hits, you won't have unwanted slack in the line. Your other hand is now free to pull in line as required. This retrieving action is called _stripping in_ line.

A Good Backhand Is Invaluable

Looking through all the fishing books out there, the lack of emphasis that is placed on the backhand cast consistently surprises me. I can't for the life of me explain this situation. I think that, after the forward cast, the backhand is the most indispensable cast. Because the mechanics of it are so similar to the forward cast, it should be the very next thing you learn after you graduate from Forward Cast 101. To make a backhand cast, follow these steps:

1. **As shown in Figure 14-4, start the backhand cast by facing the target head-on (with just a slight turn to the left for rightie casters; a slight turn to the right for lefties).**

   This position has the effect of pointing your shoulder at the target when you lift your elbow in the casting motion.

2. **Begin by holding the rod out from your body with your arm crossed in front of your chest.**

3. **The backstroke is executed as you snap your wrist up, lifting your line and bending your elbow.**

   You apply power just as you do with a forward cast. Power is added to the backstroke through an arc of about 45 degrees.

4. **Stop the backstroke when the rod is at 12:00 in the plane of the cast.**

   Your elbow is raised, and your forearm points backward.

5. **As the line straightens out or you feel a slight tug, begin the power stroke and make a quick snap through a 45-degree arc.**

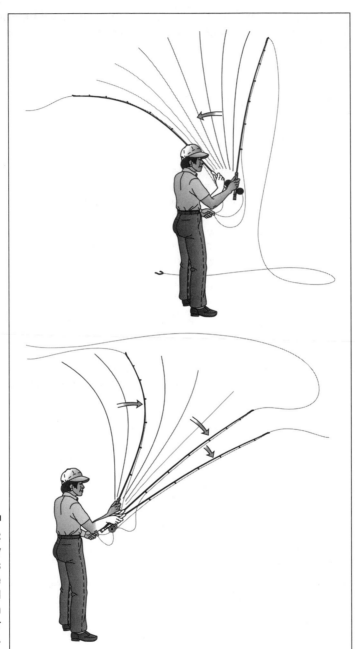

Figure 14-4:
The body
mechanics
of the
backhand
cast often
make for
accuracy.

This is a very powerful cast, almost as efficient as the forward cast. I use it when I find that a cross wind is driving my cast into my back or my hat. It is also great for two people fishing in a boat. If both of you are righties, the angler in the bow can throw a backhand cast while the angler in the stern uses an overhead cast. You are much less likely to get tangled, and the angler in the stern is much less likely to slam a hook into the angler in the bow.

Rollin' on a River

Sometimes, you may not have any room at all for a backcast, but a nice fish is within 20 feet of you. The roll cast was designed for this situation. As noted in the section about the technique of fishing a dry fly in "Drag: It's a Major Drag," later in this chapter, the roll cast is also the favorite method for picking up a fly after you fish out a cast. The roll cast relies on the surface tension of the water to *load up* (or bend) your rod, so I suggest that you try using this cast in a stream (there ain't much surface tension on a lawn). If you want to make sure that you have all the pieces of this cast together before venturing into the water, go ahead and try it on the land, but then try it on the water too.

To execute a roll cast, follow these steps:

1. **Use any cast to get about 20 feet of line out.**

   In a stream, cast upstream. On a lake, the cast's direction doesn't matter.

2. **Start with the rod at about a 45-degree angle and with your arm raised as shown in Figure 14-5.**

3. **Begin your backstroke, which will pull the line toward you.**

   The line shouldn't completely leave the surface of the water because the resistance that is caused by the surface tension of the water causes the rod to flex and load up.

4. **Push the rod forward and snap your wrist at the end of your stroke.**

5. **Point the rod at your target and shoot the line toward it.**

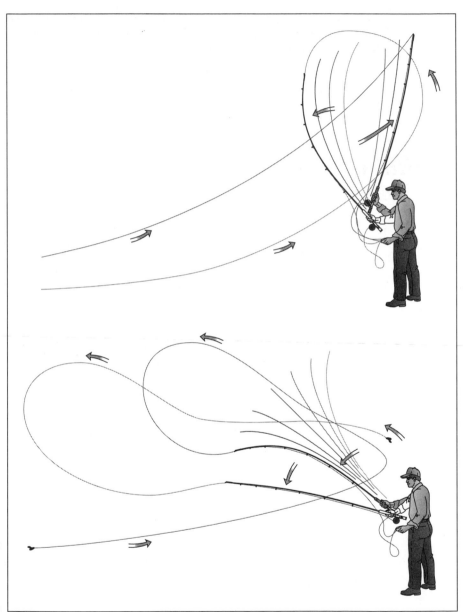

Figure 14-5:
The roll
cast.

The Double Haul

Distance doth not a fly caster make. I keep telling myself this; but like most flyrodders, I like to cast to the limits of my ability and then some. This is not great angling form. The longer the distance, the harder it is to strike properly and set the hook. However, there are times — on big rivers, by a lake, or in saltwater — when the distance caster will outfish everybody else. The technique is called *double hauling* because it adds power to your cast and also aids in handling wind.

If you want to throw a fly for serious distance, you need to learn how to double haul. This technique is one of those things that you *definitely* won't master from a book. And if you are a beginner, you won't learn it until you have the forward cast well under control. Double hauling is one of those things on which many anglers will give you advice, until one day a light bulb goes off and you say, "Now I get it!"

Let me offer you a few hints. First the principle involved: The fly rod, no matter what cast you try, uses its flex to develop line speed. The faster the line speed, the further the cast goes. What you are doing when you double haul is adding extra speed to your line — not by moving the rod faster, which would muscle the cast, but by pulling on the line and moving the line faster, as shown in Figure 14-6.

To execute the double haul, follow these steps:

1. **Strip about 15 more feet of line off your reel than you normally would and then lay out a normal cast.**

2. **With the line resting on the lawn (or water), lean forward before you start the pickup for the double haul and grab the line just behind the nearest guide.**

   Righties grab the line with the left hand; lefties grab the line with the right hand.

3. **As you lift the line with your backcast, pull sharply on the line in your hand.**

   If you continue this motion all through the power stroke of the backcast, your arm will travel through approximately six feet of distance. This travel adds tremendously to line speed.

   As the backcast unrolls, the rod pulls some of the extra line from your hand and shoots the extra line backward.

4. **Allow your casting arm to drift back as the backcast unrolls.**

5. **Just before you begin the forward cast, reach with your line hand and grab the line near the first guide.**

6. **Begin the final power stoke and pull on the line in a long, sweeping motion.**

7. **Release the line and allow it to shoot forward with your cast.**

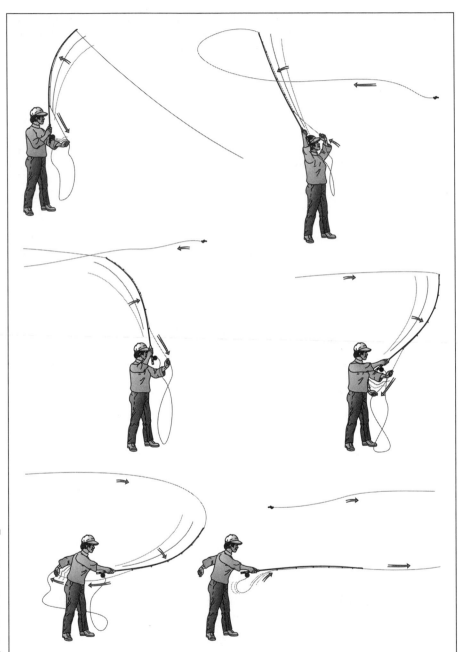

Figure 14-6:
The double haul separates the veteran from the newcomer.

When you hit one of these casts right, you will know it. As there is with a baseball bat or a golf club, there is a *sweet spot* in your rod where it performs optimally. You will feel line being pulled from your hand. When I am saltwater fishing, which is when I use the double haul the most, I love the feel of reserve power at the end of the cast. The line slaps the rod and gives one last pull as the fly reaches its destination. Knowing that you have power to spare is always nice. This reserve power shouldn't stop you from approaching as near to a fish as you can before you cast. Double haul only when you must.

The Stripping Basket

During the 1960s, the otherwise forgettable film "Man's Favorite Sport" showed Doris Day and Paula Prentiss getting Rock Hudson a complete fishing outfit. With inflatable waders and a real doofus hat, nothing could possibly have looked dorkier. But that was because stripping baskets weren't around in those days. A *stripping basket* is a basket that an angler ties around his or her waist. When casting long distances from a boat, jetty, or shore, a stripping basket, which stores your stripped in line in one safe spot, can keep your line from getting tangled, falling under a rock, or getting swept out by the surge of the waves. So at the risk of looking silly, remember there are worse things in the world than walking around with something that looks like a Rubbermaid dish drainer tied to your waist — like not catching fish!

Using a stripping basket makes the two-handed retrieve practical. If you need to imitate fast-moving bait fish, this retrieve is a great weapon to have in your arsenal.

To execute the two-handed retrieve, follow these steps:

1. **After laying out your cast, place the rod in the crook of your underarm.**

2. **Now, with your two free hands, pull in line hand-over-hand for a rapid retrieve.**

   This hand-over-hand action is as fast as anything you can do with conventional tackle.

3. **When a fish takes, righties, strike with your left hand and raise the rod in your right hand. (Lefties, do the reverse.)**

   This double-barreled maneuver drives the hook home effectively.

Drag: It's a Major Drag

Now that you have an idea of the mechanics of the major casts, it's a good time to consider the problem of *drag*. After you understand drag and how to avoid it, you will understand the principles behind the casts that follow. Pay attention. You could have the best casting form in the world, but if you have drag on your fly, you will catch nothing.

When a natural fly (one that is alive or was living) floats downstream, it moves at the speed of the current. Something that moves at a much different speed does not look natural; and if it does not look natural, fish are going to pass it up.

Here's how drag happens: Say that fish are rising, as they often do, up against the shore, and you are standing in midstream, where the water is moving more swiftly.

You present a dry fly to a rising fish with an upstream forward cast. For a few feet, you get a nice drag-free float. However, very soon the faster midstream current starts to put a belly in your relatively thick fly line, finally pulling it across current. Back in the fishing zone, where your fly is, this current action has the effect of whiplashing your fly across the current. The result is that your fly is moving in a direction that a natural fly never moves in, and it is moving at an unnatural speed. This is drag. Your chances of catching a trout are as close to absolute zero as anything ever gets in this uncertain world.

What you need is a way to cast your fly so that a trout sees it as a living insect (in other words, without drag). The following casting maneuver is designed to do just that. You will come up with some of your own casts as you follow the cardinal rule: Think about what is happening at the end of your line.

The Reach Cast

From one bank to another, any number of factors can affect the speed and direction of the flow of a river. Next to the bank, it is slower than it is in midstream. A rock or log may affect the flow. Underwater weed beds work in similar fashion to redirect and retard the flow of a river. Because of these factors, the fly caster has to deal with a number of varying speeds of current between rod and fly. To deal with these situations, the reach cast is designed to give your fly a float that looks convincing rather than dragging the fly at an unnatural speed.

The reach cast puts the line *upstream* from the fish so that when the fly is in the eating zone of the trout, the line has no slack. To execute a reach cast, follow these steps:

1. **Complete a forward cast up through the end of the power stroke.**

2. **Instead of dropping the rod tip straight down, move as far up current as you can while bending from the waist and reaching across your body with your arm.**

This cast can give you an extra six to eight feet of drag-free float. For very finicky and spooky trout, this cast also has the advantage of presenting the fly *before* the trout sees the leader. In ultra-calm, ultra-clear conditions, it may be your only way of deceiving a trout.

Note: You can combine the reach cast with any of the other casts described in this chapter. These combined casts will be a little more contorted than the forward reach cast; but when necessity calls, you will figure a way to try your own combinations. Combining these casts takes a great deal of body English.

Chapter 15

How to Strike, Fight, and Land (And Sometimes Release) Fish

. . . .

In This Chapter

▶ Striking a fish

▶ Catching a fish

▶ Fighting a fish

▶ Landing or boating a fish

▶ Releasing a fish

. . . .

*Y*ou have learned how to cast, tie knots, and pick lures and flies, but none of this makes you an angler. Anglers catch fish. In order to do that, you need to know when to strike a fish, how to fight it, how to complete the fight and land it, and then how to kill it humanely or set it free.

Should I Strike Now?

Different fish have different takes. Whereas a pike may slaughter your topwater bait, a trout may approach your fly in a daintier fashion. A bass may play with a lure. A bluefish may slam it. Some fish will take surface lures with wild abandon, yet be much more deliberate with a subsurface bait. The general rule is this: There is no *one* general rule for when to strike. To be an effective angler, you need to know your fish and its behavior.

A savage strike doesn't require a savage response from the angler. Usually, all this sort of response does is ensure that you pull your bait, lure, or fly away from the fish before you have a chance to set the hook. You need to come tight to the fish: All the slack must be gone from your line, and you must feel the weight of the fish *before* you drive the hook home.

Some fish, like the tarpon, require a couple of good, slamming strikes at this point. The trout, on the other hand, needs just a slight jerk to set the hook. With bass and pike that tend to play with the bait, you need to let them run with it for a bit. To get one securely on your hook, follow these steps:

1. **Drop the rod tip when you feel the fish take your lure or bait.**

2. **After giving the fish a little while to get the bait inside its mouth, point the rod at the fish, reel in as you drop your rod tip until you have taken up all the slack, and then lift the rod forcefully to set the hook.**

3. **Give the fish a good firm whack by lifting the rod high.**

   If you have a stiff rod with a fast tip, your fish should be on at this point.

4. **Whack it again for good measure — maybe twice more.**

Soft rods require even more forcefulness in the hook-setting motion. Some rods, although they are nice, safe casters, are too soft ever to set the hook. If you follow all of these recommendations and just can't seem to set a hook, you may need a rod with a faster tip.

Catching a Fish, or "Jeepers, It's On! Now What Do I Do?"

Having a fish on the end of your line is like any other emergency situation: If you have never been through it before, you may lose your head. Remember this piece of advice: It's an emergency for the fish, not for you. If you maintain your cool, you can win this fight. Millions of anglers have done it before you, so it isn't magic. Still, you do need to know what you are doing. Fighting and beating fish is one art where I promise you that you can learn from your mistakes because you will replay them a thousand times in your head. The better the fish, the more times you will tell yourself, "Gee, if only I'd. . . ."

And then, after you finally learn how to fight your average fish, you will hook into a big one someday, and it's a whole new ball game (with a whole *new* set of mistakes to make and learn from).

Fighting: This Is the Fun Part

Having a fish on and not knowing what to do can be a source of much anxiety. It shouldn't be. Having a fish on is the fun part of fishing. That tug. That pushing and head-shaking and throbbing. That wildness. These are the prime thrills of fishing. It's you against the fish, and the fish is in its element. That *you* will win is not a foregone conclusion (although the more fish you fight, the better your chances are). Win or lose, the fight is always a thrill. Learn to savor it.

Remember that your rod is your buddy

A good fishing rod can be a great tool *if* you remember to let it help you fight the fish. Let the rod do some of the work. It was designed to do just that. Follow the advice of Izaak Walton and keep the fish under the bend of the rod. This means that you should be holding the rod at an angle that allows it to bend. It doesn't have to bend double, but it has to bend. This flexing of the rod, more than anything else, will tire, (and eventually conquer) a fish. No matter how far the fish runs, no matter how much it jumps or shakes, the rod will flex, putting pressure on the hook, which is buried in its flesh.

The reel is working for you, too

When fighting a fish, the drag mechanism on your reel is another potential ally. If you have set the drag properly (as covered in Chapter 8), the drag acts as a brake mechanism that can further tire the fish. In most cases, the time to set the drag is before you cast. Adjusting the drag while you are fishing becomes just one more thing that you can mess up, and I don't recommend doing it.

The exception is when you are fighting a big fish in saltwater. In this case, the specially designed drag can be adjusted at certain times during the fight. My advice is this: Don't do anything unless someone with a great deal more experience than you tells you to do it. Because different kinds of fish fight differently, remember, in setting the drag, to make the punishment fit the crime. For example, a big bluefish requires more pre-set drag than a medium weakfish. Also bear in mind that drag increases the resistance working against the fish — it doesn't stop it dead in its tracks. The purpose of drag is to *tire* the fish.

Even the line is an ally

When a large fish runs off a great deal of line, the resistance of the water against the line creates even more drag. This can work in your favor if you have a sense of how much added pressure your tackle can take. Only practice will teach you this lesson.

Heads up

Heads up means that the head of the fish points up. If you are able to keep the head of the fish up, *you* are directing the fight. With its head up, the fish is disoriented and bewildered and can't see where to go (that is, it can't see a rock to slip under or a weed bed to dive for). If the fish can get its head down, you are in the position of reacting while the fish picks where it will take the fight.

Keeping the head up doesn't mean rearing back at all costs. Sometimes a little pressure to the side or from side to side will do the trick. You are in contact with the fish, and you just have to feel your way through the fight, responding to its twists and turns by pulling back, easing up, or changing direction — whatever it takes.

Let the current help you

A fish is going to run away from the pressure of hook, line, and rod. If you have hooked your fish in moving water, try to position yourself downstream from the fish. That way, the fish is not only fighting you and your tackle, it is also fighting the current. This move may not always be possible, but when it is, do it, even if you have to back out of the stream and walk downstream.

He went in the weeds: I lose

If the fish burrows into the weeds, you may well have lost it, but not always. True, if you bend the rod every which way trying to get the fish out of the weeds, you will probably break off sooner or later. However, if you point your rod tip straight at the fish, reel up tight, and start walking backwards, you *may* coax the fish out of the weeds.

Jumping

People are always telling us not to jump to conclusions. I won't pass judgment on the non-angling side of life, but if your tussle with a fish *concludes* on a jump, it can mean only one thing — the fish has jumped free, and your fight is over. It may have broken the line or shaken the hook, but either way, it's off. In most such cases, I bow (drop my rod tip) when a fish jumps. When I bow to a fish, I literally bow. I bend from the waist, drop my rod tip, and extend my arms like a waiter offering a tray full of canapes. As soon as the fish falls back to the water, I come tight again. When a fish is airborne, it may reach a point in its trajectory when all of its weight and momentum snap against the line. Without the buoyancy of the water to act as a shock absorber, this is a very good time for knots to break under the added force of gravity. A hard-mouthed fish, like a tarpon, may not be very deeply hooked to begin with. The force of a jump may be all that is needed to dislodge a hook.

Pull up, reel down

When fighting a fish, the idea is to tire the fish and to recover line that the fish has taken off the reel so that you can eventually get the fish close enough to grasp or gaff. The reeling up is the longest and most tiring part of the fight, and it's one that doesn't come naturally.

The wrong way

Most newcomers get a fish on and reel for dear life. This technique will do you no good. It can even do you harm by causing bad line twist.

The right way

As indicated in Figure 15-1, *pull up* to try to bring the fish toward you; then drop the rod tip and, as you do, reel up line. Remember: As you reel in, drop the rod tip so that you have some place to go when you pull up again.

Remember, too, that every pull up is not going to bring the fish in. Sometimes a fish will take a lot of line before you are able to recover any. Or you may have gained a great deal of line, and then the fish sees the boat and tears away on another run. Keep the pressure on — it's the only way to land the fish. Don't fiddle with the drag because, more often than not, doing so puts too much pressure on your tackle, and I can almost guarantee that you will lose the fish.

Playing the fish

You should always try to get the fish in as soon as possible, especially if you are going to release it. The longer the fish fights, the more lactic acid it builds up, and the harder it is to revive. Releasing (letting go of) a fish that you have fought to the point of exhaustion before you have spent the time to revive it often makes no sense beause the fish may well die anyway.

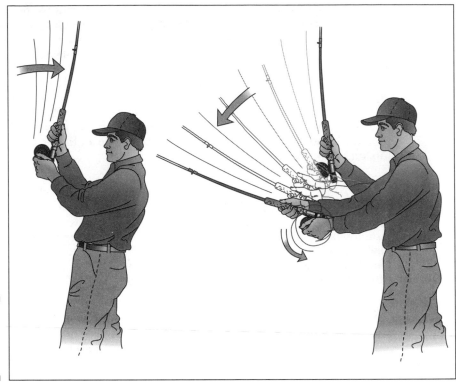

Figure 15-1:
Pumping a
fish. Pull up.
Reel down.

In the ocean, ending the fight quickly is even more important (even if you are keeping the fish) because a long, splashy fight is a great way to attract a predator (like a shark) who will end the fight for you as he takes a meal. This happened to me in the Florida Keys with a tarpon that weighed well over 100 pounds. I fought hard, but I could have fought harder and followed my guide's advice and have gotten the tarpon into the boat within ten minutes. Instead, I prolonged the fight, and my heart was broken as, two hundred yards out, I saw a tremendous commotion and then felt my line grow slack as a huge shark devoured my tarpon.

Light tackle equals a longer fight

While it is more sporty to subdue fish on lighter tackle, you need to use enough tackle to do the job. Using an outfit that doesn't let you bear down on the fish may still land you a fish after a long fight; but if the fish is totally exhausted when you land it, you didn't use heavy enough gear, or you didn't push your gear to the limit.

Landing or Boating the Fish

After you have subdued a fish, your next task is to land it or boat it. This section gives you the lay of the land (or the water) for most fish that you can land by yourself. I am going to assume that if you are going for big game, you either already know what to do or will be fishing with a guide or someone with experience. Landing a big fish is not something to do on your own with only a book as your guide, unless you are a real dummy. (It's a word my publishers asked me to avoid in this book, but I can't think of another word to describe someone who tussles with a big and dangerous game fish without actual physical help and personal experience.)

Do I need a net?

For trout and bass, "the experts" say that you definitely should have a net if you want to release fish back into the water in the hopes that they will live and reproduce. The theory behind this reasoning is that, if you use a net, the fish will be less exhausted when netted rather than landed by hand.

Having said that, I can tell you that I rarely use a net when trout fishing (or when bass fishing, for that matter). I find, at this stage of my angling career, that I can get most fish within my grasp when they still have some life in them. With trout, I reach under the belly and lift up until I am cradling the fish gently. Then I lift it out of the water. For bass, I grab the fish by the lower lip. If I am fishing a lure that has several treble hooks, I hold the line taut with my free hand and then come around with my rod hand to grasp the fish by the lower lip. If I have a really big fish, I use a net. You may want to use a net for all fish, and that's perfectly fine.

If you use a net, you should flip it over so that it is hanging in front of you as the fight concludes. Make sure the net is wet, so that you do not damage the protective mucous-like slime that coats the fish. As shown in Figure 15-2, hold the rod tip high and slip the net over the fish, tail first. Remember to keep the fish in the water until you have the net around it.

What about a gaff?

Certain things in life are designed so well that you take one look at them and you know what they are for. A gaff is one of them. It's really nothing more than a humongous hook on a long shaft. When you gaff a fish, most of the time you are going to keep it. This is not always true.

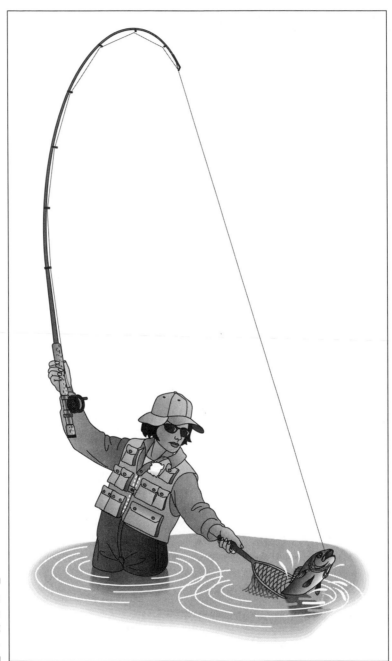

Figure 15-2:
The classic
landing net
position.

For example, a lip gaff is not quite the heavy artillery of a standard gaff, and it is often used by tarpon fishermen who want to release their catch. But for most other cases, you gaff and kill. Surf fishermen have short hand-held gaffs that are great for bluefish, but most gaffs are long-handled and are designed to be used while leaning over the side of a boat. With smaller fish (in saltwater, I would say anything up to 30 pounds), you can probably do your own gaffing. Try to gaff the fish somewhere in the head, gill, or shoulder region. With bigger fish, don't try it until an expert has shown you how.

You Can't Have Your Fishing and Eat It, Too

Fishing, like hunting, is a blood sport. But it is also very different in one significant way. After you shoot a deer or bird, it's a goner. You can't release it back into the wild. A caught fish is different: It can always be returned. So the angler has a choice: "Do I kill the fish, or do I let it go?"

The decision is up to you. Don't let anybody tell you that you are immoral if you decide to kill fish. If you intend to eat them, killing them is okay with me. However, and this is a big *however,* if we *all* killed *all* the fish we caught, fishing (in the words of Beavis and Butt-Head) would suck.

This is especially true of the glamour fish like trout. They are the top predator in their environment, and the way nature has set things up, few top predators are out there relative to animals lower down the food chain, which means that if you take a bunch of trout out of a stream, the fishing quality in that stream will *definitely* decline. The same holds for ocean-going big game, like marlin and tuna. The world just doesn't have that much big game. If you thin out the herd, there is that much less to go for next time you hunt.

I like to eat trout. I like to catch them even more, so I pretty much return all my trout to the stream. The same goes for bass. I don't care for pike, so they go back too. Walleye are great to eat and are fairly prolific, so I keep them. Flounder I keep; stripers go back. Bluefish I keep some of the time. Tarpon, bonefish, and snook all go back.

Words to fish by

"Of all the sports of capture, fishing is the most merciful. There is no need to kill unless you choose. The fish that gets away lives to be hooked another day. On the conscience of the fisherman, there are no wounded ducks, no paunch-shot deer. You catch your fish, if you don't want him, back he goes, none the worse for wear."

—Gifford Pinchot, Founder of the U.S. Forest Service and lifelong angler.

That's what I do. You can make up your own mind about what you want to do. If you are like me, you may start out killing a great number of fish. But as the years go by, you may (as I have done) kill fewer and fewer fish even as you catch more and more.

Before you catch (or release)

If you intend to release a fish, you should follow these few rules:

- ✔ Make up your mind whether to catch or release when you set the hook.
- ✔ Try to set the hook quickly so the fish cannot swallow it too deeply.
- ✔ Minimize the time of the fight. (An exhausted fish is not a strong candidate for survival.)
- ✔ Consider using barbless hooks.

After the fish is landed or boated

These tips increase a fish's chances of surviving:

- ✔ Leave the fish in the water as much as possible.
- ✔ Handle the fish as little as possible.
- ✔ Use forceps or pliers to remove the hook.
- ✔ Use a wet rag (if you have one handy) to hold the fish. (This technique causes less damage to its scales and protective coating.)
- ✔ Wet your hands before handling the fish.
- ✔ If the hook is very deep inside the fish's mouth, cut off the leader. In many cases, the hook will eventually rust out or work itself free. By the way, artificials are usually not taken deep.

Releasing a fish

Sometimes, releasing the fish is relatively easy. You simply remove the hook and the fish wiggles vigorously, which lets you know that it is ready to take off for freedom. Sometimes, the fish won't wait for you to release it. Instead, it will wriggle free and hightail it.

Often, however, the fish is totally exhausted. If you simply released it right away, you would have a belly-up, soon-to-be-dead fish on your hands. Before you *release,* you need to *revive.*

A good rule of thumb to follow in figuring out if a fish needs reviving is this: If the fish lets you hold it and doesn't struggle, revive it. After all, any self-respecting wild animal will take off like greased lightning to escape the clutches of a strange creature. To a fish, a human is a strange creature.

Reviving a fish

Follow these steps (illustrated in Figure 15-3) to help ensure that a caught-and-released fish survives:

1. **Hold the fish gently and keep it under the surface of the water.**

   Cradle it from below if you can. If you cannot, hold it gently by its sides. You may grasp some mid-size fish (salmon and stripers, for example) by the tail.

2. **If you are in heavy current, move to gentler current.**

3. **Point the fish upstream.**

   On lakes or in the ocean, however, current usually isn't a factor when reviving a fish.

4. **Move the fish backward and forward so that its gills are forced to open and close.**

   When properly done, this technique delivers oxygen to a heavily oxygen-depleted fish. Reviving the fish so that it can swim under its own steam may take a few minutes. It lets you know that it is ready to be released when it starts to wiggle.

5. **Release the fish.**

   It should swim slowly away. If it rolls over on its back and lays there, this is not a good sign. Bring the fish back under your control and continue to revive it.

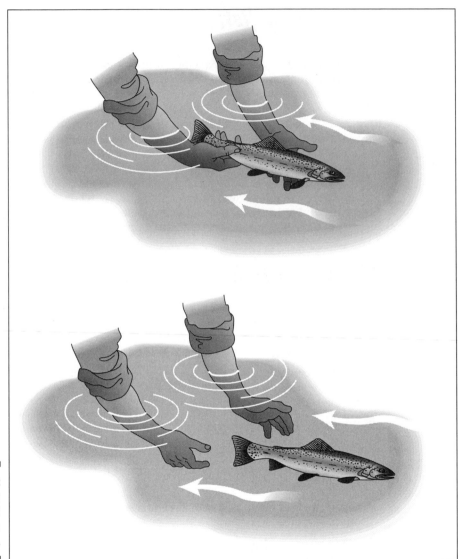

Figure 15-3:
Reviving
and
releasing a
fish.

Chapter 16

Where and When to Fish

"*R*ight Place, Wrong Time" is the name of an old rhythm and blues song. It was about boy-meets-girl, but the same is true when fisherman (or fisherwoman) meets fish. Knowing *where* the fish are and *when* they are there is as important a lesson as any. Because if the fish aren't there, it stands to reason that you aren't going to catch any.

Where

All animals that hunt — whether they are lions, humans, or striped bass — hunt the zone known as *the edge*. It could be where deep water rises to shallow, where fast current meets slow, or where grassland meets water hole. It is the place where prey lose their caution and temporarily leave the safety of their lairs to pursue food (or sometimes mate). Prey often perform these activities to the point of not being tuned into dangers. Predators lie in wait until their prey is thus exposed, and then they strike.

As an angler, or predator, you seek out your prey in those areas where they forsake security in pursuit of their basic drives. The more food around for your prey, the easier it is for you to approach.

Whatever fish you fish for and however you choose to fish, the principles in this little drama are repeated over and over without fail: The angler offers something that looks like safe food to the fish. Fish bites. Angler hooks fish.

Rivers and streams

The basic fact of life in a river or stream is moving water. Food is carried along by the current. Bait fish dart out into the current while seeking bugs, worms, and the like. Game fish move out into the current to eat the same things the bait fish eat (and they eat the bait fish, too). You should look for those places where predators can hang out in security but which are also close to the food being carried on the watery conveyor belt of the stream.

Riffle, pool, riffle

A normal free-stone river (*free-stone,* by the way, means what it says: a river with a great number of stones lying around) is made up of two areas:

- **Riffles:** Rocky areas with fast-moving water
- **Pools:** Deeper areas where the current slows

In trying to visualize a free stone stream, think of a typical mountain stream with boulders and rocks.

The other kind of stream is the *spring creek,* which as its name implies, rises from a subterranean source. It is usually more gentle and slow-moving than a free-stone river and it usually has weed beds and undercut banks.

As illustrated in Figure 16-1, a typical riffle pool system has a number of likely places for game fish, particularly bass and trout.

1. **The riffle.** In the riffle, rocks break up the current flow. Water picks up more oxygen from this turbulence and provides a rich habitat ground for insects and other aquatic life. Game fish hang out in the lee of the current, behind or directly in front of rocks or at the margins of the stream bed, where the current slows and undercut banks may offer shelter. In these conditions, with food zipping by, fish tend to strike quickly at anything that looks like food. Flyrodders want bushy, very floatworthy flies. Exact imitation is not as important as it is in slower water.

2. **The head of the pool.** As the current rushes into the head of the pool, it often digs a nice hole. Fish will hold in the depths and rise to take the food which flows through the funnel that characterizes the entry to many pools in a classic riffle pool system. Typically the current will enter in a *V*-shape. At the outside edges of the *V,* you can also prospect for fish. (They often show themselves as they feed on floating food.)

3. **Deadfalls, logs, rocks, debris.** Anything that obstructs the current offers a place for a predator to lie in wait.

4. **The middle of the pool.** This is usually the place where the current is slowest. In many rivers, it is also the place where the fishing is the slowest. You will occasionally find big fish in this part of the pool; but for the most part, little current means little edge (which means not-so-great fishing). If the current is clipping along, however, try your luck in this area. Hey, you never know.

5. **Weed beds.** These are usually found in slower streams and spring creeks. Weeds offer shelter, and they are often rich in fish food, such as freshwater shrimp and insects of all types. Predator fish hang out in or near weeds because such a location is conveniently close to their food supply.

6. **Tributaries.** Where water from a smaller stream enters a larger stream, it is usually cooler and more oxygen rich. You may well find game fish just downstream of the outlet of a feeder stream (the place where a tributary flows into a larger body of water). As far as those fish are concerned, they are at the head of a pool.

7. **Spring holes.** Subsurface springs beneath rivers and creeks bring cool water in the hot weather and warmer water in the cold weather. Often, the water temperature of a spring is close to the optimum for fish activity. Wherever you find an underwater spring, you may find nice fish. How do you know where a subsurface spring is? Someone tells you, or you figure it out after fishing a particular stretch of stream in all conditions. Say it's the middle of a heat wave in the summer, and you catch a few fish at a particular spot in the depths of a pool. The odds are you have hit upon the location of a spring hole. Mark it and remember it next year when heat strikes again.

8. **Eddies.** The *hydrodynamics* of some pools — that is, the physics of the water flow as it interacts with the structure of the pool — creates calm areas that collect many of the dead insects and shellfish that float downstream. The pickings are easy, so in the case of trout, you will see very gentle feeding activity. A delicate casting hand and a quiet approach can reward you with nice fish.

9. **Shade.** Bankside trees offer shade, a thing that fish seek on bright sunny days. Shade also offers fish some protection from the view of predatory hawks, eagles, and ospreys.

Bankside trees and shrubs offer rich habitat for all kinds of insects. As mentioned in Chapter 4, aquatic insects hatch out of the water and often spend a day or two in the trees and shrubs before returning to mate over the water. So if you see mayflies in the shrubs during the day, look for a spinner fall nearby at night. Also, trees and bushes that are in bloom attract nonaquatic insects that sometimes find their way into the water.

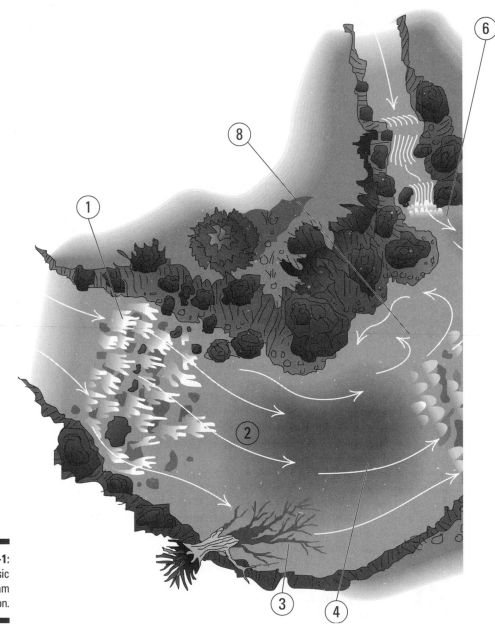

Figure 16-1:
The classic
front-stream
configuration.

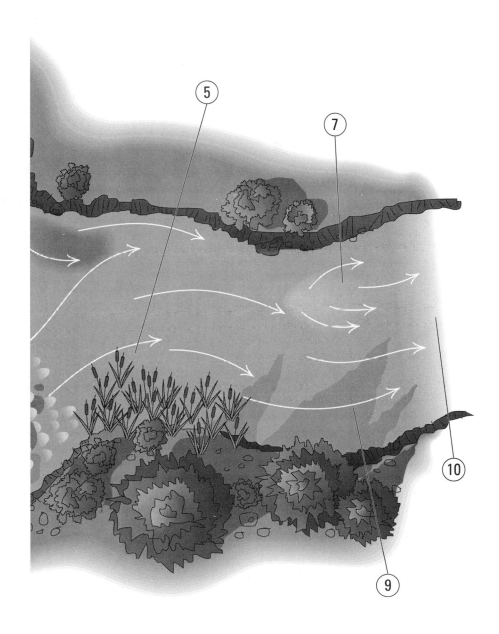

Catastrophic drift — far from a catastrophe

Sometimes the insect or shellfish population can outgrow the capacity of a particular weed bed. When this happens, whole battalions of little organisms abandon their native weed pocket and take to the current in search of new food. This activity is known as *catastrophic drift*. If this happens while you are on the stream, you will be treated to a major feeding frenzy. The upside is that the fish are feeding like crazy. The downside is, with so much food in the water, the odds aren't great they will take whatever you are throwing at them. Still, a feeding frenzy brought about by catastrophic drift provides a unique fishing opportunity.

10. **The tail.** As the water leaves the pool to enter another riffle, it often shallows out and gets very glassy and slick. When a great deal of insect activity takes place, game fish often venture into this shallow water and slash about. These circumstances provide for tricky fishing, and the fish can be spooky (but exciting in a special way). I can't really describe this situation other than to say that the water looks pregnant with the possibility of good fishing.

Taking on a big river

The first time you step into a huge river like the Yellowstone, you will find so much fishy looking water that you really won't know where to start. I have found that the best thing to do in these cases is to think of a really big river as a bunch of smaller rivers.

- If there is an island in the middle of a big river, treat each channel as if it were a separate smaller river.

- Treat the island as if it were a big rock in the middle of a stream. Fish will hang just upstream and just downstream of the island, where there is some protection from the current.

- If you are fishing from the bank and a current line (the edge of the current) is about 20 feet out from the bank, fish the 20 feet of river between the current and the bank as a separate stream.

By breaking the big problem down into separate parts, you can tackle the task at hand in manageable bites.

Dead water: don't waste your time

When fishing a lazy river with big bends and slow deep pools (the Delaware River in New York State is one such river and almost any Ozark stream would be another), remember that trout and bass concentrate in areas where there is some current. Those long, slow, mid-pool stretches look like inviting spots to fish, but nine times out of ten — make that ninety- nine million times out of ninety-nine million and one — you will not catch anything in this kind of water. If you are floating downstream in a boat or canoe, pass by such a pool and save your casting for water that fits the fish-holding profile. (Unless, of course, you see a fish.)

Lakes and reservoirs

Lakes and reservoirs are both standing bodies of water with a few important differences.

- ✔ A reservoir is a more recent creation than a lake. (After all, most lakes have been around since the last Ice Age, but reservoirs are man-made and are relatively recent creations.) Reservoirs haven't had time to evolve all the subtle habitat features of a good old-fashioned lake.

- ✔ Reservoirs can have their level raised or lowered and are, therefore, subject to tremendous fluctuations in depth. Not only does this fluctuation have the obvious effect of determining how much water is available for the fish to hang out in, it also means that significant parts of the reservoir bottom can dry out in periods of low water, affecting the long-term survival of shallow-water bait fish, insects, shellfish, and aquatic vegetation.

A promise from the author (and a picture, too)

I promise that I won't give you a diagram full of little fish marks and 30 different kind of structures to look for. If you have ever read a how-to fishing book before, you know what I am talking about. "Fish for walleye on drop-offs. Try bass over gravely bottoms. Look for northerns by weedy shores." Such suggestions are all true; but collectively, they are a big chunk to swallow in one gulp.

It's much better, I think, to remember the idea of *the edge* (mentioned earlier in this chapter in the section titled "Where"). Look for current, changes in depth, shelter, or anything that breaks up the uniform character of the water. When you discover an edge, realize that game fish and bait fish have to deal with it in various ways. Some fish feed on one side of it. Some lurk on the other side.

I guess this whole concept does require a picture after all, but I'll keep it simple.

Figure 16-2 represents a lake that exists nowhere but in a fishing book. It has a little bit of everything that you might find in any lake from the Arctic Circle to Patagonia.

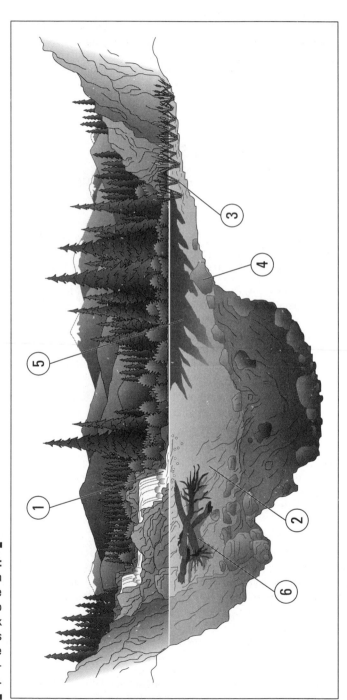

Figure 16-2:
Turn
the page
sideways to
take a look
at this
all-purpose
super-
typical lake.

1. **Inlets and outlets:** Wherever water flows into or out of a lake, bait follows, and game fish concentrate to feed.

2. **Drop-offs:** Wherever the structure goes from shallow to deeper, you may find game fish lurking in water that is in a comfortable temperature zone. This usually puts game fish *under* bait fish (which they can ambush from below).

3. **Weed beds:** Weeds can be a haven for bait fish, a breeding ground for crustaceans and insects, and (because of these assets) a magnet for game fish. Weed beds also offer a place for game fish to hide from prey and predators.

4. **Rocky points:** Rocky points can block the wind, divert a current, and offer shade. In other words, rocky points provide classic edges.

5. **Shade:** Trees on the banks and lily pads in the shallows offer shade (which affects water temperature). Shade affects the view of dangerous predators, like herons and raccoons, and that limits their ability to prey on game fish.

6. **Underwater stuff:** Sunken islands, drowned trees, and fallen trees offer structure, which translates into hiding places for predators and habitat for bait.

Birds

Feeding birds are always a sign that bait is available — whether it is in the form of insects or bait fish. This situation is a no-brainer. Fish where the birds are.

Other bird signs are more subtle. For example, a blue heron (or any other wading bird that is known to feed on bait fish) is a promising sign for anglers. If you see such a bird hanging around the same pool day after day, chances are that Mr. Heron knows that this pool is a regular food source. (You can count on Mr. Game Fish to have reached the same conclusion.)

Deep thoughts

"How deep should I fish?" This is a question that only the fish can answer. Obviously, you need to fish where the fish are. Water temperature has a great deal to do with their location. If you can figure out where the water is at the optimum temperature level, that's a good place to start fishing. Some electronic devices take the water temperature at various depths, but (as with all electronic devices) they cost money.

A do-it-yourself temperature gauge

You don't always need a sophisticated gauge for reading temperatures at different depths. Say you want to find out what the temperature is at ten feet. Here's a simple way to do that:

1. **Tie an inexpensive (but accurate) outdoor thermometer to the end of a line.**

2. **Let out ten feet of line (you can guesstimate this) and attach a bobber to the line at the ten-foot point.**

3. **Then put the thermometer in the water, let the thermometer sink, and take a reading.**

   To check the temperature at other depths, just let out five more feet of line (for example), move the bobber five feet up the line, and you get a fifteen foot reading, and so on.

Forget about the deep blue sea

If you fish on the ocean, chances are that you won't start by venturing out 10, 20, or 100 miles to blue water all on your own. For one thing, the exorbitant cost of a boat and gear for this type of fishing is beyond the reach of most beginning anglers — make that most anglers, including yours truly. Most of your fishing will be done closer to shore in shallower water (less than a hundred feet of depth). When you narrow your search field down to this strip of shallow coastal waters, the overwhelmingly big ocean begins to take on the characteristics of a combination of river and lake.

It's like robbing a bank

When the notorious stick-up man, Willie Sutton, was asked why he robbed banks, he gave a sensible answer: "Because that's where the money is." If you want to catch fish, go where the bait is. Think of the ocean as a bank filled not with money but with bait. Just as when fishing in a stream or lake, the first thing to look for is feeding fish. The second thing to look for is bait. And the third thing to look for (actually it's two things) is current and structure.

Tides are the key

Anyone with any ocean angling experience knows that tides are critically important. There are two high tides and two low tides each day. For the angler, this means roughly dividing the day into six hours of *incoming* water and six hours of *outgoing* water (followed by six more hours of incoming water and six more hours of outgoing water). When the tide is moving, you will find a current coming in and out of creeks, back bays, and the like. Treat this current just as you would treat a river or stream, and fish the moving tide accordingly. If a current sweeps by a rocky outcropping, look for fish just as if they were holding behind a subsurface rock in a trout stream.

Here are some additional tidal tips:

- Try to fish when the tide is moving. At *slack tide* — in other words, still water at the end of a tide — there is very little action that would cause bait to concentrate. Consequently there is nothing to concentrate game fish.

- On an outgoing tide, position yourself just outside creek mouths, bay mouths, and harbor mouths. That is where the bait (and the fish) will be as the tide recedes.

- On an incoming tide, you will often find fish just inside of bay and harbor mouths. Most anglers, however, find this situation to be less of a sure bet than finding fish on an outgoing tide.

- At low tide, examine exposed flats to see the contours of the bottom. You will find holes, troughs, and subsurface structure to check out later during high tide.

- When fishing shallow flats, the incoming tide will often bring nice fish out of deeper water as they follow bait onto the flats.

- As in stream fishing, structure attracts game fish. At high tide, try rocky jetties that attract fish to nooks and crannies.

- Be mindful of the phase of the moon. The full moon will bring abnormally high and low tides. This situation will affect ocean access and safety. Know the territory, especially at night!

It's a big lake

The tides make the ocean behave like a stream. But the ocean is also a very big lake. As you would in a lake, look for structure, drop-offs, and channels. Weed beds hold food and hide predators. Underwater wrecks provide all kinds of hidey-holes.

It's what's underneath that counts

Sometimes, tides or storms will carry big mats of floating weeds and grasses along with them. Bait fish and shellfish are often in and around these mats. Floating weeds and grasses also cut down on light. All of these factors combine to make a spot that may hold a concentration of game fish.

Look at the birdie

If you see a battalion of diving gulls all bunched up together, you can bet there are bait fish underneath them. What happens is this: Game fish encircle the bait fish and force them to the surface; and then, while the bait fish are penned up, the gulls have easy pickings. My advice is this: Follow the birds. My other advice: Follow the bird (as in *one* bird). Sometimes, a lone bird diving repeatedly in the same place indicates that a feeding striper or a cruising sailfish is nearby. Check it out.

Don't trust terns. *Terns* are little birds, very much like swallows. You will see them dipping and diving along the shore. While diving gulls are a pretty sure bet as a sign of game fish, terns are a 50-50 shot. If you get under a flock of terns and cast a few times but catch nothing, move on. All that commotion means that the terns have found food but the game fish haven't.

Temperature counts, too

Fish when the water is at the right temperature and you will catch fish. Fish when the water is the wrong temperature and you will catch nothing. It's that simple. As in freshwater fishing, a thermometer (or a more-sophisticated electronic monitor) is one of the most practical angling aids you can buy. As noted in Chapters 9 and 10, all fish have an optimum temperature range. Seek it out.

When

The quick answer to the question "When do I fish?" is simple: Whenever you get the chance. Most of the time, you can find a way to catch *something.* You may not be able to fish for the big guys, or you may have to forget about some of the glamour fish and go for panfish, flounder, or whatever. Still, it's fishing. The other thing to remember is this: Game fish don't go to sleep during the day; they just go to different places. Sometimes, they go to deeper water. Sometimes, they visit reefs or nooks in a rocky shore. But they are *somewhere,* and they can be caught if you know where to go and how to fish. The important thing is to fish whenever you can.

If it is true that the early bird gets the worm, it is also probably true that the early worm gets the fish. (And the late worm, too.) In other words, long experience has shown that dawn and dusk are very productive times. When the world changes over from those animals on night duty to those that come out in the daytime, you have another one of those edges that I spoke about earlier in this chapter. This particular edge is not a physical edge, but an edge in time. The important thing about all edges is that they are *transition* zones, and some creatures have a natural advantage in making that transition. The skillful predator exploits that advantage. Just as the trout grows bold and loses caution when many mayflies are on the water, many predators grow bolder in dim light. Maybe, in dim light, the bait fish feel that they are less visible; they get a little cocky, and the game fish know that the pickings will be good. Anglers observe this behavior, and that's when *they* are on the water.

Stars and stripers

At the turn of the century, millions of immigrants' first landfall in America was on Ellis Island, through which nearly 20 million future Americans passed. A causeway connects Ellis Island with the New Jersey shore. About ten years ago, I was fishing there with Captain Joe Shastay, the pioneering fishing guide in New York Harbor. The causeway runs over a shallow flat where you can pick up schoolie stripers (up to 5 pounds). You can use a trout or freshwater bass rig for these guys. We arrived at sunset on December 23, which was a cold but windless winter evening. I rigged up. Joe took the temperature of the water at the end of the outgoing tide. It was cold — about 45°F.

"Water from the mountains upstate," Joe said. "A little cold for bass. Wait 'til the tide turns."

Within the hour, just as Joe had predicted, I began to see feeding fish all around. What happened was, the incoming tide had brought in warmer ocean water (49°F), and the stripers turned on. Fishing under those conditions was like flipping an on/off switch. I cast and caught, cast and caught, and cast and caught (maybe 50 fish). The fishing couldn't have been more productive.

The best of times

Sometimes, the fish totally ignore the rules and come out to feed when all the books say they have no business being out and about. But of course, if fish didn't make fatal mistakes like that, no one would ever catch them. For most fish, most of the time, here's when you want to be fishing:

- At dawn and dusk.
- On cloudy overcast days (which have similar light conditions to dawn and dusk).
- For trout, fish the pleasant time of the day. Water temperature in spring and fall is usually optimal for insect activity in the warmest part of the day. In the summer, the prime insect time is when things cool down a bit.
- Apple blossom time. For shad, for trout, for smallmouth bass, and probably for a good many other fish, the locals will tell you, "Don't fish until the dogwood blooms," or "Wait until the redbud leaves are as big as squirrel ears." What these tips all mean is that generations of anglers have noticed that when the spring really starts to put some early flowers and leaves out, it is a sign that the air and water are warming. This is when fish are going to stir from their winter doldrums.

The worst of times

In my opinion, you can hang it up right after a big barometric swing (though there are some anglers who have exactly the opposite opinion). Time and time again, it has been my experience that a change in the weather means that fish are going to need some time to adjust to the change. A Finnish fisheries biologist (whom I ran into years ago while fishing with the Rapala brothers on one of the lakes near their hometown) said that it was his belief that bait fish don't have sophisticated organs to compensate for pressure. He believed that a falling barometer meant that bait (or at least Finnish bait) had to go deeper to equalize pressure. When the bait fish went deeper into the water, the game fish followed, and anglers who were using top water plugs and dry flies were out of luck. According to his theory, a rising barometer should have the opposite effect and should make for good topwater action, but I have never noticed that effect. If you play the odds, my advice is give the fish a little time to adjust to a change in the weather.

"If you don't fish at night, you won't catch big fish"

If you hang around Montauk Point, you will hear that the hard-core guys (supposedly the guys who catch the big babies) fish in the middle of the night, dressed in a wet suits and using miners' lamps for illumination. I can tell you right now that I have seen 50-pound striped bass pulled out of the surf at nine o'clock in the morning under a bright sun. I have seen such striped bass on top of the water, boiling under bait all through clear fall days. It's a great time to fish. So, no, you don't have to fish when it is dark to have a chance to catch big fish.

However . . .

You will catch more fish in low-light conditions than you will catch in the heat of the day. You will catch more fish on cloudy days than you will catch on sunlit ones. You will have a much better chance in shallow water when darkness provides bait fish with the feeling, but not always the reality, of security from predatory game fish.

A Few Tips That Didn't Fit Anywhere Else

Here are a couple of pointers that I want you to remember. All of them have to do with getting your offering to the fish without scaring the fish away. Remember, scared fish don't eat! And if they don't eat, they don't take whatever it is you are throwing at them.

Where do they all go?

I had always wondered where fish go to after their early morning feed. One day I found out. We were fishing for stripers out on Gardiners Bay at the tip of Long Island. Gardiners Bay has a very long, skinny sand bar that was created by the killer hurricane of 1938 that boiled up out of the Gulf Stream, causing hundreds of deaths. We were catching bluefish in very skinny water. We could see their fins waving as they positioned themselves down tide of the bait. The blues were feeding as if they were trout holding below a riffle. Then, when the tide turned, they disappeared. We moved to the other side of the bar, thinking that the blues had changed position.

Our guide, Paul Dixon, picked up his push pole and began moving us parallel to the beach, about a hundred yards out.

We found no feeding activity anywhere along the shore. The surface was calm. But when we reached about four feet of depth — not much depth, but enough relative to the shallows on the shore — I began to see stripers. As Paul poled over them, they darted like a school of minnows. For the next mile and a half, we passed over thousands and thousands of stripers. We even caught a few. So the next time anyone tells you fish disappear after sunrise, remember that all the fish in the world could be just a little further offshore.

Stay calm

You see a fish that is finning quietly just below the surface. (No scene is more enticing to an angler, nor more likely to make a fish feel skittish). When approaching a fish like this (in fact, when moving through *any* water where you think you might find fish), keep these four simple rules in mind:

Take it slow

The faster you move, the more likely you are to make a disturbance. In really calm water, moving slowly is a matter of taking a step, waiting a second for the waves to subside, and then taking another step. The same goes for rowing your boat or canoe — do it slowly and steadily.

Quiet, please

Be careful about banging your oars, scraping rocks with your boots, or walking with heavy footfalls. Sound really does travel well underwater, and it transfers very well between land (underwater rocks, riverbanks, and beaches) and the water. Take it easy, and if you must do anything, do it quietly.

Stay out of sight

In most cases, if you can see the fish, the fish can see you. This rule is not always true, however. For example, if you are downstream of a rising trout, it will probably not notice you. The basic rule is this: Stay out of the line of sight of wary fish. Here are some tips you can follow to do that:

✔ **Blend into the background:** Although you don't need full camouflage, wearing clothing that is the same color as the background against which the fish will see you is a good idea. (Remember that fish are not used to seeing fluorescent exercise outfits in their usual environment.)

✔ **Keep a low profile:** Just like the guy who wants to keep his head on his shoulders while hiding in a foxhole, the angler should stay low and out of sight.

Really — I mean it — be quiet!

I just want to emphasize how important it is to stay cool, calm, collected, and *quiet*. The more enticing the fish, the harder keeping quiet may be; but the only way that you are going to be sure not to scare off a trophy fish is by being quiet.

Fish near, then far

Everyone likes to cast as far as he or she can. This feat can really impress your friends. The fish, however, couldn't care less. All the fish cares about is this: "Does that thing with a hook attached to it look like food that I want to eat?" If that thing with the hook does look like edible food, you want to make sure that you have done nothing else to put the fish on its guard, so disturb as little water as possible. The best way to tackle a stretch of water is to fish the water that is nearest to you and then fish progressively further with each cast. If you do it the other way round, any fish that is close in is going to have been through a great deal of distracting commotion by the time that you are ready to cast to him.

Fish the clock

In keeping with the last hint, *fishing the clock* is a way to fish the water methodically and to get the most out of each position. Say you are standing in a stream, prospecting for trout with a dry fly. Before you slap your line on the water at the most upstream position, you can work your way up to it and cover many possible trout holding spots (or *lies*) in between. You begin by casting along an angle that is downstream. Fish out that cast and then angle your next cast a little more upstream. In this way, your fly, lure, or bait is in prime fishing water for about a half dozen casting angles rather than just one. The same goes for the wet-fly fisherman who casts downstream. First, carve out a pie-shaped wedge and fish that, starting more closely in and then casting progressively farther away.

Chapter 17

Getting There: Walking, Driving, or Floating

. . . .

In This Chapter

▶ Learning your range as a walker

▶ Wading without going under

▶ Boating without going broke

▶ Getting grandpa down to the river

. . . .

*G*oing fishing, for most of us, involves going somewhere. It could be just down to the stream, two hours away by car, or clear across the lake. Wherever you go fishing, you have to get from here to there. (Having a way to get back also helps.)

Walking

An angler on foot is like a foot soldier. You need to be prepared to transport equipment for fast changing weather, for food and water needs, and (after you get to the scene of the battle) for combat. To carry all of this gear, you have to balance two variables:

 ✔ **Pack light:** There is a law of physics (or at least a law of the physics of anglers) that every pound that you pack to go fishing feels like two pounds coming back. Take only what you need.

 ✔ **Pack completely:** If you are not comfortable, you will be miserable. The cold feels colder, the wet feels wetter, and hunger and thirst seem more insistent. Think of what you will need and make sure that you take it with you.

How far is too far?

You look at the map and it shows two miles to the stream you plan to fish. So you figure "Two miles in; two miles out: No big deal." But it is a big deal if those two returning miles are on an uphill grade, in the dark, on an un- marked path, in a snaky area, with landowners who like to sight in their deer rifles before going to bed. Also, after you get to the fishing spot in the first place, you have to fish. Often, this means a good deal of wading, stream- crossing, and rock-hopping, all of which can be very tiring. Bottom line: Think about how far you can reasonably walk — then cut that distance in half. Then see how it all works out. The *worst* thing that can happen if you follow this advice is you will have more time to fish.

Just like Wee Willie Keeler

Old time baseball great Wee Willie Keeler compiled a .345 lifetime average by spraying singles all over the place. His philosophy was, "Hit em where they ain't." I have the same philosophy of fishing: Try to find a place to fish that has few anglers. Sometimes doing so means nothing more than taking a few minutes to cross the stream to reach the side that is less fished. Sometimes it means walking farther. Sometimes it means using a little psychology, as I learned on a trip to a much-fished section of Yellowstone Park (see the following sidebar).

There only needs to be water at the end

Don't ask me why, but it is a law of fishing psychology that anglers will walk miles *along* a stream in preference to crossing a half mile of land. I saw this happen on Slough Creek (one of the greatest trout streams in the world) in Yellowstone Park. I was really anxious for my wife and kids to see this stream because the fish are so big and are often quite catchable.

When we left the parking lot at Slough Creek, we walked and walked, and we found fisher- men in every good spot. Rather than horn in on someone else's vacation, we went back to our cabin in the Lamar Valley, parked the car, and trudged a half mile in the hot sun to get to the Lamar river. We had a mile of terrific trout stream and two hours of fishing all to our- selves with native cutthroat rising to Pale Morning Duns.

What I learned that day is this: Your average walking angler likes to get to water as soon as he or she can. It's like a security blanket. After reaching the stream, this same angler is con- tent to walk along the bank for miles. But that's just the quickest way to the water, not the quickest way to the fishing. Sometimes, like what happened to us on the The Lamar, the shortest way to the good water is across dry land.

Say please!

You would be surprised to find how much private water is accessible to you if you ask. Just as importantly, you need to ask in the right way. Many landowners freely give permission if you follow these simple suggestions:

- ✔ **Try and look human:** If you just rolled out of your sleeping bag, didn't brush your teeth, and forgot to comb your hair, you will look like an escapee from a chain gang and you will be treated as such. Try and neaten up before you knock on a landowner's door.

- ✔ **Please and thank you, Ma'am:** Manners count. Calling people Sir or Ma'am and remembering to say please and thank you go a long way.

- ✔ **Have a plan for your catch:** If you are fishing catch-and-release, tell the landowners. They may be happy to hear that you are not depleting their resource. Or you can also offer to bring some fish back for their pan if they would like.

- ✔ **Don't screw it up for the rest of us:** Be a good guest so that the rest of us can approach the same landowners after your visit. That means obvious stuff like *don't litter.* (If you can carry it in, you can carry it out.) It also means *leave every gate the way that you found it.* If it is open, leave it open. If it is closed, leave it closed. There's nothing like having a fisherman lose some livestock to turn a landowner off.

Getting back

If you are in a new place and the path is so-so, don't wait until dark to start the walk back. One of these times, you may lose your way, and being lost in the woods at night will remind you of what it was like to be a scared four-year-old in a strange, dark house. Make a mental note of how much time it took to get to the stream and leave that same amount of time to get back *while it is still light.*

Clothing tips

I don't mean to sound like your mother, but I feel compelled to tell you how to dress and what to bring. Okay, I guess I do mean to sound like your Mom.

Stay warm

Although the sun may be hot while you're fishing, the air is usually going to be cold on the way back. Pack a sweater or polypropylene (fuzzy synthetic) pullover.

These boots were made for wadin'

Wading boots are not always the best walking shoes. If you have a long way to go, sometimes putting your waders in your backpack and putting on a fresh pair of boots or shoes for the walk out is easier. Or if you have stocking-foot waders, you may just want to take them off and walk out in your wading boots. Because you can pretty much count on stumbling into a berry patch one night, you will also be saving yourself from the heartbreak of punctured waders.

Seeing where you are going helps

Pack a flashlight and test it before you go fishing. While I'm on the subject, take some matches in a case that will keep them dry. This isn't for light, but for fire. Take my word for it: One of these days, when you are cold, wet, and lost, you will bless a nice, warm, cozy fire.

Wading

Even though wading is just walking, it requires much more skill and care than walking down the street does. First, you are often dealing with the force of moving water. Second, you can't see the ground in front of you that well. And third, underwater rocks and plants can be slippery. For all of these reasons, there is one cardinal rule of wading: *Take it slow!*

Come to think of it, there is a second cardinal rule: Test the footing in front of you before you take the weight off your back foot.

Drop-offs, unseen rocks, and current surges are often invisible, so you need to wade slowly and cautiously, one foot at a time.

Thy rod and thy staff

I do most of my wading without a staff, but there are times when one really helps, either as a probing device or as a third leg.

Although a stick lying around on the ground may make a serviceable wading staff, what do you do with it after you are in the middle of the stream? For greater convenience, many people like commercial wading staffs that can be tied to a belt. If you can't find such a staff, a cheap and easy alternative is a ski pole with the little rubber circle cut off of the bottom. I say *cheap,* because in the summertime, ski poles are not a hot ticket, and you can often pick up a bunch at bargain-basement prices. Because many trout fishing destinations are also at or near ski resorts, you are very likely to find some ski poles right in the town where you are fishing.

Thy friend, too

You would think that if one person can easily slip and fall in a stream, then linking two people is a sure recipe for a dunking. But the opposite is true. By linking arms together, two anglers can actually gain strength and stability. If one of you is a stronger wader, that person should take the upstream position because that is the more difficult one. (This is also a good way to get a new angler a little more used to handling moving water.)

Think like a fish

When a fish is hooked and it wants to use the force of the current to fight you, it turns broadside to the current. This may work fine for a fish trying to escape. For an angler trying to wade, it is precisely the wrong thing to do. You want to present the thinnest silhouette possible. In other words, stand sideways to present a more streamlined surface to the rushing water. I realize that some of us older anglers may have a shape that looks more like a soup spoon than a steak knife, but sideways is still the most efficient way to deal with the physics of moving water.

Lead with your rear

You see a nice fish rising behind a midstream rock. Inch by inch you begin to wade across the treacherous stream. It's slow going, but you are slowly getting in position for that perfect cast. And then the bottom drops sharply and you realize there is no way you are going to make it. Whatever you do, don't turn around and wade out! This action simply presents the broadest part of your body to the flow, and it is a great way to get knocked off your feet. Just take your time and back out, inch by inch.

If you fall

One of these days, you are going to take a tumble into the water. If you are careful, you will tumble much less often than you think. In 25 years of angling, I have fallen into the stream exactly twice. I've come close to falling more often than that, but in terms of bona fide butt-soakings, that's it. That makes me lucky. If you fall in, you should be able to right yourself pretty quickly. It helps if you keep your waders tightly cinched with a belt. If the current does take you, don't fight it: The river always wins. If possible, keep your feet in front of you so that if some part of you strikes a rock, it probably won't be your head. Although taking an involuntary ride is a little scary, try and remember that most dunkings will leave you in calm water in less than half a minute. And if you just can't manage to stay safe and hold on to your rod, let the rod go. After all, you can buy a new rod faster than the rod can buy a new you.

Boating

This book costs $19.99 in the U.S. The cost of a fishing boat can range anywhere from the couple-hundred-dollars class up to the hundred-thousand-plus class. If you are a beginning boater, this is not the place to get the last word on such a big decision. However, there are a few first words.

Canoes

A canoe is one of those things that you look at and you know exactly what it is supposed to do. It is perfectly designed to slice through the water. In a stream or a lake, it is the form of locomotion that will usually take you the furthest and fastest with the least amount of muscle power. Because it can ride on the top of most cars without much fuss, it is also an extremely practical way to increase your range as a fisherman. Good as canoes are, however, they are not designed to do a couple of things:

- A canoe is not made for standing. Sitting is fine — standing will tip it quicker than you can say "Yikes, I'm falling!"

- A canoe is not designed for heavy winds and choppy water. Of course, in the hands of an expert, you'd be amazed at how a canoe can handle angry water; but for most of us, most of the time, a canoe works well when going *with* the current and *not* into heavy wind and choppy water.

Johnboats

Johnboats are also spelled *jonboats*. (You would expect that someone named John was involved with the invention of the johnboat. Actually, the inventor was a Missourian named Owen Swinney. Go figure!) After the canoe, this is probably the most popular design for angling. Johnboats originated on the lazy, meandering rivers of the Ozarks; and in many ways, the original design resembled canoes in that they were narrow and tippy. The modern design is stubbier and more stable, and the addition of an outboard motor more than compensates for the loss in hydrodynamic efficiency. Set a johnboat in a gently flowing river and it will pretty nearly guide itself downstream. Its shallow draft (in other words, it doesn't ride low in the water) also makes it a good choice for a cut-rate flats boat for the saltwater and back-bay angler, but it is not my first choice for heavy water.

Bigger boats

When you talk about boats that run longer than 16 feet, you are dealing with boats that no longer offer the option of *practical* oar propulsion. (Although oars or paddles may help in a pinch, boats this long are designed to be propelled by motors.) For most anglers in most situations, a motor boat means a boat with an *outboard* motor. Through long trial and error, a number of designs have come to be the preferred boat for most anglers. I think if you buy a boat that was designed on your home waters, for your home waters, you can be fairly assured that it will serve you well in local conditions.

How much vee?

A vee-shaped prow is great for cutting through choppy water. It also adds length that the angler can't utilize very well. For most inshore conditions, the Mako design is a great all-rounder. The more snub-nosed Boston Whaler is also terrific and versatile. The Whaler offers more practical space for its size. In angling terms, this practical space is known as *the fishing platform*.

How big?

A big boat with a big motor is impressive. It is also expensive. Your boat should be *just* big enough to do the kind of fishing you want to do. For most lake fishing and inshore fishing (which includes places as rough as Montauk Point), you should never need anything more than a 23-footer. The *sportfisherman* is a bigger boat with a special design for more long-distance big-water fishing; but if you're a beginner, you are probably not going out tomorrow to buy a sportfisherman.

How many people can I cram in?

Never cram a boat. A boat is designed to carry a certain amount of weight and *no more*. Don't mess around with the capacity of your boat. The formula that Al McClane used to figure out the safe capacity of the average boat carrying average sized (150-pound) people is

$$\frac{\text{Length x Width x Depth}}{20} = \text{Number of People}$$

Better fishing through electricity

I don't love big outboard motors. They do their job, but they are loud, messy, and bulky. An electric motor, on the other hand, *feels* like a fishing tool. It enables the lone angler to sneak up silently on bass and pike, wall-eye, and even lake-dwelling trout. An electric motor is silent and frees up both hands for fishing. They even work on canoes. Definitely not for long-distance propulsion, they are perfect for up-close work in the all-important fishing zone.

Can I survive without electronic gear?

Survive, yes; catch fish, maybe. Although you may not need a console that looks like the bridge of the Starship Enterprise, you would do well to have a depth finder of some kind. Having a depth finder is good for two reasons:

- ✔ It is important to know the depth of the water so that your boat will clear underwater obstacles.
- ✔ Depth and changes in contour of the lake bed are both important indicators of the presence of game fish. If you know how to read it, a simple depth finder can be a powerful fish-finding tool. For a little more expense, a device that visualizes and graphs the water and bottom underneath the boat is very useful.

Okay, I boated the tuna. Now where am I?

One of the easiest things an angler can do on the water is get lost. You fight a big fish, he turns you around a couple of times, all of a sudden you forget which way you were pointing, and you are up the creek without a paddle. Actually, you are usually out at sea without a clue. Now, thanks to 24 satellites circling the globe at a cost of 20 billion dollars (give or take a few bil), you can locate yourself by using the same technology employed by the U.S. Department of Defense. This technology is called GPS (Global Positioning System), and it is the greatest invention ever for the directionally challenged. With prices coming down, as they do with all high-tech items, a direction finder is a worthwhile investment. And if you don't think so now, get lost once and then let's talk about it.

Belly boats: The low tech route

The *belly boat* (or *float tube*), which is basically an inner tube with a seat and two holes for your legs, is a wonderful way to add to your mobility in deep pools, back bays, and lake shores. Spending a day floating down a spring creek, sneaking up on feeding trout, watching the clouds drift by — this is the kind of fishing that can clean your bad vibes out in a hurry. If you fish with a belly boat on a lake, I advise wearing some fins over your waders to help you move around.

Driving: Do I Really Need Four-Wheel Drive?

For 99.9 percent of your fishing, any car will get you there. In certain cases, four-wheel drive is absolutely necessary; but I own a regular car, I've always owned a regular car, and I fish a lot. If you are a surf fisherman, then, yes: Four-wheel drive is a great blessing. Having chased schools of bass and bluefish down a half mile or so of beach, I am green with envy toward the guys in the Cherokees and Blazers as they go tearing after the fish. Likewise, on a hot day in the Rockies, a four-wheel drive is a lifesaver for covering the miles of rough road you find on many ranches. So the answer really is this: You can get plenty of great fishing without a four-wheel drive, but, if you have one anyway, it helps.

Old guys, bass, and the New York Yankees

The first time I ever used a belly boat was with the late John Groth, one of the greatest angling artists of this century. John, a city kid from Chicago, loved to fish; and in his later years, he bought a place out on the east end of Long Island. But because he no longer had the mobility and stamina to handle the surf, he just ignored the autumn run of stripers and blues. Instead, he headed for the string of clear ponds that run down the spine of Long Island, deep in the pine forests.

On this one afternoon, we had the most beautiful pond (actually a small lake) all to ourselves. John fired up his corncob pipe and waded into the water. As he puffed and kicked himself into position, he looked like Popeye imitating a locomotive. All through the warm October afternoon, we caught nice largemouth on popping bugs. I had a couple bologna sandwiches in one of the pockets of the float tube, a cold beer in another, and my little portable radio tuned to the Yankees-Royals play-off game. There is a beer commercial (that I am sure you have seen) in which a bunch of actors (pretending to be fishermen) gather around the campfire at day's end, pop a couple of beers, and say, "It doesn't get any better than this."

Those beer guys weren't on the pond with old John that day.

A Little Help from Their Friends

Many of the places and techniques mentioned in this book are fine *if* you are an able-bodied angler. But many older anglers (and those with one kind of disability or another) may have some difficulty finding the same kind of access to quality fishing. I am happy to report that all this is beginning to change. An organization called Project Access has been started by Joan Stoliar of New York City with the express purpose of providing fishing opportunities to the elderly and disabled. What a great idea!

As Joan, who is a major-league angler in her own right, put it, "This is not just a good deed for disabled anglers. It's for the rest of us, too. Think about all those friends and relations who can't fish because they can't get down to the stream. We are all missing out on some great fishing companions."

So Joan, with the help of two of the most active fly-rod organizations, Theodore Gordon Flyfishers and Trout Unlimited, set about trying to create access for their disabled and elderly friends. A number of sites were found on the Beaverkill River in the Catskills, and on a few weekends in the spring, the clubs had an outing during which they cleared and graded paths for wheelchair access. The results have sparked a nationwide movement to provide access for all.

Think about what you can do in your town. If you have a local fire truck, it may be filling up down at a river or at a lake. Guess what? Access for fire trucks may also serve as access for wheelchairs. Why not talk to the fire department folks about putting their truck access on some of the best fishing pools on the river? That way, when their trucks are done drinking, Grandpa can get down to the stream with his rod.

For information on Project Access sites or if you want to create one in your town, you can reach Project Access by e-mail at Info@ProjectAccess.com or Webmaster@ProjectAccess.com.

If you don't have e-mail, the regular old postal address is Project Access, Box 299, Village Station, New York, NY 10014.

Chapter 18
Dress for Success

· ·

· ·

*1*f you are dressed for the weather, you can pretty much fish in any conditions. If you are not dressed well, I guarantee you will be miserable. The cold feels colder. The heat feels like the inside of a Weber Kettle, and the wet gets into your bones and stays there for days. Even though we live in gear-obsessed times, you don't need all that much to dress comfortably. I'm not promising that you'll look great, but who's looking anyway? The fish don't care. Even though there has been a move afoot recently to introduce style into fishing gear, I am totally opposed to mixing fashion and fishing. Keep it simple!

Weather changes from day to day and, even more importantly for the angler, it changes *during* the day. Mornings are cool, afternoons are hot, cold fronts blow through, showers start and stop. The one thing you can usually depend on is some change in the weather during a fishing session. This means that no matter how you are dressed when you start fishing, you will have to put on or take off clothes at some point. Make sure you have what you need on hand.

What Burlesque Shows and Anglers Have in Common

Long ago, striptease artists discovered that the more *layers* they took off, the more the audience liked the show. It's the same with angling. By that, I don't mean that you do a Demi Moore impression while you take your waders off. What I do mean is that by dressing in layers, you can put on or take off articles of clothing as the day goes along and still stay comfortable.

Most of the time I start out the day wearing a t-shirt, with a turtleneck over it, followed by a fleecy pullover. And if it is windy, a rain jacket as a wind-breaker. When it's cooler, I wear a wool shirt over the turtleneck, and when it's warmer, I just wear a long-sleeve cotton shirt over the t-shirt. Jeans when it's cool; shorts when it's hot.

Your basic clothes arsenal

This basic setup will serve you in most places, most of the time. The only time I modify it is when it is ultra-hot, like in the tropics when there is no chance of anything remotely cool happening *or,* at the opposite end of the weather spectrum, when it's cold and going to stay that way, like for in-stance, Lake Michigan in November. But let's leave the extremes for a second and talk about being prepared for weather from about 40°F to 90°F, which is the range at which most of us fish.

- ✔ **Underwear:** Regular old cotton t-shirt and shorts.

- ✔ **A long-sleeve cotton turtleneck:** This gives overall covering of your torso and protects neck and chest from wind (which you can pretty much always count on in a boat).

- ✔ **Long johns bottoms:** In particular I like the silk ones. They are light, cheap, and warm. Even if you don't need them while fishing, they take up little space and you will be glad you have them when your jeans are wet and you haven't brought spare clothes for the drive home (but I don't advise going into a 7-11 or bar when that is all you are wearing).

- ✔ **Hiking or athletic shorts (with pockets):** Have them in your gym bag in case it's a warm day. This means bring a gym bag with a change of clothes.

- ✔ **Jeans or khakis:** There's a reason that people just naturally wear them when given a choice. They're comfortable, they break the wind, they keep the sun off, and so on. Some experts have a thing against cotton because it feels cold when it is wet. My solution is to have an extra pair.

- ✔ **Long-sleeve cotton shirt (warmish weather):** When it's hot, I always wear a long-sleeve cotton shirt to keep the sun off. At this stage of the game, I think most of you know that prolonged exposure to the sun is hell on unprotected skin. And fishing is a pastime that gives you about as much sun as any human activity.

- ✔ **Long-sleeve wool shirt (cold weather):** Wool stays warm even when it's wet. For early spring and autumn fishing, I prefer it to cotton.

- ✔ **Fleece pullover (Polartec, Polarfleece):** There are a lot of brand names for that soft, fleecy synthetic material that most outdoor stores sell these days. I think that this is one of the few great synthetic things.

✔ **Rain jacket:** You can buy very high-tech, very expensive rain jackets that "breathe." That sounds good, but the only thing that I have ever found that keeps you dry in an all-day soaker is a *completely imperme-able* rain jacket. I always have one along when I am on a boat, not just for rain, but also to break the wind when you're making a move from one fishing spot to another. Get one that fits *over* your fishing vest. Make sure it has a hood. Waist-high is the best length for wading anglers.

If you don't feel like shelling out for a rain jacket, or if you forget yours, you can make a poncho out of a lawn-size garbage bag. Cut holes for the head and arms and, in a pinch, you're in business.

Does color make a difference?

If you can see the fish, the fish can see you — so, yes, color does make a difference. If you blend into the background, you will scare fewer fish. English fishermen wear green for the same reason that Robin Hood did: they blend into the background. In the American West, tans and browns work well. Out on the shallow ocean flats, you are going to look like a big silhouette, no matter what you do. Stay low and far away.

You Can't Fish without a Hat

They say that 40 percent of your body heat is lost through your head. In my opinion, anglers who don't wear a hat are also losing 40 percent of their brainpower. You need a hat when you fish. It keeps your brains from baking when the sun is out. It keeps the rain off. It shields your eyes so that you can see what the fish are doing when the sun is low in the sky — which is, coincidentally, the best time of the day to fish. The most popular hat is a plain old baseball cap, and that is what I wear most of the time. Some anglers prefer a long-billed hat, and this is a good idea for early morning and late afternoon fishing.

Dorky but not dumb

What the baseball cap design lacks is any sun protection of the neck and ears. Enter the most dweebish looking hat ever invented, the *Flats* hat. It was devised for fishing the sun-drenched bonefish flats of the Caribbean. It also has a long bill that is especially helpful in shielding your eyes from late afternoon and early morning sun, when it's particularly important to see well because that is when so much good fishing takes place. Recently they have started to make these hats with a chin strap — another silly-looking but practical feature, which I am sure you will seek out after your lose your ninth or tenth hat by having it blown off your head while speeding along in a boat.

Right next to the wine glasses

I have always treated baseball hats like baseball mitts. They just get older and more worn and full of salt stains from perspiration. My neighbor's teenage son taught me how to use the dishwasher to clean my favorite hat. You just put in on the upper tray, where you usually put cups and glasses, and run the washer normally. The hat will still be wet when the cycle is through, but don't put it in the dryer. Just let it air dry and your hat may not look brand new, but you (or your spouse) will see a large improvement in its general funkiness.

More shade

The long-billed hat is not the only possibility for fishermen. In very hot, direct sun, where you are fishing in the heat of the day, I like an open-weave straw hat with a reasonably wide brim. It throws shade on your head and shoulders and is well ventilated to let cooling breezes through.

Waders

If you are going to do any stream wading or surf casting, you need *waders*. The first thing you need to know about them is that they all leak sooner or later. It doesn't matter how much you pay or how well you take care of them, they are going to leak. Sometimes you will be able to find the leak and patch it, and sometimes you are just going to have to shell out for another pair.

- **The boot foot:** A one-piece chest-high outfit. The boot is attached to the legs. This is the most convenient design for dressing in a hurry. It is also the *only* design for surf casting because there is no way for sand or pebbles to find their way into the boot.

- **The stocking foot:** Stocking-foot waders (which are also chest high) do not come with a boot attached, so they require wading shoes. Many anglers prefer this because they say a sturdy wading boot gives them extra support while wading. On the minus side, they take a long time to put on and take off. Once they are on, you are basically committed to staying in waders until you are done fishing for the day. To prevent abrasion of the stocking foot, you should always wear a pair of wading socks *over* the foot of the wader.

- **Hip boots:** Great for fishing in streams in the summer. You can't get in nearly as deep as you can with chest-high waders, but if the river never gets that deep, why roast inside of chest waders?

Face it, waders are an inconvenience. You wouldn't wear them if you didn't have to. There is a range of wader materials that vary in durability and comfort.

✔ **Neoprene:** This is the material used in wet suits. If you are fishing in cold waters, neoprenes are the waders of choice. Walking around in them on a hot day, you will feel like a baked potato in a microwave oven. And they are devilish when they spring a leak: you have more chance of pitching a perfect game in the major leagues than you do of finding a pin-sized hole in neoprenes. So why get them? As I said, they are the *only* thing to fish in when the water is cold, below 60°F.

✔ **Rubber and rubberized:** When I started fishing, I bought rubberized canvas. You can still buy this material, and it works as well as it always did — which is pretty good. It doesn't get high marks in the mobility department, but it still moves more freely than the rubber waders that have lived in the trunk of my car since 1984. That pair cost $39.95, and although they are not super comfortable, they are indestructible.

✔ **Flyweights:** Lightweight rubberized synthetic. Great for traveling because they can roll up very tightly in your duffel bag. They offer no insulation, but a pair of sweatpants and thick wool socks worn under them help.

✔ **Breathables:** Made of Gore-Tex and its clones. These are the new kids on the block. Pretty pricey but ultra-comfortable. The jury is still out on durability.

A Lesson from Skin Divers

In the heat of the summer, I prefer to wet wade if at all possible. I started out using sneakers, but took a couple of spills on slippery rocks. If you have stocking foot waders, then you probably have wading shoes. Wear them over a pair or two of heavy socks. While fishing in the South Pacific a few years ago, I picked up a pair of the felt-bottom shoes used by pearl divers when they walk on sharp coral reefs. These "reef-walkers" are now found in most dive shops and a few tackle stores. The current generation of these little rubber booties, more costly than the nine dollar pair I bought in the town of Banana on Christmas Island, usually zip up the side and are snug enough to keep out sand and gravel.

Belts with suspenders

When I was a kid, we always had a laugh at the "old guys" who wore belts and suspenders. I still think it's kind of overkill for streetwear, but with most waders it's a must. You wear suspenders to hold up your waders, and the belt keeps water from rushing in if you get a dunking. This is a serious safety precaution. You can drown if your waders fill up.

Feltless free fall

You can buy waders and boots without felt soles, but you shouldn't. When rocks are covered with algae, wet leaves, dead seaweed, or unidentifiable slime, they are very slippery. Felt is clingier and helps counteract the slipperiness. Felt also wears out after a few years and you have to replace it. It's worth it. Felt is cheap. A broken fishing rod or bent reel is not.

Cleats are neat

A couple of years ago, I was fishing on a jetty that juts into the Atlantic. The guys on the end were deep into a run of false albacore. When I saw about half a dozen rods bent over, I felt compelled to hop the big jetty rocks to make my way out to the fishing. I was wearing felt, but it didn't matter. I hit a slippery spot and took a hellacious fall, right on my casting arm. Somehow I managed to grab onto a rock before an incoming wave swept me right off the jetty. I was lucky (although it took a couple of days and a lot of aspirin before I felt unsore enough to feel even remotely lucky). If I had been smart, I would have worn a pair of strap-on cleats. There are a few different kinds that you can buy. One is like a pair of rubbers with metal cleats on the bottom. They are murder to get on, but they never slip off. I prefer Korkers, which are more like a sandal with studs on the bottom. Either way, the metal makes for a very sure grip when it rubs up against stone. If I don't have them I just won't go out on a jetty anymore. They are also very helpful when wading a strong river like the Yellowstone.

Duct tape, the wader wonder

I have one mounted fish on my wall. He's a 6³/₄-pound brook trout with a bite taken out of his tail, no doubt in his careless youth. I caught him on a stream in Labrador in early August. When I hooked him, I worked my way over to the side of the stream to continue the fight where I had a chance of winning. This required me to fanny walk across a number of midstream boulders. As luck would have it, one of those boulders had a sharp edge that tore a five-inch gash in my flyweight waders. When I had calmed down from the excitement of my gorgeous brookie, reality set in. When you're in the middle of Labrador and the nearest store is over a hundred miles away, you can't just hop in the truck and get a wader repair kit at the nearest tackle shop (and there are no roads there anyway). I did have a roll of gaffer's tape, also known as duct tape, that lived in my duffel bag since I had worked as a gofer on local film crews. The first thing they teach you on a production is how to rip gaffer's tape with your teeth. It has a thousand and one uses on films and it earned a thousand and one thank-you's from me when I ripped off a piece and ran it alongside the gash in my waders. I got another two full seasons out of them, and in the end, it was the seams and not my patch that gave out. Moral of the story: Always carry a roll of duct tape on a fishing trip.

Vests

Vests are such a common sight that it's hard to imagine fishing without them. Yet until Lee Wulff had the bright idea of sewing some blue jeans pockets onto a denim vest about 60 years ago, there were no fishing vests. You can buy vests with a gazillion pockets and you can stuff every one of those pockets. And you can also make sure that you have every possible gizmo hanging off the little snaps and rings that many vests have. I know that some of you will because fishing, like every other pastime, has its share of gear freaks. However, I recommend that you take as *little* as possible in your vest.

There are five features to look for in a vest:

> ✓ **Two large outer pockets suitable for holding a box of lures or flies:** The pockets should open and fasten *from the top*. If your vest has pockets that open on the side, you will forget to zip up one day and eventually you will lose a box of expensive flies or lures.

- **Four inner pockets:** These are smaller, and it's okay if they only have velcro and no zippers. I like to put a box of split shot in one pocket, tippet or leader material in another, and bug repellent in another.

- **Four small outer pockets:** One should have a zipper for an extra car key. The rest are for a small box to carry flies, floatant, and this and that.

- **A metal ring:** I tie my clippers onto this. They do make retractable pin-on gadgets that are designed as clipper holders, but I have broken every one I ever bought and lost my clippers each time. I save old fly line for these kinds of jobs. I tie my clippers on with them. Fly line is also a free alternative to Croakers for holding your sunglasses when you want to keep them handy.

- **Outside back pouch:** Put your rain jacket in here, or maybe your lunch, water bottle, extra reel, and so on.

Sunglasses Make a Difference

You need sunglasses. On a sunny day, you will suffer much less eye fatigue if you wear them. But even more importantly, *polarized* glasses cut down on glare and enable you to see down into the water. You will see fish that are just not visible to the naked eye. And if you can see them, you have a much better chance of catching them. Polarized glasses provide the most assistance in seeing into the water when the sun is high in the sky. When it is low, the surface looks like one continuous, glaring sheet. Polarized lenses cut that glare and let you pick out a dry fly. As the light gets lower, you face a trade-off, because even though you are cutting glare, you are also letting in less light. At some point, you just can't find your fly anymore. When this happens, I try to fish without my sunglasses, but to tell you the truth, it rarely works. As for color, I fish with gray lenses that are said not to change the true colors of things. Many saltwater anglers prefer brown and amber, especially on the flats.

Ten things to keep in your vest

- **Sunscreen:** Use it for *all* daytime fishing.

- **Insect repellent:** You will feel like a real genius the next time you walk two miles to the fishing and the bugs are out in force *if you bring something to keep them from biting you.*

- **Clippers:** For cutting leader and trimming knots, clippers are preferable to teeth because clippers don't need to go to the dentist.

- **Thermometer:** Fish bite at certain temperatures and not at others. A thermometer tells you if you are wasting your time. Many tackle shops sell inexpensive thermometers designed to withstand being tossed about in vests and tackle boxes.

- **A plastic garbage bag:** You may not keep fish as a rule, but every so often you will want to, and who needs a vest full of fish slime? You don't need a lawn-size Hefty Bag; a wastebasket liner is more like it.

- **Forceps:** They help remove hooks more easily. This is good for the catch-and-release angler who wants to get the fish back in the water in a hurry. And it's always good for dealing with fish with sharp teeth.

- **Rain jacket:** It doesn't take up much room and it makes a big difference, especially when it rains!

- **Spare car key:** Everybody loses the car key sometimes. It's a bummer if this happens when it's dark and cold by the side of a trout stream 20 miles from home.

- **Flashlight:** They make small flashlights that you can clip on and aim so that you have two free hands for knot tying, removing hooks, and so forth. Then, on the way to the car, you can see where you are going. Don't leave home without this item!

- **First aid kit:** With the current boom in outdoor sports, it's easy to find a compact first aid kit. Buy one and keep it in your vest or tackle box at all times. In fact, if you have both a vest and a tackle box, buy two kits. You may never need them, but if and when you do, you will be most appreciative. If you are allergic, make sure you have something to treat severe allergic reactions of the type that are triggered by bee stings or other insects' bites.

Part IV
Eating

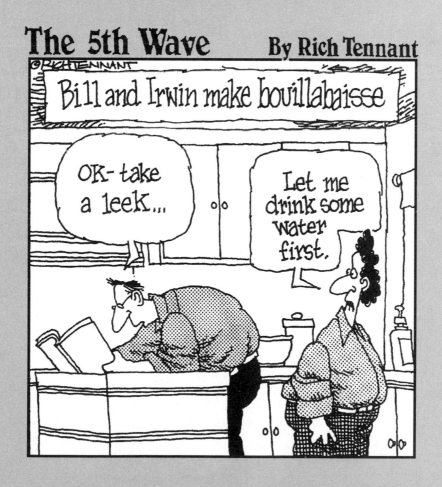

In this part . . .

Chapter 19 covers storing and cleaning your catch. I even show you how to cut fish into fillets and steaks. Chapter 20 contains some great tips for cooking fish, and I've also thrown in my ten favorite fish recipes. Chapter 21 offers some tips on photographing and mounting your trophy catches.

Chapter 19

Cleaning and Storing Your Catch

● ●

In This Chapter

▶ Scaling, gutting, and filleting fish

▶ Cleaning and not getting yelled at

▶ Keeping fish from getting that "fishy" taste

● ●

C leaning fish is not the most fun part of fishing. On a cold night, standing at the dock and filleting a mess of bluefish is a miserable, smelly job. But if you want to eat fish, you have to clean the fish, unless of course you are a parent, in which case my strong suggestion is, have your kids clean the fish.

Instant Karma

For the sake of good eating as well as being a nice person, you really should kill the fish right away (the exception is if you have a live well on your boat that is big enough to hold fish and keep them alive). It is not a good thing to leave the fish to flop and squirm and suffocate, whether it's in your creel, in an ice chest, or lying on the sand at the beach. There are two great advantages to killing quickly if you want to eat the fish.

✔ A quick kill allows you to dress the fish at the peak of freshness. All those guts can affect the flavor of the fish if you leave them in there all day.

✔ As with tomatoes or peaches or any foodstuff, bruised tissue is mealy. A dead fish will not flop around and bruise its flesh trying to escape.

Being a good executioner

I recommend that you buy yourself a small club called a *fish priest.* Then, once you have a fish you want to eat, you whack it over the head a couple of times. If you're out on the salt and you have brought in a bigger fish (up to 50 pounds or so), an old bowling pin serves wonderfully as a club. *Don't* try to kill any really big game until you have seen it done and participated in the kill with some experts. The object is to kill the fish, not the angler.

Storing and transporting

If there is anything that smells worse than bad fish, I don't want to know about it. But there is another side to this: Part of the reason that fish can turn so quickly is that they are so delicate. Handled with proper tender loving care, a well-cooked fish is one of the freshest-tasting things you can eat. A. J. McClane once explained the smell of fresh fish by saying that all fish, when kept properly fresh, will smell a little bit like a cucumber that you just sliced open. I never thought about it before, but once I started sticking my nose into the fish cooler, I noticed that McClane was right.

There are a number of schools of thought on the question of when to clean fish and how to store them. Take your pick.

- **Willow creel:** The willow creel is a classic for a reason. The weave of the willow branches allows air to circulate, which is what you want. If you use a willow creel, the accepted old-timey way to keep fish is to line the bottom of the creel with green grass and then to put a layer of grass between the layers of fish. This method is good for a few hours (no more) in hot weather.

- **Canvas creel:** Less pricey than willow creels. These usually have a washable plastic liner inside a canvas outer bag. If you dip the creel in water and get it good and soaked, evaporation will help cool fish. As with the willow creel, the canvas creel is for the freshwater angler.

- **Ice chest:** Open the chest, put the dead fish in. Close the chest.

- **Live well:** You will find these on many boats. A live well is a compartment through which water passes. In most cases, you can keep fish alive in them for hours.

- **A stringer:** A piece of string, rope, or specially designed set of metal clips passed through one gill of the fish. You can keep a mess of fish alive this way by tying one end of the string to your boat and putting the other end (with all the fish on it) back in the water. This is more of a freshwater tactic. I don't recommend it in the ocean because big game fish on the prowl will treat your stringer as a nice big gob of live bait.

Cleaning: Or, Why God Made Day-Old Newspapers

Fish cleaning can be a kitchen-destroying operation: scales flying everywhere, drying and sticking to everything, and guts sliding off the counter and clogging up the sink. Speaking from long and tragic experience, I can tell you that part of the reason that many wives secretly hope that their husbands come home fishless is that they do not want to deal with the mess. Guess what — it doesn't have to be that messy. My advice to you is that whenever possible, you clean the fish *before* you bring it into the kitchen.

You only need one tool to dress most fish: a good knife. My favorite is the Dexter, an American-made carbon steel knife that retails for less than $20. It sharpens easily, holds an edge fairly well, and performs double duty for vegetable slicing, cheese slicing, and any other general chopping or slicing chore. I also have a Martini, which is a very thin Finnish fillet knife that also works well as an all-rounder — but in the end, the Dexter works the best. Its blade is thin and with a slight curve that works well for filleting tasks, and it has enough oomph to cut through the backbone of a larger fish when you are making steaks. I wish it came with a sheath or holder, but it doesn't. Most anglers fashion a case out of two pieces of cardboard taped together.

Scaling

Although every fish has scales, not every fish needs to be scaled. The scales on a trout, for example, are so small that you don't have to worry about them. In fact, you wouldn't know there were any scales on a trout if someone like me hadn't told you. *Note:* If you are going to fillet the fish *and remove the skin,* there is no need to scale. Otherwise, here's what you do:

1. **First, take some newspaper and lay out about four spreads.**

2. **Run the knife against the grain of the scale.**

   (*Note:* They do make specialized fish scalers, which are probably worth the small investment, but you will probably end up losing yours, as I did mine.)

   Your motion should be firm enough to remove the scales, but not so strong that they go flying all over the place.

3. **When you have finished scaling, lift the fish and peel back the top sheet of paper. Lay the fish down on the next (clean) sheet of newspaper and throw out the top sheet with the scales.**

4. **Rinse the fish.**

Gutting

You gut a fish to get rid of the organs in the body cavity. These are filled with all kinds of gunk, including digestive juices. For this reason you want to exercise care in slitting open the belly. It's less messy and keeps the flesh fresher if you don't pierce the organs while gutting.

1. **With the blade pointed toward the head, pierce the stomach cavity and make a slit toward the head. Try not to make too deep a cut, just enough to get through the top layer of skin and flesh.**

2. **Now pointing the knife toward the tail, completely open the stomach cavity.**

3. **Reach in and pull out the guts.**

4. **Detach the gills with the knife, or simply pull away.**

5. **Wrap the guts in the top sheet of paper and discard.**

Filleting

It takes a certain amount of touch to fillet a fish, but expending a little more effort at the cleaning stage is worth it because it means no bones at the eating stage. When you get the hang of filleting, you can zip through a pile of fish pretty quickly, and it gives you a sense of accomplishment that you can do something as well as the old-timers.

Don't worry too much if you don't get absolutely all the meat off the fish when you first start filleting. The idea at the beginning is to get *some*. If you skin the fish, as recommended, you do not have to scale it first. Obviously, if you are going to use the skin, scale it unless you like to eat scales. Figure 19-1 shows the basics of filleting a small fish (up to about 5 pounds).

1. **Cut off the head just behind the gills.**

2. **Hold the fish by the tail. With the knife blade pointing away from you and across the body of the fish, begin to cut toward the head (or at least where the head used to be). Use the backbone to guide your knife.**

3. **To take the skin off, begin by holding the fillet by the tail, skin side down.**

4. **Hold the knife crosswise across the fillet and insert the knife between the skin and the flesh. Don't worry if you don't get this perfect at first.**

5. **While holding the skin, cut in the direction of the former head.**

When you have a larger fish, the tail-to-head method of filleting can be a little awkward. In this case opening the fish like a book is an effective method, as shown in Figure 19-2.

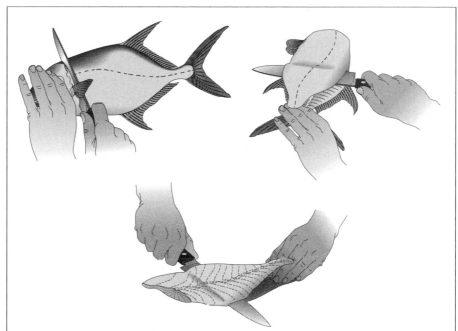

Figure 19-1:
Filleting a
small fish.

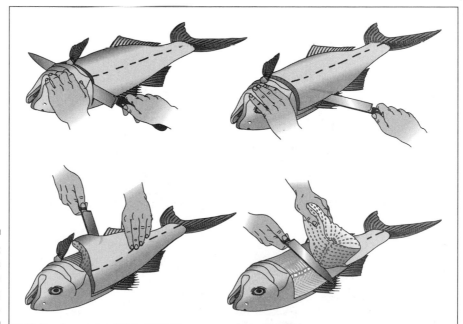

Figure 19-2:
Try this
technique
for filleting
larger fish.

Follow these steps (shown in Figure 19-2) to fillet a larger fish:

1. **Make a deep cut just behind the gills (about halfway through the thickness of the fish).**

2. **Cut a slit a few inches in length along the top of the fish (the dorsal side).**

3. **Using the tip of the knife, separate the flesh from the bones, as illustrated. The fish should open up just like a book.**

4. **When completely open, finish cutting away the fillet by moving the knife along the "spine of the book."**

Cutting steaks

I am not a big fan of the current fashion at expensive and fashionable restaurants where one part of the meal is named after another: Fish Sorbet, Fruit Soup, Rack of Turnip. However, *fish steak* is an old and time-honored phrase. Many people don't go in for cooking fish steaks because they are too dry. My advice to you: Make thinner steaks, an inch or less.

You can use a Dexter for making steaks or a wide-bladed chef's knife (the kind chefs use on TV when they chop vegetables). Figure 19-3 walks you through the steps of cutting fish steaks.

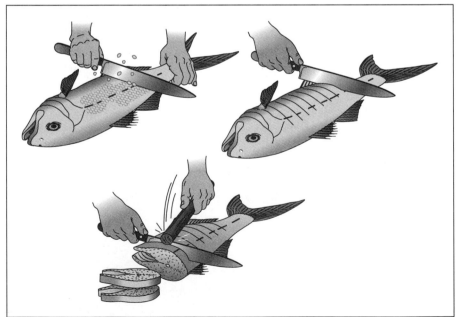

Figure 19-3:
Cutting a
fish into
steaks.

Simple and great

One of the most memorable fish meals I have had was in Northern Labrador, fishing for big brookies. Our guide, Howard Guptiel, had kept a "small" brookie for lunch: 4 lbs. This was no fish for pan-frying. Instead, he fried up some un-Canadian bacon, so that there was some fat left over. Then he dredged the brookie steaks in a little flour and fried them in the grease. The flesh was as orange as a hunting vest. The hot, salty fat and some ground black pepper were all it needed. I learned that day that freshness will do for flavor what youth does for looks (that is, you don't have to do much messing around to get a good result). The fish was so good, in fact, that I brought home two more small fish to make for my grandfather's 85th birthday. Grandpa was a great fish eater and, since fish were held in high esteem in Poland at the turn of the century, he told me an old Russian proverb about making do with what you have: "If no fish, then lobster will do." True words that also reflect the way I feel about fish — which I love — and lobster, although good, is really just a big insect as far as its sporting qualities are concerned.

1. **Scale the fish.**

2. **Make a row of cuts crosswise along the fish. Space the cuts so that they are the thickness of the steaks.**

3. **Cut down to the backbone.**

4. **With a mallet, a rolling pin, or a thick branch, strike the back of the knife blade so that it goes through the backbone.**

   This is not the place to perfect a big swing for your rock-breaking technique in case you ever end up on a chain gang. A short chop should do it.

5. **If your stroke doesn't completely detach the steak, continue to cut through the flesh and skin until the steak falls away from the rest of the fish.**

Freezing

Frozen fish does not have the consistency of flesh that has never been frozen. The physics behind this are simple. Living cells are filled with water. Water expands when frozen, and this expansion breaks down tissue. However, if you are not going to eat fish right away — like within a day — then I recommend freezing. It keeps the fish tasting fresh. For example, many people have told me they don't like the taste of bluefish. It's too oily, they say, or too "fishy." What they are really referring to is the taste of fish oil that has come in contact with the air and turned rancid. Bluefish has a lot of oil, so unless you cook it on the day you catch it, it will have that oily, fishy taste. Freezing stops this process short and preserves the fresh taste. I usually freeze fish that I have filleted first. Wrap each fillet in wax paper. Store them in a Ziploc bag, keeping the fillets flat.

Chapter 20

Cooking, Eating
(And Sometimes Drinking)

. . . .

In This Chapter

▶ Fish cooking basics

▶ Frying

▶ Poaching

▶ Broiling

▶ Roasting

▶ My favorite fish recipes

. . . .

*I*f people hadn't started eating fish a long time ago, I doubt that anyone would have had the bright idea of fishing for them just for the fun of it. Now, of course, we know what a kick it is to have a good fish on the line whether we keep it or throw it back. Still, at the root of it all, there is the quest for food, and fish is a great food.

Is It Done Yet?

Fish is cooked or it isn't. There is no such thing as a medium-cooked fish. It really is an on-off switch. One minute the fish is milky looking, semi-transparent, and hard to cut with a fork. Then, just like that, the flesh turns opaque and a fork will flake it easily: the fish is done.

I know it like the back — I mean front — of my hand

Tom Colicchio, who is a gonzo fishing addict, is also the chef at one of New York's top restaurants, Gramercy Tavern. One night, after a long day on the Delaware River, a bunch of us gathered round the campfire while Tom whipped up a rack of veal to go with some wild mushrooms and ramps that we had gathered. Using nothing more than a simple mess kit, he turned out a gourmet meal in about a half hour. I noticed the way he tested the meat for doneness by prodding it with his finger. The same technique can also be used to test the doneness of fish or any cooked flesh for that matter.

First, hold out your hand with the palm facing you. Move your thumb so that it's butted up against the rest of the fingers. Check out the little lump of flesh where the base of the thumb pushes up a mound in the palm. Poke that area with the index finger of your other hand. That's how meat feels when it is uncooked or very rare.

Now spread your fingers. The mound of flesh disappears. Take the index finger of your other hand and prod the same place again. It resists. That's what cooked flesh feels like.

Ten minutes to the inch

You can't always poke fish this way to test it. For example, when you are deep frying, how could you possibly stick your finger in there? The best guestimate method I know was originally published by the Canadian Fisheries Board, and it is very simple. Whether you boil, fry, poach, or broil, you should cook fish no longer than *ten minutes for each inch of thickness*. What this means is that you measure the fish at its thickest part and multiply it by ten minutes for each inch. The one exception is charcoal broiling. In this case, use the ten minutes to the inch rule as a rough guide. The intensity of the fire and the closeness of the fish to the fire will lengthen or, more often, shorten the cooking time.

The more experienced cooks among you will no doubt have reckoned that the Canadian Fish rule means the thin part of the fillet is going to be done before the fat part. You're right. However most fillets are pretty uniform in thickness, as are all steaks, so I usually don't worry about it.

A neat way to even up the thickness of fillets that have a long thin "tail" is simply to flip the tail over so that the thin end of the fillet is doubled up, which means it will respond to heating the same way that a thicker piece would. Thanks to chef Susan Spicer of Dayona in New Orleans for this tip.

Marinate with Caution

Everybody likes marinated food. Garlic, salt, wine, soy sauce, lemon juice — all the classic marinating ingredients — sound so good. A duck or a cut of venison can sometimes be marinated for days to the benefit of the completed dish. Marinating is used to give flavor and/or to tenderize tough cuts of meat. Basically, there is no such thing as a tough cut of fish. So by all means, pile on the lemon juice, the white wine, the teriyaki sauce, but half an hour of marinating will give it more than enough flavor without giving your fish the consistency of a wet paper towel.

Fearless Frying

Crispy, crunchy, salty. Show me someone who doesn't like fried fish and I will show you someone who is possibly an extraterrestrial. The big trick with frying is *hot oil.* If the oil isn't hot enough, the coating will absorb a lot of grease, and you have yourself a potential stomachache with some nice heartburn thrown in for good measure. With hot oil, the crust is crisp light and non-greasy.

I am one of those people who needs to mind my cholesterol intake, so I don't use Crisco anymore, but you can, and it does a great frying job because it has a high smoking point, which means the oil can get good and hot. I cook a lot with olive oil these days, which takes a fair amount of heat before it smokes.

The best fish frying recipe I know is also the first one I learned. I was in the Florida Keys and I had caught a nice grouper. The captain, whose name I forget, gave me this recipe, which I have used ever since. He also told me that the best cure for seasickness was to wrap both arms around an oak tree.

Fried Fish
Serves 4

> *1 cup (250 mL) flour*
>
> *1 teaspoon (5 mL) salt*
>
> *1 tap ground black pepper*
>
> *1 cup (250 mL) buttermilk*
>
> *1 cup (250 mL) cornmeal*
>
> *8 fillets of fish, trimmed to four inches in length*

1. **Season the flour with salt and pepper; then dredge fillets in flour.**

2. **Shake off excess flour and, one at a time, dip fillets in buttermilk; then dredge in cornmeal.**

3. **As each fillet is done, put it in a preheated cast-iron pan with about an inch of oil, very hot.**

4. **After about 2 minutes (see the aforementioned Canadian Fisheries Board rule), use tongs to turn fish.**

5. **Fry another 2 minutes; then remove and drain on paper towels.**

Poaching Allowed

If people know you are an angler and you get married, I guarantee one of your friends will give you a fish poacher, one of those long pots with a little rack inside to lift out the poached fish. It's a good thing to have, but I can honestly say I don't know anybody who ever bought a fish poacher on their own. You can poach fish without one, but a poacher sure makes the job a lot easier.

Poaching is a method of cooking fish that is well suited to delicate flesh (and most fish is pretty delicate). It allows the flavor and texture of the fish to come through. If the fish is absolutely fresh, you might want to serve it with nothing more than steamed potatoes. Once you've poached the fish, you can serve it hot or cold. For me, cold poached fish with some dill or mustard mayonnaise is pretty hard to beat.

Poached Fish
Serves 4

> *1 large fillet*
>
> *poaching liquid to cover fish (recipe follows)*

Making poaching liquid (fish stock)

> *4 cups (1 L) water or dry white wine*
>
> *fish bones and head*
>
> *1 carrot*
>
> *1 onion*
>
> *1 celery stalk*
>
> *$^1/_2$ teaspoon (2.5 mL) salt*
>
> *10 black peppercorns*
>
> *sprig of parsley*

1. **After filleting fish, discard guts. Put skeleton and head in pot with other ingredients.**

2. **Simmer 20 minutes.**

3. **Strain and save the liquid; discard remaining ingredients.**

Poaching the fish

Now that you have fish stock, you can actually poach the fish:

1. **Place fish on poaching rack in poacher.**

   If you don't have a poacher, any pan big enough to hold the fish will do.

2. **Cover fish with stock.**

3. **Bring to boil and then simmer.**

4. **Simmer 10 minutes per inch of thickness.**

5. **When the fish is done, lift it out of the broth using the two handles on the poaching rack.**

   If you don't have a poacher, stick a couple of slotted spatulas underneath the fish and gently lift it out so that it doesn't break apart.

6. **Garnish with parsley or dill and serve with mustard sauce, homemade mayonnaise, salsa, or anything else with a little tang and taste to it that catches your fancy.**

   Experiment because fish prepared this way is kind of like chicken: It picks up the flavor of whatever you serve it with.

Broiling

Salty, crusty, and peppery. Broiled fish when you order it in a restaurant is a lot of fun. When you make it at home, however, it never seems to come out that way because your broiler most likely isn't as hot as one of those gas-powered top-broilers that they use in restaurants. So if you are even able to get that nice crust on top, by the time you do, the fish is as dry as an un-oiled baseball mitt. I forget about broiling unless I can make fish on the barbecue, which brings up a whole other set of problems.

Help! My fish is broke

If you barbecue, fish fillets tend to break apart and fall through the slots on the grill. However, there is a product that came out on the market in the last few years that has virtually revolutionized my fish-grilling life. It's cheap, uncomplicated, and it works, which are three unusual things to find in a new product these days. It's called a Griffo Grill, and the simple original version (which I haven't seen lately) is nothing more than heavy window screening that you lay on top of your grill. Flipping is no longer an anxious game of waiting and seeing if the fish is going to fall apart. The recent, more jazzed up version is a piece of enameled steel with pea-size holes. The principle is the same in both models: Little holes to let the radiant heat through are small enough to keep fish flakes from falling off.

Broiled Fish

fish (fillets or steaks)

salt

black pepper

olive oil

paprika (optional)

lemon juice (optional)

1. **Brush fillets or fish steaks with oil.**

2. **Salt and pepper to taste. Dust with paprika if you want to get a nice red and black charred look.**

3. **Place on hot grill — 10 minutes per inch of thickness.**

4. **Remove from grill and squeeze lemon juice on fish.**

Hey, the skin sticks to the grill! What do I do?

There is basically no way that I know of to keep pieces of skin from sticking to the grill. Don't cook with the skin on your fillets if this bothers you.

Baking and Roasting

There are no special tips or techniques here. The fish goes in the oven preheated to 350° and cooks ten minutes per inch. The real art is in the ingredients, a few of which are listed in the recipes that follow.

My Favorite Fish Recipes

The following recipes aren't the only ones by a long shot, but they are a really good spectrum of techniques. Once you have mastered these, experiment to your heart's content. If you hit on any great ones, let me know.

Extremely Fresh Trout (Truite au Bleu)

A very impressive way to make trout. When you do it correctly, the skin turns a deep blue that never ceases to amaze people, much to the delight of the chef. Best of all, it is a no-brainer. For the fish, it is literally a no-brainer because the recipe calls for killing the fish with a sharp blow to the head just before cooking.

> *1 quart (1 L) fish stock (see the section on poached fish)*
>
> *¹/₂ cup (125 mL) vinegar*

1. **Bring stock to boil in a poaching pan (or any pan, if no poaching pan is available).**
2. **Kill the live trout with a sharp blow to the head.**
3. *Immediately* **gut the fish.**
4. *Immediately* **plunge the trout into the boiling stock. When it returns to the boil, remove from heat and cover for 5-8 minutes.**

   The eyeballs turn white and pop out when the fish is done. Kids have a lot of comments on this step in the recipe.

5. **Remove the fish by lifting out the poaching rack (or by using a pair of slotted spatulas) and serve.**

Door County Fish Boil

Door County is a very long and thin peninsula that sticks out into Lake Michigan just above Greenbay, Wisconsin. Generations of commercial fishermen have made their living hauling their catch out of the rich lake waters. This recipe, which I have modified for the home cook, originated in a shore dinner that the fishing boat captains used to make for their crews and families. The original recipe calls for 20 pounds of potatoes and 20 pounds of lake trout, but the lamprey eels that made their way into the lake a half a century ago did such a good job of decimating the lakers that nowadays, everyone makes this dish with whitefish chunks. Also, the original fish boil takes place outside over a really big fire. The last step in this recipe calls for the cook to throw the contents of a #10 can filled with gasoline onto the fire. This produces a super-hot fireball, and the water in the kettle boils over, taking any fish oils or dirt with it. My advice to you is don't throw gasoline on your indoor range. Serves 4 hungry diners or six "pickers."

> *2 lbs (1 Kg) medium red potatoes, scrubbed and cut in half*
>
> *4 white fish steaks, $^1/_2$ pound (250 g) each (This recipe also works well with striped bass and probably a lot of other fish that I haven't tried.)*
>
> *8 small onions, peeled*
>
> *2 quarts (2 L) water*
>
> *2 tablespoons (30 mL) kosher salt*
>
> *black pepper to taste*
>
> *2 tablespoons (30 mL) chopped parsley*

1. **In a large stock pot, combine the potatoes and onions with 2 quarts water (enough to cover the vegetables by 2 inches). Stir in salt and bring to a boil. Cook for about 15 minutes with the pot partially covered until the potatoes are almost tender when pierced with a fork.**

2. **Arrange the fish in a single layer on top of the vegetables. (Don't worry if the fish isn't entirely covered by the water.) Lower heat to moderate and cook until the whitefish flakes easily (about 10 minutes).**

3. **Using a slotted spoon, transfer the whitefish to a large, warm platter. Spoon the potatoes and onions around the fish. Sprinkle with parsley and black pepper to taste. Serve with melted butter and lemon wedges alongside.**

Gasper Goo Court Bouillon

Man, woman, and child . . . all Cajuns cook. And just as universally, all Cajuns have fishing and hunting camps they go to every chance they get. Some of these camps are nicer than my house, and some are just a shack in a small clearing. All of them share one feature, however, and that is what Cajuns call an Old Black Pot, but which the rest of us call a Dutch oven — a heavy cast-iron pot for cooking soups and stews. This recipe was shown to me by an ex-Mississippi riverboat pilot named Alan Zeringue. Along with another old-time swamper named Connie Serrette, Alan nets freshwater drum — the Cajuns call it gasper goo — in the fast moving Atchafalaya river in western

Louisiana. You can make this recipe with any firm-fleshed fish, adding water or white wine to cover the fish. You don't need to do this with goo because it gives up a lot of water during the cooking process.

Serves 6 to 8

4 lbs (2 Kg) gaspergoo fillet

$^1/_3$ cup (83 mL) oil

1 bell pepper

4 cloves garlic

2 large onions

1 celery stalk

3 8-ounce (250-g) cans Hunts tomato sauce

1 cup green onion tops (scallion tops)

salt and cayenne pepper to taste

1. **Chop vegetables and sauté for 5 minutes in cast-iron pot.**
2. **Add tomato sauce and simmer for 30 minutes.**
3. **Meanwhile, season fish to taste, and don't be shy with the cayenne. It not only adds zip, but it also pulls flavor out of the other ingredients.**
4. **Add fish, cover, and simmer for 45 minutes.**
5. **Add chopped green onion tops 5 minutes before stew finishes simmering.**
6. **Serve with white rice.**

Poached Whiting with Littleneck Clams

In the wintertime, there isn't a whole lot of fishing going on in the northeastern U.S.; however, you will meet other die-hard anglers on the party boats that are usually the only game in town for anglers. I love to go out from the old fishing village at Sheepshead Bay in Brooklyn. I don't think anyone could ever run into a more varied group of anglers speaking more languages than you do on one of these boats. An old Sicilian gave me this recipe for whiting on one of those 60° days that brings out the fishermen and women and helps to lighten the sentence of a New York February.

Serves 4

>*4 whole, gutted whitings*
>
>*1 dozen scrubbed littleneck clams*
>
>*¹/₂ cup (125 mL) white wine*
>
>*1 clove garlic peeled*
>
>*¹/₄ cup (62.5 mL) chopped parsley*

1. **Place fish in the Dutch oven and surround them with clams. Add garlic. Pour in wine and bring to simmer.**

2. **When the liquid begins to simmer, cover the pot and continue the low simmer for 10 to 12 minutes. The clams will steam open and add their broth to the cooking liquid.**

3. **When the whiting is done, add the fresh chopped parsley. Put the fish in a wide flat bowl with a few clams. Pour broth in the bowls and serve with a crusty French or Italian bread.**

Halibut Stew with Red Wine Sauce

They say that red wine is for meat and white wine is for fish. This recipe is yet another reason I want to meet that famous "they" because, as you will see when you taste this marvelous recipe, "they" don't know what "they" are talking about. Thanks for this dish go to my good friend and cooking buddy Bryan Miller, author of *Cooking For Dummies* and the former Restaurant Critic of *The New York Times*.

Serves 4

>*2 tablespoons (30 mL) butter*
>
>*¹/₂ pound (250 Kg) small mushrooms; if large, cut into quarters*
>
>*¹/₂ cup (125 mL) finely chopped onion*
>
>*¹/₄ cup (62.5 mL) finely chopped shallots*
>
>*¹/₄ cup (62.5 mL) finely chopped carrots*
>
>*¹/₄ cup (62.5 mL) finely chopped celery*
>
>*1 teaspoon (5 mL) finely chopped garlic*
>
>*2 teaspoons (10 mL) chopped fresh thyme or 1 teaspoon dried*
>
>*1 bay leaf*
>
>*2 tablespoons (30 mL) flour*
>
>*1¹/₂ cups (375 mL) dry red wine*

1 cup (250 mL) fresh fish broth (see the poaching recipe) or bottled clam juice

2 cloves

1¹/₂ pounds (750 g) halibut fillets cut into ¹/₂-inch (1.25-cm) cubes

Salt and freshly ground pepper to taste

2 tablespoons (30 mL) cognac

2 tablespoons (30 mL) finely chopped parsley

1. **Heat the butter in a saucepan and add the mushrooms, onion, shallots, carrots, celery, garlic, thyme, and bay leaf. Stir until the onion is wilted.**

2. **Add the flour and stir. Add the wine, fish broth, and cloves, stirring with a wire whisk. Bring to a boil. Simmer for 20 minutes and reduce liquid to about 1³/₄ cups (425 mL).**

3. **Add the fish, salt, and pepper, stirring gently so that the fish is coated with the sauce. Simmer for about 5 minutes and add the cognac. Sprinkle with parsley and serve.**

Reddened Blackfish

Blackening, unless it's done right, is a perfect way to take good food and use it to fumigate your house with smoke. James Graham, a great fish and game chef in Lafayette, Louisiana, came up with an alternative. He calls it bronzed fish. Northeasterners might try this with a blackfish fillet, or West coasters can try it with white sea bass. After all, if we have been eating blackened redfish for all these years, then why not some reddened blackfish? Actually, you can use any fish for this technique. The result is a quick, clean, beautiful red-gold crust of powerful spices.

You can get blackening spices pre-mixed in many stores these days, but just in case, I am including a spice recipe that I found in an excellent cookbook called *Cajun Men Cook,* which you may order through The Beaver Club, P.O. Box 2744, Lafayette, LA., 70502.

Blackening (or bronzing) spices

1 teaspoon (5 mL) onion powder

³/₄ teaspoon (3.75 mL) oregano

³/₄ teaspoon (3.75 mL) thyme

1 teaspoon (5 mL) black pepper

1 teaspoon (5 mL) white pepper

1 teaspoon (5 mL) cayenne pepper

2 teaspoons (10 mL) salt

4 teaspoons (20 mL) paprika

1 teaspoon (5 mL) granulated garlic powder

Combine the seasoning in a bowl and mix well.

Bronzing the fish

¹/₈ cup (30 mL) corn, peanut, or olive oil

4 fillets of white-fleshed fish (redfish, blackfish, weakfish, snapper, dolphin, and so on)

Lemon wedges

1. **Rinse the fillets and pat dry. Dredge in seasoning. Set aside.**

2. **Cover pan with 1/8 inch (3 mm) of oil and heat over medium high flame. When the oil is good and hot but not yet smoking, fry the fillets for 2 to 3 minutes on each side.**

3. **Remove fillets from heat and serve with fresh lemon wedges.**

Speckled Trout, Islamorada Style

Islamorada, in the Florida Keys, is one of the best fishing-friendly towns in the U.S. The best dining, or at least my favorite, has always been at Manny & Isa's. It's a simple road house run by a Guatemalan couple who raise their own key limes (for their sublime key lime pie).

The chef has a light hand with fried fish, and I always try some, served with fried plantains and a salad. There are two sauces, both homemade, that are plunked down with the fish: one of green chilies and garlic; the other of tomato, mint, garlic, and chili peppers. Try them and the words "tartar sauce" may disappear from your vocabulary.

This dish gets its zip from my version of Manny & Isa's tomato mint sauce. Topped off with frizzled onions or leeks, it looks like a real restaurant dish. As with many of these recipes, any white fleshed fish will do if you can't get specks or weakfish.

The fish

Serves 4

2 large fillets of speckled trout, skinned

2 tablespoons (30 mL) olive oil

salt

pepper

1. **Brush fillets with olive oil; add salt and pepper to taste.**
2. **Grill over hot coals, turning once.**

The salsa

1 diced chili pepper

2 cloves diced garlic

1 diced shallot or scallion

2 ripe tomatoes, peeled, seeded, and chopped (or, if you don't feel like peeling and seeding, just chop the tomatoes)

¹/₄ cup (62.5 mL) chopped fresh mint

¹/₄ cup (62.5 mL) white wine or lemon juice (or both)

2 teaspoons (10 mL) olive oil

1. **Sauté chili pepper for 1 minute in hot olive oil. Then add garlic and shallots for another minute.**
2. **Add chopped tomatoes and simmer for a few minutes until most of the liquid has evaporated.**
3. **Add mint, stir, and pour salsa over the cooked fillets.**
4. **Deglaze the pan with wine and/or lemon juice, pour over fish, and serve.**

Great South Bay Roast Striper

No turkey or standing rib roast ever arrived at the table to more oohs and aahs than this dish, a large striper, stuffed with minced local shellfish.

This meal, or rather, the idea for the meal began as I was visiting my friend Neil Ganek's take-out shop (Petite Crevette or The Little Shrimp) on Atlantic Avenue in Brooklyn. Ganek, who served a hitch as a tank driver in his native Yugoslavia, got his discharge at the age of 19 and took off to see the world, cooking on a succession of tramp steamers for nearly six years.

To make the meal, we all trooped to Barry Kanavy's bay house, out in Long Island's Great South Bay. It is a perfect headquarters for fishing and hunting activities, and what makes it even more fun is that Barry won it in a card game, although when I ask him what he was holding, he claims not to remember. "It was a long night and we had a few," he recalls.

The most tricky part of this dish (which serves eight) is removing the skeleton from the uncooked fish, which you do by cutting from the top: First, slit the fish along the backbone. Then cut and separate the two fillets from the spine. Snip the backbone and remove the skeleton. Next, cut open the stomach from the top and remove the innards.

For the stuffing

> *1¹/₂ cups (375 mL) scallops*
>
> *1 dozen oysters*
>
> *1 dozen clams*
>
> *1¹/₂ cups (375 mL) crab meat*
>
> *1 shallot*
>
> *2 cloves garlic*
>
> *3 egg whites*
>
> *1 cup (250 mL) bread crumbs*
>
> *1 tablespoon (15mL) Dijon mustard*
>
> *2 tablespoons (30 mL) applejack (or brandy)*

1. **Dice the shellfish.**

2. **Sauté the shallot and garlic cloves and add to the shellfish. Combine in a large bowl with egg whites, bread crumbs, mustard, and applejack.**

For the fish

> *1 striped bass, 6 to 8 pounds (3 to 4 Kg)*
>
> *¹/₄ cup (62.5 mL) olive oil*
>
> *juice of 2 limes and 2 lemons*
>
> *basil, rosemary, thyme (to taste)*
>
> *1 teaspoon (5 mL) crushed red pepper flakes (optional)*

1. **Stuff the bass and sprinkle with olive oil and lemon juice.**
2. **Add remaining spices and lime juice to pan.**
3. **Roast at 375˚F for approximately 1 hour.**
4. **Serve on a big platter, cutting the bass crosswise like a big sausage.**

Hey, How about the Fisherman?

Putting food on the table is one of the great satisfactions of angling, but putting food in your stomach while you're fishing ranks right up there. For some reason, the person who normally eats one sandwich between breakfast and dinner, can scarf up three or four in a day on the water, plus candy bars, nuts, dried fruit, and more candy bars. Pay attention to food and drink and you will spend a more pleasurable day with rod and reel. Pangs of hunger and thirst are particularly annoying when you're five miles up a stream or ten miles out at sea.

Salt + water = happiness

Most of us fish in the warmer months, which also means that most of us are going to perspire more and develop a powerful thirst. Take plenty of liquids. I find that nothing beats cold water. When I take along a cooler, I will sometimes save space by putting in a couple of water bottles that I have kept in the freezer. As the ice melts over the course of the day, I get refreshing cold water, and at the same time, the rest of my food is chilled.

Lauri Rapala's nursery rhyme

Enzo Rapala, the son of the inventor of the famed Rapala lure, once took me fishing on a Finnish lake using a boat just like his dad's, a canoe-like boat with oars called a soutavene. While we trolled around for trout, Enzo recited a poem that his dad used to like in the old days. It's about fishermen and the food they catch.

Row the boat, row the boat

Hear the creaking oars

Cast the net

Through the weeds

Pull the catch ashore.

There's a tail for the mate

Who pulls the fish in

A belly for the cook who boils him

But only a fish head for the fisherman.

If you are going out for a whole day, take two quarts of water. If you are wearing a fishing vest, two 16-ounce bottles are all you can comfortably carry. In either case, drink a good amount of water before you begin fishing.

You're out in the Rocky Mountains. It's a beautiful day. There's snow on the mountain tops and wildflowers along the stream bank. You've been fishing in the hot dry air for two hours and you decided to sit down for a rest. You're thirsty. The water looks really refreshing, right out of a Busch Beer commercial. As they say in my part of Brooklyn, "fuhged abowdit." High mountain streams often carry a bacterium known as *giardia* that can make you awfully sick. Bring your drinks in with you.

A product plug (honestly, they didn't pay me a thing)

When it's really hot, if you are like me, you are going to sweat buckets. Sometimes losing all those salts and fluids makes me feel like quitting at midday. My solution is Gatorade. Not only does it slake your thirst, but it also replenishes the salts and minerals that come pouring out of you when you sweat a lot. I drink a whole 16-ounce bottle before I go fishing and then take along two quart bottles for the day. I don't get so tired anymore.

Beer, wine, booze

Most serious anglers that I know do their drinking after they fish. There's nothing the matter with a beer on a hot day. Come to think of it, there is probably nothing better, but alcohol tends to slow me down, and I want to be sharp when that world-record bass gently taps my worm.

So as far as drinking and driving a boat go, I think there are cheaper ways to commit suicide.

Road rules

The greatest naval hero in English history, Lord Nelson, once said, "East of Gibraltar, all men are bachelors." Since Nelson had a live-in girlfriend in Italy while his wife was in England, I can understand what prompted him to develop this philosophy. Fishing trips are a little bit like this for people who are watching their waistlines or their fat intake. They may treat butter like the plague when they are home, but once they go fishing, they can't get enough of thick sandwiches, piled high with artery clogging cold cuts and slices of fat-rich cheese. There are two schools of thought on this. The Pig Out school says that you should treat fishing as a special treat, a dispensation from having to eat a healthy diet in the "real world." The Guilty Conscience school says "Don't do it." I come down squarely in the middle. If you are going out for a day's fishing, a big old hero sandwich will probably bring you so much pleasure that I say go for it. On the other hand, a week of Big Macs, fried eggs, and steaks is not necessary. You can eat tuna sandwiches, roast vegetables, soups, baked beans, salads, cold cereal, fruit, pretzels, sardines, and so on. And, oh yeah, you can also cook up a few fish.

Some sandwich thoughts

I am taking it for granted that you already know how to make a sandwich. Over the years, I have found just a few common-sense things that have resulted in better sandwich eating or at least less sandwich disasters in the bottom of the cooler.

Wrap small and tight

A big hero sandwich looks great, but you will not normally eat it all at once. Then you are in the position of having to rewrap it, which hardly anyone ever does properly, and the result is a lot of salami, lettuce, and tomato bits rolling around the cooler or the back of your vest. Cut the sandwich into smaller pieces and wrap each piece individually. I use wax paper for wrapping and then I put everything inside a Ziploc bag.

Dry is good

While soggy bread may be good for bait, it's lousy on a sandwich. Remember that a sandwich to take along on a fishing trip is not the same as a sandwich that you make at half-time while watching the game on TV. Often, you are not going to eat your fishing sandwich for a few hours. That mayonnaise that tastes so good on a ham sandwich in the den is going to squoosh right through the bread when you unwrap your sandwich at the stream. Sliced tomatoes will soak through the crustiest, freshest roll. My solution is to cut down on the wet stuff, and if I absolutely need some, then I spread it right on the meat and cover it with a piece of lettuce or a slice of cheese.

A sandwich that always works

Like a lot of things that I like in fishing, this is a tip that I picked up from Jack Allen, my bass guide in the Everglades. It satisfies those hunger pangs, has plenty of salt, and answers a craving for sweetness. Not exactly gourmet stuff, but then, we're talking about a fishing trip, not a food tour.

Peanut Butter and Honey

A couple of shmears of peanut butter

1 tablespoon (15 mL) honey

2 slices bread

2 slices bacon (optional)

1 sliced banana (optional)

1. **Spread the peanut butter on the bread.**
2. **Dribble the honey on the peanut butter and *lightly* spread.**
3. **If you like, add banana slices or crisp bacon.**

Chapter 21

Alternatives to Eating: Photography and Mounting

*T*homas Edison was once asked about what went into the glamorous job of being an amazing inventor. He replied, "99 percent perspiration, 1 percent inspiration." Fishing is kind of like that. You spend almost all of your time *trying* to catch fish, and the actual amount of fish-on-the-line time is very small by comparison. So how do you make the memories last?

A God-Given Talent

Very few of us are born with the natural ability to catch fish consistently, but most of us have a native talent to take lousy pictures. Any number of disasters can happen, starting with the fact that when *you* catch a big fish, you are probably so excited that you can almost guarantee that you are going to mess up the photo of the catch of a lifetime. If you want to take a photograph of a great fish and you are the one who caught the fish, let your fishing partner do the shutter snapping.

Or maybe you should ask a pro for some photography advice. Actually, you don't have to, because I did. The pro is Richard Franklin, an excellent angler whose photos have appeared in many publications including *The New York Times, Field & Stream, Flyfisherman,* and others.

Are you keeping the fish?

You must first decide if you are going to kill your fish or not. If you are not going to kill it, there's a whole list of special tips in Chapter 15 and later in this chapter, all of which involve getting the fish free and back in the water in the minimum amount of time. If you are going to kill the fish, then time isn't such a crucial factor, although you don't want to prolong the agony of your catch unnecessarily.

This is not the 19th Century anymore

Hardly anyone ever takes photos the way they used to back in the early days of photography. You know the ones I am talking about — all those photos of stiff, unsmiling people staring into the lens with all the warmth and happiness of someone who has just swallowed a live toad. Today, we want some action, some facial expression (a smile is never wrong). But fishing shots haven't changed all that much. Way back in the old days, you saw a guy standing next to a long stringer of dead fish, or holding up a fish by the jaw, or standing next to a big dead game fish hanging on a meat hook back at the dock. That was fine when photos were the only way of keeping a record. Today, a snapshot isn't such a big deal. Cameras are easier to use, film is relatively cheap, and we all appreciate photos with a little art to them where the subjects don't look like early arrivals at an embalmer's convention.

Your basic photo

When you can, follow the basic rule of photography — position the sun over your (the photographer's) shoulder so that it illuminates your subject.

Flash bulbs work in the day, too

It's easy for me to tell you to get the sun over your shoulder, but there are times when the sun doesn't want to go over your shoulder. You could be stuck on a riverbank looking into the sun. Or it might be high noon and the sun is directly overhead. In cases like this, use a flash to *fill in* the shadows on your subject.

How to make a big fish look small

In you mind's eye, you remember everything about where you caught that big fish. You can see it very vividly: the trees in the background, the mountains in the distance, the boat under you, your trusty pointer sleeping at your feet, your kid saying "I don't care about the fish, Daddy. I'm tired and I want to go home." Don't try to capture all this on film. You will end up with a photograph where everything looks small and dinky. Instead, remember that anyone looking at your picture will respond to two things: the fish and a human being. Concentrate on those two elements and have them occupy as much of the photo as you can.

One of the most effective tools for good picture taking is a wide-angle lens. Some automatic cameras have a wide-angle function included. With a wide angle, you can get closer to your subject, which makes the fish that the angler is holding up look a lot bigger in the foreground. You might think this is cheating, but it's not. All it does is ensure that the fish in the photo looks as big, as nice, and as exciting as the fish in your memory. Boaters take note — a wide-angle is the only effective way to get the boat *and* the subject in the picture without having to leave the boat to get the shot.

Is it okay to use automatic cameras?

More and more cameras now do more and more of the work, leaving less opportunities for messing up to the photographer. Of course, real photographic artists may want the ability to make their own choice of lenses, exposures, and so on. But for most of us, most of the time, all we want is the best picture with the least fuss. If this is your outlook, automatic everything is great. For myself, and this tells you how serious I am as a photographer, I prefer those cameras that come with the film already in them so all you have to do is take the pictures and drop the camera off at the developer and that's that.

Of course, as with everything else, there are more and less expensive automatic cameras. If you want to (and are able to) spend a few extra bucks, look for the following features:

✔ Autofocus gets your subject looking sharp without a lot of unnecessary fiddling around while your fish tries to squirm out of your hands. Remember to point the camera at the *most important* thing first because that is what it will focus on. Then lock the focus and finish composing your shot.

✔ A simple zoom function will give you more choices, especially close-up capability.

Polarize

In Chapter 18, I recommend polarized lenses for your sunglasses. For the same reason, a polarizing filter is always a good idea when you are taking pictures on the water. Not only does it cut down on glare, but it also enhances the richness of the colors in the scene. Also, a polarizing filter will let your camera see into the water to capture the look of a clear lake, or a glimpse of a trout feeding in a pool. This last type of shot is always exciting because it gives a look into the world of the fish when it is totally unafraid and going about its business.

The wet look

Whenever the food magazines that I write for shoot pictures of fruits and vegetables, they always make sure they are wet. This goes double for fish pictures. In general, a fish looks best when you photograph it fresh out of the water. The wetness makes the colors pop and gives an overall sheen to the fish. A dry fish looks as exciting "as a dead fish."

Ice is nice, too

Ice gives a picture that same glistening quality that water does, and it adds some sparkle of its own. A few fish on ice in a chest makes a very inviting photo. Obviously, you don't want to do this with fish that you plan on releasing.

Shoot where the action is

I have a mess of pictures of me with fish. In all honesty, they are just a bunch of mug shots of a grinning goon. Happy, but pretty goofy. I much prefer pictures where the angler is caught in action:

- During the fight when the rod is bent. There is a story in this kind of photo, and people find it naturally interesting.
- Landing the fish, when the viewer gets to savor some of the anticipation and excitement of the moment.
- Releasing the fish. This presents the fish and the angler in the fish's environment. As with the fight, this is a photo that expresses a story.

Catch, shoot, and release

The point of catch and release is that the fish survives. The point of shooting a picture is to give you something more tangible than a memory. Here are some things to keep in mind if you want to give your fish a fighting chance at surviving. Remember, anybody can take a picture of a dead fish. Getting the shot and letting the fish go requires a little more finesse.

✔ Since shooting a photo of a fish involves keeping it out of the water, you are adding stress to an already stressful situation. So speed helps — both in landing and in shooting.

✔ As long as you hold the fish in the water, facing upstream (if there is a current), the fish will survive a long, long time. When you want to snap a picture, lift the fish out of the water, supporting its body as you do so. (Remember, the fish's internal organs are normally supported by the buoyancy of water.)

✔ If you have a friend helping you, let the friend hold the fish in the water until you are ready to snap a picture. Focus on your friend's hands (so you don't have to focus when the fish is in the air) and then have your friend lift the fish for your shot.

One for the Wall

If you are like most anglers — and I am assuming that you are — then I am also assuming that when you finally catch that big fish, there are two surprises in store for you:

✔ Just like George Perry when he caught his record largemouth, you will probably be totally unprepared for a monster, and it will involve a good amount of dumb luck on your part if and when you land the fish of a lifetime.

✔ After a nail-biting fight, you will finally land the fish, and you will have no idea what to do with it in order to get it to the taxidermist in something resembling reasonable shape.

The good news is that you are not trying to preserve something for future generations of scientists to have as a perfect specimen of a fish species. All you want is a fishlike thing hanging on your wall. So even though you may have a detailed list of instructions buried at the bottom of your tackle box telling you how to handle the fish properly for perfect preservation, my bet is the taxidermist will look in his book under "Ready-mix fish colors" and give you the same treatment he has meted out to the thousands of relatives of your fish that he has handled over the years.

Try this if you can

The better you handle your fish, the better chance your mount has of looking like the fish that you caught. Here are a few tips:

✔ Photograph the fish as soon as you can. This will give your taxidermist the most accurate record of the appearance of your fish.

- If possible, lay the fish out flat, put it in a sealed plastic bag (or at least one that has as much air as possible squeezed out of it) and immediately freeze the fish.

- If freezing is impossible, cover the fish with a wet cloth to preserve the sheen and colors of the skin and put the fish in your cooler, laying it as flat as possible.

- If you don't have a freezer or ice, try to keep the fish alive and in the water, tethering it with a stringer through the jaw.

- Write down where and when you caught the fish; what kind of bait, fly, or lure you used; your name, address, and phone number; and your fishing license number. This will help with conservation officers, customs officials, and your taxidermist. While fish switching may not be as upsetting as having your baby switched in the maternity ward, it is nice to know that the beautiful fish hanging on the wall is definitely, positively the fish that you caught.

Don't overdo it

A person with mounted fish covering every square inch of wall in the TV room may or may not be a good fisherman. What in fact he is (I say *he* because it is guys who are most often afflicted by this show-off personality defect) is someone who has a "Hey, look at me!" problem. A few nice trophies are impressive. A wall full of them is just a lot of dead fish that someone else should have been given the chance to catch. In fishing, as in life, the proper sporting attitude should be "Leave some for the next person."

Part V
The Part of Tens

The 5th Wave   By Rich Tennant

"Someone should tell Phil he's sautéing three of my lures in that pan of onions and garlic."

In this part . . .

1 present a bunch of top-ten lists. You get my favorite Internet sites, my favorite fishing books, and my favorite places to fish.

Chapter 22

Fishing as an Interactive Sport: Ten Stops on the Internet

● ●

In This Chapter

▶ What the weather is like where the fishing is

▶ What shape the streams are in *before* you fish

▶ How to find the right outfitter for you

▶ When the next tide will be

● ●

*T*he Internet is like one of those bulletin boards at the supermarket full of ads for handymen, house painting, free kittens, garage sales, old boats, and church trips: you have to wade through a lot of (unorganized) stuff before you find anything that is remotely useful. There's a lot of junk out on the Web, and you can waste time surfing it as effectively as any time wasting thing I can think of. Still there are a few spots that I find genuinely useful.

The United States Geological Survey

http://webserver.cr.usgs.gov/public/monty/

The United States Geologic Service maintains a site with a number of good weather links, including

✔ U.S. forecasts by zone and region from the National Weather Service

✔ An interactive weather browser

✔ Maps of U.S. overlaid with Infrared, Radar, Satellite photos

Coastal Marine Forecasts

http://www.weather.bnl.gov/

This site provides coastal marine forecasts from Boston to Washington as well as the southeastern U.S. These forecasts include easy-to-read charts with surface analysis, sea conditions, and temperature.

Real-Time Water Data

http://h2o.usgs.gov/public/realtime.html

Another USGS site that gives real-time stream conditions for most of the United States' fishable rivers. This is a great site to check out when you are in an area that requires lots of driving from river to river. Although I hate most graphs, the ones at this site are actually quite good.

Tide Predictions

http://www.ceob.nos.noaa.gov/tideframe.html

Maintained by NOAA (the same folks who make the coastal marine broadcasts), this site provides a nationwide table that tracks tides and predicts the next high and low tides.

J.P.'s Fishing Page

http://www.geo.mtu.edu/~jsuchosk/fish/fishpage

This is the first fishing page that I found on the Web, and it is still a good one for *useful* links. I don't know who J.P. is, but I applaud his keeping his links list to a manageable size.

The Anadromous Page

http://www.peak.org

Actually, this page deals with all kinds of fishing, not just anadromous fish like salmon. It's a well organized set of links with fairly up-to-date fishing reports, discussions of environmental issues, recipes, outfitters, gear, and so on. Plus a good internal search engine to help you find specific information.

GORP (Great Outdoors Recreation Pages)

http://www.gorp.com/gorp/activity/ecoint.htm

The Mother of All Links. This Web page is supposedly broken down into a number of areas, but it all looks like one big list to me. It lists many, many interesting sites. If you want to blow an afternoon clicking away at fishing links, there is something here for everybody.

Angler's Online

http://www.inetmkt.com/fishpage/index.html

Just to give you a choice, this page is the other Mother of All Links. It's a little bit of a hodge podge like GORP, but it's still pretty useful. This site has links for current fishing reports, weather, tackle, and magazines, plus a good site-wide search engine.

Saltwater Fishing Questions and Answers

rec.outdoors.fishing.saltwater

This well frequented newsgroup provides a place where you can post questions and get answers from fellow anglers. The same holds true for the newsgroups that follow.

Fly-Fishing Questions and Answers

rec.outdoors.fishing.fly

This site records a lot of hits every day (that is, it gets a lot of visitors) and is a very good place to get questions answered. It's also a pretty civil site. In other words, differing opinions don't automatically get flamed.

Bass Fishing

rec.outdoors.fishing.bass

This newsgroup doesn't get a lot of traffic, but if you post a question, it will get an answer. Regular members seem to come from all over, which means that you will be dealing with people who understand your local conditions. I find this newsgroup to be a lot better than many of the bass Web sites, which are overly commercialized.

AltaVista: A Very Useful Site to Help Find Other Useful Sites

http://www.altavista.digital.com

The Internet has a bunch of sites designed specifically to help you search out what you're looking for. As of this writing, the very best one (and easiest to use) is maintained by Digital Corporation. Your Web browser will probably suggest a few others as well, and you should feel free to try them. I am pretty sold on AltaVista.

The Women's Fishing Partnership

http://www.eskimo.com/~baubo/wfp.html

For all the women anglers out there, you now have your own Web site with links to many of the womens' fishing organizations that are springing up all over the country. This site also contains plenty of links to useful sites for nonwomen anglers.

Chapter 23
Ten Gotta-Have Books

In This Chapter

▶ The one book every angler *needs*

▶ How to tie every knot ever tied (or at least it seems that way)

There may be more fish in the sea than there are fishing books, but there sure are a lot of books about fishing. Any short list will leave out zillions of good books, but you have to start somewhere. For now, you might as well start here. While these books won't teach you everything you need to know about fishing, they sure won't steer you wrong.

Numero Uno

McClanes' New Standard Fishing Encyclopedia and International Angling Guide (enlarged and revised Second Edition) by A.J. McClane; 1974, Henry Holt.

If you had only one book, this is the one. It's the first place to go for anything to do with any kind of fishing. The research is great, the writing is a joy, and the information is accurate.

Very Small and Very Good

Streamside Guide to Naturals and Their Imitations by Art Flick; 1969, Crown Publishers.

Everybody knows that trout fishing with a fly can be very complicated, but it took Art Flick's wonderfully small and straightforward book to show that it can also be simplified. His explanation of why, when, and how certain flies work is crystal clear, and his advice to forget 90 percent of the fly imitations out there is about the single best piece of advice I have seen in print.

No Loose Ends

Practical Fishing Knots by Mark Sosin and Lefty Kreh; 1991, Lyons & Burford.

I don't know of two men who have fished more or more productively than these authors. Every angler needs to know a few knots. This book has every knot you could possibly need. The drawings are clear, and so are the instructions.

The Last Word on the End of Your Line

Hook, Line, and Sinker, The Complete Angler's Guide to Terminal Tackle by Gary Soucie; 1994, Holt.

All the kinds of hooks, lures, swivels, snaps, and leaders. I didn't know you could say so much about this topic until I read this book. I also never dreamed you could say it so well. The definitive work on the subject.

Unsnobby and Undifficult

The Orvis Guide to Fly-fishing by Tom Rosenbauer; 1984, Lyons and Burford.

So many fly-fishing books make you well aware of how much the author thinks he knows and how much you don't know. Not Rosenbauer's. His book is complete, informative, and has a very accessible voice and attitude.

If Trout Had a Bible

Trout by Ray Bergman; 1991, Outlet Book Company.

Originally written in 1938 by the fishing editor of *Outdoor Life,* this is the classic American book about all aspects of trout fishing. It has a very readable style and a very even-handed treatment of all methods of angling for trout. If you are not interested in trout fishing, then you still should have some Bergman in your library, in which case, my recommendation is *Just Fishing.*

A Lot Better than Karl Marx

Curtis Creek Manifesto by Sheridan Anderson 1976, Frank Amato.

A comic book, but a very good one that many have used as a simple introduction to fly-fishing. It helps if you were a hippy way back when (but it is
not absolutely necessary) in order to enjoy this concise, amusing, and, to
use a term from the *Sgt. Pepper* days, right-on book.

Very Pretty Pictures and Useful, Too

The Lore Of Sportfishing by Tre Tryckare and E.Cagner; 1976, Crown
Publishers.

An American version of a European book that you see in bookstores from
time to time. Great plates and amazing illustrations. Kind of a thinner
version of some of the material in McClane's Encyclopedia. The color prints
of all the world's game fish are worth the price alone.

How the Other Guy (or Fish) Sees It

Through the Fish's Eye: An Angler's Guide to Gamefish by Mark Sosin and John
Clark; 1973, Harper & Row.

Once again Sosin, this time with Jack Clark, delves into an overlooked area
and comes up with a methodical presentation of an important and little-
understood subject. It's great to know how to cast or to know a whole lot
about lures, but first you must understand the fish, and this book seeks to
explain that critical first step to angling success. My thanks to Dave Allerton
at Florida State University for turning me on to this book.

A Fishopedia

Freshwater Angler Series by various authors; Cy Decosse Books.

Every decade has its richly illustrated series of how-to fishing books. For
clarity and simplicity, as well as enough (but not too much) accurate
information, this is an excellent beginner's reference library. Titles include
Advanced Bass, Panfish, Largemouth, Smallmouth, and *Artificial Lures.*

Chapter 24
Ten Gotta Reads

*W*e fish to eat, but we like fishing for a lot more than the food it provides. Likewise, there are many books that teach us how to catch fish, but just as important are those books that teach us how to catch fishing fever.

Imitated by Everyone, Equaled by No One

In Our Time by Ernest Hemingway; 1996, Scribner Paperback.

When Nick Adams got off the train at St. Ignace (the beginning of "Big Two Hearted River"), modern fishing writers had a model against which all other angling literature in this century would be judged. Hemingway's fishing writing is astonishingly real and intimate.

He Got the Bass Some Respect

The Book of the Black Bass by James Alexander Henshall; 1970, Bass Anglers Sportsman Society of America.

About the only thing people know about this book (if they know anything at all) is that it has the famous line that calls the smallmouth "inch for inch and pound for pound the gamest fish that swims." There is a whole lot more about bass and the art of angling in this learned and information-filled book. After a hundred years, the info still holds up, and the writing is great.

A Guy Who Knew How to Live and How to Fish

Superior Fishing by Robert Barnwell Roosevelt; 1985, Minnesota Historical Society Press.

Teddy's uncle, a great gourmet, conservationist, and ladies' man. He brought the rainbow trout to the eastern part of the U.S. and exported stripers and shad to the west. He was also a funny, perceptive writer who lived to fish. *Superior Fishing* is the story of a trip that he took with a snooty French nobleman to the waters of the Ojibway and Chippewa. Don't miss the camping grocery list at the end.

Better Than Ahab, and a Better Fisherman, Too

Striper: A Story of Fish and Man by John N. Cole; 1989, Lyons & Burford; drawings by Marvin Kuhn.

Ex-commercial fisherman and founder of *The Maine Times,* Cole's affection and respect for the great game fish of the northeastern U.S. comes through in his tight and rich prose. I guarantee you'll want to read his other great love letter to a fish, *Tarpon Quest.*

You Say You Want to Be a Fishing Guide?

Ninety Two In The Shade by Thomas McGuane; 1995, Vintage Books.

A novel full of sex, drugs, rock and roll . . . and bonefish. McGuane's sporting writing (both fishing and hunting) is modern, sometimes off the wall, but always precise and passionate. He's probably the best current angling writer (now that A.J. McClane is gone).

The Next Best Thing to Fishing

Fishing with McClane by A.J. McClane (edited by George Reiger); 1975, Prentice Hall.

What can I say? You have probably noticed by now that I am very partial to McClane, but he was the best. Look at it this way: There are titanic headline makers like Babe Ruth, and then there are guys who have more grace and finesse than anyone before or since. By that line of reasoning, McClane was the Joe Dimaggio of angling writing, and this collection of 30 years of *Field & Stream* articles is a good indication why.

Fly-Fishing in a Whole New Light

The Fly and the Fish by John Atherton; 1971, Freshet Press.

Atherton was an artist and well acquainted with the properties of light and water. His discussion of why flies work and his application of this knowledge was a true inspiration to me early in my angling career. He has some great stories about the classic waters of Canada and the northeastern U.S.

Is Your River Crowded? Thank Norman

A River Runs through It by Norman MacLean; 1973, University of Chicago Press.

Definitely the most famous fishing book of the last 20 years. MacLean was a very good writer who knew both fishing and human beings. He loved Montana, and it comes through in this book, which spawned Robert Redford's movie, which spawned the current fly-fishing boom.

A Good Old Book from the Good Old Days

Going Fishing by Negley Farson; 1943, Harcourt Brace.

"This is the story of some rods and the places they take you to," begins this world-hopping collection of fishing stories that stretch from New Jersey to the Caspian Sea. Farson was a great angler and observer, and this book, if you can find it, is great for its enthusiasm and for its demonstration that if you keep your eyes and ears open, you can learn something of use from every new fisherman. The late Arnold Gingrich, founder of *Esquire* magazine, called this "one of the six underestimated books."

Sometimes, Nice Guys Finish First

Trout Madness by Robert Traver; 1960, St Martin's Press.

Traver, whose real name was John Voelker, was a small-town district attorney and judge in Michigan's upper peninsula. When he wrote the thriller *Anatomy of a Murder,* it brought him enough money to retire and trout fish at his little cabin in the woods. The full title of his book is *Trout Madness, being a dissertation on the symptoms and pathology of this incurable disease by one of its victims.* I understand the disease, and I also think Traver understood you, me, and anyone who loves to fish.

Traver also wrote another terrific book, *Trout Magic,* which has a passage in it that certainly describes the way I feel about fishing:

> I fish because I love to: because I love the environs where trout are found, which are invariably beautiful, and hate the environs where crowds of people are found, which are invariably ugly; because of all the television commercials, cocktail parties and assorted social posturing I thus escape: because in a world where most men seem to spend their lives doing things they hate, my fishing is at once an endless source of delight and an act of small rebellion: because trout do not lie or cheat and cannot be bought or bribed or impressed by power, but respond only to quietude and humility and endless patience; because I suspect that men are going along this way for the last time and I, for one don't want to waste the trip: because mercifully there are no telephones on trout waters; because only in the woods can I find solitude without loneliness; because bourbon out of an old tin cup always tastes better out there; because maybe one day I will catch a mermaid; and finally, not because I regard fishing as being so terribly important, but because I suspect that so many of the other concerns of men are equally unimportant — and not nearly so much fun.

Chapter 25
My Ten Favorite Places

*O*f all the places I have fished in the world, the places listed in this chapter are the ones I have enjoyed the most. Some I have been to only once, and some I go back to time after time. Some have scenery and some have none, but all have given me great fishing pleasure.

The River of Grass

The Freshwater Everglades, Florida, U.S.

Stretching from Lake Okechobee south to the mangrove-dotted brackish waters just north of Florida Bay, these stands of waving sawgrass criss-crossed by bass-filled canals offer dependable action for spunky largemouth, as well as a way to escape the crowds of "Condomallia" (which is my name for Florida's east coast). The Sawgrass, Holiday Park, and Loxahatchee refuges all offer angling access.

To the Point

Montauk Point, New York, U.S.

At the tip of Long Island, not far from the Gulf Stream. Pretty much every striper, bluefish, tuna, marlin, weakfish, and shark in the northwestern Atlantic has to pass by this rocky outcropping twice a year: once on the northern migration and once on the return southern trip in the fall. Ditto the schools of bait on which these great game fish feed. From the shore or from a boat, this is one of the world's great angling spots.

Papa Fished Here

Key West, Florida, U.S.

Hemingway lived here for a reason: great fishing. But while he was interested in marlin, I love Key West in the blistering hot months of late spring and early summer, when the tiny palolo worms hatch out of the coral and bring up the huge tarpon in a feeding frenzy that looks like a pod of the world's biggest trout in a mayfly hatch.

Blueprint for a Perfect Stream

Slough Creek, Yellowstone Park, U.S.

I am partial to this beautiful mountain meadow stream because my wife and I spent our honeymoon there. I have also fished for big and gorgeous cutthroat with my daughter in its clear pools. With no trees to obstruct your backcast and very little in the way of subsurface obstructions to wrap your line, this is a great place to land a big trout on very light tackle.

The Hottest Fish

The Missouri River, Montana, U.S.

The section of the Missouri below the dam at the confluence at Three Forks is a mind-bogglingly rich spring creek full of the big heads of football-sized trout gorging themselves on unending hatches of all kinds of insects. These are tough fish, super tough, but they are also amazingly strong. When people say "hot fish," these Missouri River trout come to mind.

Down a Lazy River

The Meramec River, Missouri, U.S.

I could have just as easily named a half dozen other Ozark streams (The Current, Jacks Fork, Gasconade, Black, and Big Rivers). These lazy, meandering, limestone-enriched rivers are easy to float by yourself and full of great smallmouth bass on their home range, and I will take a native fish on its home turf over a transplant any day.

Far but Fine

The Quillen River, Patagonia, Argentina

This river will not appear in any other top ten, I guarantee. If you go all the way to Argentina (and every trout fisherman and woman should try to get there sometime) there are easier-to-get-to and more famous rivers. I like the Quillen because it is a little river that is easy to size-up and negotiate all by yourself. It is also full of trout that have seen very few flies or lures, so a well presented cast in a fishy looking place should take a fish. Miles and miles of river, all to yourself.

We Wish You a Merry Kiritimati

Christmas Island, Kiribati Republic

Due south of Hawaii, just a scosh north of the Equator, this is the best bonefishing I have ever seen. White coral flats stretching for miles and miles and zillions of tailing bonefish. No excuses about "I couldn't see them" or "They were so spooky." You will catch bonefish here — everyone does.

It All Started Here (or Nearby)

The River Test, England

There aren't many spring creeks in the world where you can catch brown trout and salmon. In this picture-postcard stream about an hour south of London, you will find both. Also, in late spring, there is a hatch of humongous mayflies (the only bug the English refer to as The Mayfly) that brings up big fish. I wish they stocked this stream less, but still, it's pretty, and Izaak Walton fished here, too.

Big City Bass

Ellis Island, New York Harbor, U.S.

On Christmas Eve, when the incoming tide brings warmer water, the die-hard flyrodder can still get his or her last licks in under the causeway that leads from Ellis Island to Jersey City. With the skyline of Manhattan as a backdrop and the city all decked out in Christmas lights, this is great fishing at a magic time.

Chapter 26
Ten Shots at Big Fish

*N*o matter how many times you hear people say they don't care if they catch big fish, you can bet that once they do, you won't hear the end of it. Big fish are just plain exciting. If you want to catch big ones, go where the big ones are.

Very Big-League Trout

Brown Trout: Egg Harbor, Wisconsin, U.S.

There are a number of places in the world where you can catch really big trout (Tierra del Fuego, the White River in Arkansas), but I think that the Great Lakes offer the best chance for big fish. I like Door County, Wisconsin, because in the fall, when the spawning urge is upon them, the really big guys congregate close to shore. Hard to catch, but they are all big and they are definitely there.

When You Get Tired of Disney World

Largemouth Bass: Ocala National Forest, Florida, U.S.

There are a few places where you can catch big bass with some frequency. The southern California lakes all produce monsters. Likewise, new reservoirs in the southern U.S. (or newly drained and refilled reservoirs and impoundments) often yield big fish for a few years, but if you want to go to a place where big bass occur *naturally,* then central Florida has the weather and the water to grow big bigmouths.

Ugly but Big

Northern Pike: Manitoba, Canada

A rule of thumb in my part of the world (the northern hemisphere) is "Go north for big fish." At the limits of their range, most North American game fish tend to grow bigger, and this is certainly true of northern pike. I have caught them up to 18 pounds on a fly in northern Labrador. But that was when I was fishing for brookies. For consistently big fish, the pike lakes of Manitoba are currently the best producers.

Bronzed Beauties

Smallmouth Bass: The Tennessee Rivers and Tributaries, Tennessee and Alabama, U.S.

This is the home range of the smallmouth, and it suits them fine with swift flowing rivers with plenty of food and a long growing season. I have also had good luck up in the St. Lawrence. Remember, smallmouth don't grow as large as largemouth. Four pounds is a great fish anywhere, and five is a trophy.

Great Looks, Short on Brains

Brook Trout: Labrador, Canada

In the Minipi Lake system, giant brookies gorge themselves on equally giant mayflys during the short growing season. They put on a lot of weight fast. Four pounds is nothing to write home about. You will catch them every day, and catching a 9-pounder is doable, though rare.

Striper Heaven

Striped Bass: Montauk, Long Island, U.S.

From Thanksgiving until the second week of December, the herring are in strong, and the last — and biggest — of the bass move through with them. Fifteen to 25 pound fish can be caught consistently by flyrodders and pluggers alike. All you have to do is be there.

When You Have Eaten Your Fill

Walleye: Saginaw Bay, Michigan, U.S.

There are not many places where you have a chance of encountering, much less catching, a 10-pound walleye. Saginaw Bay is one of them. Along with Ontario Canada's Bay of Quinte, this is the Great Lakes destination for bigger walleye. My only problem is I would much rather eat a walleye than hang one on the wall.

Ambush at the Pass

Tarpon: Boca Grand, Florida, U.S.

For years, the serious tarpon guys (the ones on the lookout for the elusive 200-pounder on a fly) have frequented this pass on the west coast of Florida. The big fish materialize around Easter and keep coming through early June.

Caution, Bears Gorging Themselves!

Chinook Salmon: Kenai Peninsula, Alaska, U.S.

There is a reason that the big bears love to fish in Alaska's Kenai Peninsula: The biggest run of the biggest Pacific Salmon are found here. A 50-pound fish isn't unrealistic, and 70-pound trophies come out with greater frequency here than almost any place in the world.

A Guy Can Dream, Can't He?

Marlin: Great Barrier Reef, Australia

I know this is more than a day's drive for most of us, but if you want to catch a true fantasy fish, then try September through December off of northeastern Australia. I could have listed the bluefin tuna of Canada's maritime provinces or the sailfish of Panama here just as well, but somehow, a gigantic marlin seemed like the right one to put on the all-time wish list.

Index

• C •

Notes

Notes

Notes

Notes

Notes

Notes

Notes

Notes

IDG BOOKS WORLDWIDE REGISTRATION CARD

Title of this book: Fishing For Dummies™

My overall rating of this book: ❏ Very good [1] ❏ Good [2] ❏ Satisfactory [3] ❏ Fair [4] ❏ Poor [5]

How I first heard about this book:

❏ Found in bookstore; name: [6] _____   ❏ Book review: [7] _____

❏ Advertisement: [8] _____   ❏ Catalog: [9] _____

❏ Word of mouth; heard about book from friend, co-worker, etc.: [10] _____   ❏ Other: [11] _____

What I liked most about this book:

_____

_____

What I would change, add, delete, etc., in future editions of this book:

_____

_____

Other comments:

_____

Number of computer books I purchase in a year: ❏ 1 [12]   ❏ 2-5 [13]   ❏ 6-10 [14]   ❏ More than 10 [15]

I would characterize my computer skills as: ❏ Beginner [16] ❏ Intermediate [17] ❏ Advanced [18] ❏ Professional [19]

I use ❏ DOS [20] ❏ Windows [21] ❏ OS/2 [22] ❏ Unix [23] ❏ Macintosh [24] ❏ Other: [25]_____
                                                                                                (please specify)

I would be interested in new books on the following subjects:
(please check all that apply, and use the spaces provided to identify specific software)

❏ Word processing: [26] _____   ❏ Spreadsheets: [27] _____

❏ Data bases: [28] _____   ❏ Desktop publishing: [29] _____

❏ File Utilities: [30] _____   ❏ Money management: [31] _____

❏ Networking: [32] _____   ❏ Programming languages: [33] _____

❏ Other: [34] _____

I use a PC at (please check all that apply): ❏ home [35] ❏ work [36] ❏ school [37] ❏ other: [38] _____

The disks I prefer to use are ❏ 5.25 [39] ❏ 3.5 [40] ❏ other: [41]_____

I have a CD ROM: ❏ yes [42]   ❏ no [43]

I plan to buy or upgrade computer hardware this year: ❏ yes [44]   ❏ no [45]

I plan to buy or upgrade computer software this year: ❏ yes [46]   ❏ no [47]

Name: _____   Business title: [48] _____   Type of Business: [49] _____

Address (❏ home [50] ❏ work [51] /Company name: _____)

Street/Suite# _____

City [52]/State [53]/Zipcode [54]: _____   Country [55] _____

❏ **I liked this book!** You may quote me by name in future
IDG Books Worldwide promotional materials.

My daytime phone number is _____

IDG BOOKS

THE WORLD OF
COMPUTER
KNOWLEDGE